WOMEN ARTISTS AND WRITERS

In this provocative and richly interdisciplinary study Bridget Elliott and Jo-Ann Wallace reappraise the literary and artistic contribution of women to modernism and in particular the self representation and construction of artistic identity. Taking a comparative case study approach, the authors examine the ways in which women, including Natalie Barney, Virginia Woolf, Vanessa Bell and Gertrude Stein responded to modernism, and the manner in which their work has been positioned in relation to that of men.

Women Artists and Writers makes an important contribution to twentieth-century cultural history, and puts forward a powerful case against the academic 'disciplining' of cultural production into departments of Art History and English Studies which has served to marginalize the work of female modernists. This book will be essential reading for all women's studies specialists and anyone interested in the cultural production of art and literature.

Bridget Elliott is Associate Professor of Art and Design at the University of Alberta. She has written extensively in the areas of nineteenth and twentieth-century British and French art, cinema and popular culture.

Jo-Ann Wallace is Associate Professor of English at the University of Alberta. She has written widely on the subjects of women's literary modernism, feminist cinema and film theory, and nineteenth-century children's literature.

Natalie Barney as the little page with Renée Vivien. Location of original unknown. Published in Jean Chalon, *Portrait of a Seductress: The World of Natalie Barney*, trans. Carol Barko (New York: Crown, 1979).

WOMEN ARTISTS AND WRITERS

Modernist (im)positionings

Bridget Elliott and Jo-Ann Wallace

London and New York

First published 1994
by Routledge
11 New Fetter Lane, London EC4P 4EE

Simultaneously published in the USA and Canada
by Routledge
29 West 35th Street, New York, NY 10001

© 1994 Bridget Elliott and Jo-Ann Wallace

Typeset in Garamond by Solidus (Bristol) Limited

Printed and bound in Great Britain by
Biddles Ltd, Guildford and King's Lynn

Printed on acid free paper

British Library Cataloguing in Publication Data
A catalogue record for this book is available from the British Library

Library of Congress Cataloging in Publication Data
Elliott, Bridget
Women Artists and Writers: Modernist (im)positionings / Bridget
Elliott and Jo-Ann Wallace.
p.   cm.
Includes bibliographical references and index.
1. Feminism and the arts. 2. Modernism (Art) 3. Arts,
Modern–20th century. 4. Women artists–Biography. I. Wallace, Jo-Ann.
II. Title.
NX180.F4E44   1994
700'.82–dc20   93–44533

ISBN 0–415–05365–X (hbk)
ISBN 0–415–05366–8 (pbk)

This book is lovingly dedicated to our grandmothers and mothers.

Muriel (Surr) Elliott
Lilian (Richards) Royce
Lois Constance (Royce) Elliott

Helen Aiken (Bookless) (Wallace) Toal
Doris Ellen (Neale) Cotton
Patricia Ann (Cotton) Wallace

)

CONTENTS

CONTENTS

FIGURES

FIGURES

ACKNOWLEDGEMENTS

Intellectual work never takes place in a vacuum and this book is no exception. We would like to thank the other members of our inter-disciplinary reading group – Yu-shih Chen, David Cooper, Martin Lefebvre, Ray Morrow, Tony Purdy, Nasrin Rahimieh, and Stephen Slemon – for providing a stimulating intellectual environment over the past four years. The students in our 1992 graduate seminar on "Gender and the modernist avant-garde" shared in many of the discussions surrounding issues in this book. Librarians at the following institutions were helpful in locating source materials and permissions: British Library; National Art Library, Victoria and Albert Museum; Museum of Modern Art Library, New York City; Henry W. and Albert A. Berg Collection, New York Public Library; Archives of American Art, Smithsonian Institution; and Special Collections, University of Maryland at College Park Libraries. Special thanks to Danuta Woronowicz for help in preparing the final typescript and to our editors, Sue Roe and Talia Rodgers, for their support and patience. This project was funded by the Social Sciences and Humanities Research Council of Canada, and by the Support for the Advancement of Scholarship and Central Research Funds of the University of Alberta.

For permission to quote from Djuna Barnes's *The Book of Repulsive Women* and from her unpublished letter to Natalie Barney we are grateful to the Authors League Fund of America as literary executor of the Estate of Djuna Barnes and the Rare Books and Literary Manuscripts Collection of the College Park Libraries, University of Maryland. For permission to quote from Vanessa Bell's unpublished letters to Virginia Woolf we are grateful to Professor Quentin Bell and R.A. Marler. For permission to quote from Ezra Pound's "Hugh Selwyn Mauberley" (*Personae*, copyright 1926 by Ezra Pound) we are grateful to New Directions Press and Faber & Faber, Ltd. For permission to quote from Man Ray's and Natalie Barney's unpublished letters to Gertrude Stein we are grateful to the Yale Collection of American Literature, Beinecke Rare Book Room and Manuscript Library, Yale University. Chapter 2 of this book, "Fleurs du mal or second-hand roses?: Natalie Barney, Romaine Brooks, and the 'originality of the avant-garde,'" originally appeared in a substantially different form in *Feminist Review* 40 (1992).

Every effort has been made to obtain permission to use copyright material.

1

WHOSE MODERNISM?

The subtitle of our book, *Modernist (im)positionings*, evokes both a discourse and a strategy. The discourse is that of modernism as it has been constructed in the visual and literary arts. The strategy is, but only in part, that of a feminist recovery of "lost" or neglected women writers and artists. Our use of the portmanteau word "(im)positionings" is meant not *only* to invoke the reevaluation of writers like Natalie Barney or artists like Nina Hamnett ("imposing" them on an academy which has refused to recognize the degree of their contributions to "modernism"), but also to suggest our commitment to rethinking modernism as a discursive and historical *field*. This means re-examining the critical reception even of now canonical writers and artists like Virginia Woolf, Gertrude Stein, and Marie Laurencin. Rather than regarding them as privileged individuals whose genius assured them a place in a largely masculine modernist canon, we want to explore more broadly the conditions of their work. What were their material and financial resources? What kinds of audiences did their work attract or reach? What kind of effect did this have on their aesthetic decisions? How did they position themselves and how were they positioned *in relation to* the avant-garde, alternate women's communities, and the geographical centres or peripheries of modernist production? How does a fuller understanding of women's position within modernism alter our understanding of modernism as a discursive field?

We are influenced here by Pierre Bourdieu's work on the field of cultural production and the ways in which the cultural necessarily participates in or reflects the political. Because it is "occupied by objects and practices with minimum use-value," the cultural is also "a field in which *par excellence* the struggle is governed by a pure logic of difference or distinction, a pure logic of positionality" (Garnham and Williams 1986: 124).[1] Furthermore, as Bourdieu argues, "Specifically aesthetic conflicts about the legitimate vision of the world, ... about what deserves to be represented and the right way to represent it, are political conflicts (appearing in their most euphemized form) for the power to impose the dominant definitions of reality, and social reality in particular" (Bourdieu 1986: 154–55). What we want to borrow from

Bourdieu is the possibility of understanding "modernism" as just such a cultural field, one which must be further understood as the evolving product of a continuing struggle for certain kinds of symbolic power (Bourdieu 1986: 159). This means examining the ways in which women artists, writers, publishers, and gallery owners in London, New York, and Paris negotiated and competed – with men, but also with each other – for the power to define a modern aesthetics and poetics. However, it also means examining current institutional investments in "modernism." What is *at stake* for English studies and art history in their various disciplinary representations of "modernism"? As feminist scholars, how do we negotiate our own "positioning" *in relation to* the still largely masculinist academy, the work of an earlier generation of feminist researchers, the larger women's community beyond the university, and, not least, the women whose lives and work are the focus of this book? As cross-disciplinary, collaborative writers how do we negotiate competing disciplinary claims? Whose "modernism," whose terminology, whose theory? Bourdieu's approach will help us to articulate some of our questions and to understand what is at stake for the field of modernism, for the women we are studying, and for feminist interventions in our respective disciplines. However, we also need to supplement his work, for while his theory of symbolic power and cultural reproduction is premised upon a theory of class (or "habitus"), he largely neglects to take gender into account either theoretically or empirically. Nonetheless, and as Toril Moi points out, a feminist supplement to Bourdieu's theory "permits us to grasp the immense *variability* of gender as a social factor" (Moi 1991: 1035). Since the women who form the basis of this study are all differently positioned – in terms of class, financial resources, education, and sexual orientation – in relation to each other and to the larger field of "modernism," their gender inflects the production and reception of their work in very different ways.

In calling "modernism" a discursive or a cultural field, and in placing the term within inverted commas, we want to suggest that there is no innate or unproblematic modernism whose history can simply be uncovered. In imposing and positioning women within the literary and art historical discourses of modernism, we are not recovering a more authentic or a "truer" modernism. We hope instead to expose some of the ways in which cultural fields are constructed and especially the ways in which gender influences and informs those constructions. The "modernist" period provides an especially promising framework for such an inquiry, for one of its paradoxical characteristics is the degree to which so many of its practitioners and its subsequent historians have self-consciously participated in the construction of various hegemonic "modernisms." In the next four sections of this chapter we outline the ways in which modernism has been variously configured within the fields of literary and art historical studies; the chapter concludes with a brief introduction to the eight women who comprise our case studies.

FORMAL CONFIGURATIONS

As one interdisciplinary critic of "modernism" notes, "The common thread for anyone who yearns to be Modern, whatever the medium, is the ability to *refurbish the language of his [sic] art*, whether through disruption and new formations, or through colors, tones, sound sequences, visual effects, neologisms" (Karl 1988: xi; our emphasis). Certainly "modernism" has traditionally been constructed less as a period than as a style or a series of formal interrogations, and this has had profound implications for any assessment of women's cultural production within "modernism." This is further complicated by the different dating of "modernism" within various disciplines. In English literary studies, the "modernist" period is usually defined as covering 1890 to 1939, with the 1920s as the period of "high modernism;" in the visual arts, a formalist notion of "modernism" is equated with the rise of avant-garde artistic groups preoccupied with visual perception and aesthetic innovation, often taking the form of an emphasis on abstraction. Broadly speaking, the period of such avant-gardism extends from the mid-nineteenth century (e.g. Impressionism) through to the third quarter of the twentieth century (e.g. Abstract Expressionism, Minimalism).[2] In terms of art criticism, the rise of a formalist "modernism" is almost invariably associated with the Bloomsbury aesthetics of Roger Fry and Clive Bell. In his various activities as curator, writer, painter, educator, and collector, Roger Fry sought to rid British aesthetic taste of its latent Victorianism by promoting works of art that embodied an internal formal purity which did not relate to the moral responsibilities of actual existence.[3] As Simon Watney points out, Fry's thinking generated a two-tiered system involving imagery which was instinctive and disinterested as opposed to that which was social and symbolic. Only the former qualified as art by evoking purely disinterested aesthetic emotions and not raising the mundane spectres of subject matter, social usage, and representational content. Fry utilized these evaluative criteria for measuring past art by tracing a tradition that extended from Giotto, Byzantine mosaics, Piero Della Francesca, Poussin, and Cézanne to the French Post-Impressionists (Watney 1980: 4).

It should be emphasized that Fry organized the First and Second Post Impressionist exhibitions (1910 and 1912) and wrote his most influential critical essays during the 1910s and 1920s. During this period his ideas were popularized in Clive Bell's *Art*, which largely simplified Fry's notions of the aesthetic hypothesis and the appreciation of "significant form."[4] This was also the period when the discipline of art history was institutionalized through the launching of journals such as the *Burlington Magazine* (for which Fry often wrote) and the establishment of art history courses at British academic institutions such as the Courtauld Institute of Art at the University of London. Fry's influential position within the British arts establishment and his emphasis on the internal development of the artistic tradition help explain why his ideas proved so appealing to the newly emerging profession of art history.

Clement Greenberg, perhaps the best known apologist for "modernism" in the visual arts, was indebted to many of Roger Fry's ideas which he expanded into a more systematic theory of internal change and development in modern art.[5] In the course of indirectly acknowledging his debt to Fry and Bell, Greenberg also argued that although the notion of "pure" (or modernist) poetry emerged earlier than "pure" painting, a "pure" art criticism preceded its literary counterpart and actually influenced writers (Greenberg 1961: 240). In such (in)famous essays as "Modernist painting" and "Avant-garde and kitsch" Greenberg provides perhaps the most definitive rationale for the formalist "modernist" project in the visual arts. In the following passage from his 1965 essay, "Modernist painting," he emphasizes the self-criticism and disciplinary purity of "modernism" across the arts:

> The essence of Modernism lies, as I see it, in the use of the characteristic methods of a discipline to criticize the discipline itself – not in order to subvert it, but to entrench it more firmly in its area of competence.... It quickly emerged that the unique and proper area of competence of each art coincided with all that was unique to the nature of its medium. The task of self-criticism became to eliminate from the effects of each art any and every effect that might conceivably be borrowed from or by the medium of any other art. Thereby each art would be rendered "pure", and in its "purity" find the guarantee of its standards of quality as well as of its independence.
>
> (Greenberg 1984: 5–6)

According to Greenberg, such rigorous self-criticism and purification was necessary in order to counter the "levelling" effects of academicism, commercialism, and, especially, mass production – trends which Greenberg subsumes under the label of "kitsch" (Greenberg 1961: 9).[6] Because it is unreflectingly imitative and infinitely reproducible, characteristics which ensure its accessibility to "the masses," kitsch is more susceptible to propagandistic manipulation and thus to being a tool of fascistic regimes. The function of the modernist avant-garde, therefore, was "to find a path along which it would be possible to keep culture *moving* in the midst of ideological confusion and violence" (5). One effect of the new disciplinary purity was that "subject matter or content [became] something to be avoided like a plague" (5).

The establishment of a recognizably English-language literary modernism is usually attributed to the influence of poet and philosopher T.E. Hulme and the impresario efforts of Ezra Pound. In his much quoted essay, "Romanticism and classicism" (published posthumously and alternately dated 1913/14 or 1911/12; see Levenson 1984: 81–87), Hulme anticipated a "classical revival" of poetry grounded in "a new technique, a new convention." He

4

called for a poetry which would be emotionally "reserved" as well as "dry and hard" (as opposed to the "dampness" of the Romantics), producing "accurate, precise and definite description." Significantly, Hulme drew an analogy between the precise craftsmanship of the architect and the classical poet; like the architect, the poet is a "man who simply can't bear the idea of 'approximately.' He will get the exact curve of what he sees whether it be an object or an idea in the mind." In classical poetry the "subject doesn't matter;" the real struggle is with language, which the poet must hold fixed to his purpose (Hulme 1924: passim). Correspondences between Fry's aesthetics and Hulme's poetics are obvious and the effects were similar. Hulme's poetics were adapted and popularized by Ezra Pound who – together with F.S. Flint, Richard Aldington, and H.D. – established the relatively small and short-lived but enormously influential Imagist movement (see Zach 1976). Pound also provided a credo for what would become "high modernism" in his emphasis on technical or formal experimentation, best summed up in his demand of writers to "make it new" and in his catechism-like "Credo" which asserts, in part, "I believe in technique as the test of a man's sincerity" (Pound 1968: 9).

While there is no single literary critic of "modernism" who holds as central a place in English studies as Clement Greenberg does in art history, it is nonetheless possible to suggest a composite definition and justification of formalist literary "modernism" by drawing on the work of Irving Howe, Harry Levin, and Stephen Spender.[7] Levin's elegiac "What was modernism?" (1960) sets what will become a familiar tone. In that essay he marks the passing of a homogeneous and cross-disciplinary movement, a generation of "giants" whose creative energies climaxed in 1922 – an *annus mirabilis* of modernist production (619) – and whose hallmark was a devotion to "craftsmanship" (626) coupled with an "uncompromising intellectuality" (628). Levin's elegiac tone – the sense that he is commemorating a past greatness and coherence – is, in part, also ascribed to modernism itself. All three critics emphasize the time-consciousness of "modernism" – its sense of "nowness" (Levin 1960: 621), of "historical impasse" or "apocalyptic *cul de sac*" (Howe 1967: 15), its distrust of progress and its confrontation of the present with the past (Spender 1963: x, 71–78).[8]

Spender describes the "predicament" of modernism as "that of past consciousness living in the present;" "with his intellect [the modern] is committed to criticizing that present by applying to it his realization of the past" (78).[9] Spender is careful to distinguish between what he calls "contemporaries" and "moderns," suggesting that "contemporaries" still adhere to a Victorian belief in progress while "moderns" distrust progress and "view the results of science as a catastrophe to the values of past civilization" (x). Unlike the "contemporary," who may still believe in the efficacy of political action, the "modern" looks to art to *fuse* past and present (78) and to restore a lost sense of coherence. According to Spender, this helps to account for the modernist emphasis upon formal experimentation. The modern world can only be healed by an artistic vision which "restores wholeness to the fragmentation, even by realizing it as disaster, as the waste land, or night town" (81). That is, the self-referentiality and self-sufficiency of modernist art and literature *enact* a wholeness which is missing from the external world.

Thus traditional literary critical and art historical constructions of "modernism" share a causal emphasis upon a sense of historical and cultural impasse. Of equal interest, however, is a shared critical rhetoric which constructs the "modernist" enterprise as a heroic, if doomed, last stand in a losing battle against the forces of what Levin revealingly calls "domestication" (615). Examples of such heightened rhetoric abound: "modernism must always struggle but never quite triumph, and then, after a time, must struggle in order not to triumph" (Howe 1967: 13); "while some of [modernism's] lights are still among us, before they have all been extinguished, we should ask ourselves why they have burned with such pyrotechnic distinction" (Levin 1960: 620); "since the avant-garde forms the only living culture we now have, the survival in the near future of culture in general is thus threatened" (Greenberg 1961: 8). The questions which remain unasked in traditional/formalist configurations of "modernism" are: *whose* culture is threatened? is a modernist sense of historical impasse shared, or is it gender, class, and race specific? did formal experimentation *mean* the same thing to women and men artists, or to the women and men who viewed or read their work? did women feel the same need to restore a lost cultural coherence? whose interests did "modernism" (and its critics) serve?

INSTITUTIONAL CONFIGURATIONS

Within the last decade, there has emerged a second generation of "modernist" critics which has been far less interested in sketching in the broad outlines of *a* modernist movement; instead, they want to expose the diversity *within* "modernism" and to explore "modernism's" institutional alliances and strategies. That is, to what degree was "modernism" self-consciously constructed by its practitioners and by its critics, and how did various social and market forces help shape the practices of "modernism"? Or, as the editors of *Modern Art and Modernism* phrase it, the task now is "to examine both the circumstances under which modern art has been produced, and those under which critical theories and forms of interpretation have themselves been produced" (Frascina and Harrison 1982: 1). Peter Bürger's *Theory of the Avant-Garde* (1984; orig. pub. 1974) is perhaps the most obvious example of what we are calling a second generation re-reading of "modernism," although, given the clear distinction Bürger draws between "modernism" and "the avant-garde," he would be unhappy with our description. We will return in Chapter 2 to discuss in more detail the ways in which a consideration of gender blurs clear distinctions between an "avant-garde" and a "modernist" aesthetics. Here we want to emphasize instead the revisionary quality of Bürger's work which the title of his book, echoing as it does Renato Poggioli's *The Theory of the Avant-Garde* (1968; orig. pub. 1962), clearly suggests. Poggioli's book was published in the same decade as the formalist modernisms of Greenberg, Howe, Levin, and Spender; like theirs, his methodology is "synthetic," emphasizing broad "tendencies and ideas" (Poggioli 1968: 3) in the creation of a field. Bürger's analysis resists Poggioli's broad strokes and emphasizes instead the specificity of what he calls the historical avant-garde movements – primarily Dadaism, Surrealism, and the Russian avant-gardes after the October Revolution (Bürger 1984: 109, fn. 4). What distinguishes the avant-garde, according to Bürger, is its awareness and critique of art as an institution and its demand that art be reintegrated into the praxis of life. By "art as an institution" Bürger means "the productive and distributive apparatus" and "the ideas about art that prevail at a given time and that determine the reception of works" (22). His methodology, which he characterizes as dialectical, has much to offer a feminist analysis of "modernism." Unlike dogmatic criticism (which is oppositional in its strategy), dialectical criticism is aware not only of its indebtedness to the work upon which it builds (in our case, the recuperative work of an earlier generation of feminist scholars), but also of its own historical and institutional embeddedness. This is also one reason why we believe that cross-disciplinary work, with its tendency to "make strange" or to "defamiliarize" disciplinary assumptions, is of crucial importance in the production of feminist knowledge. (The ramifications both of the professionalization of the arts during the "modernist" period and the concurrent entry of women into such professions as the academy will be the focus of Chapter 3.)

Two other examples of the analysis of modernist institutional networks and practices are Michael Levenson's *A Genealogy of Modernism: A Study of English Literary Doctrine 1908–1922* (1984) and Lawrence Rainey's "The price of modernism: reconsidering the publication of *The Waste Land*" (1989).[10] Each explodes the myth of modernist homogeneity through the careful reconstruction of a particular moment and place of modernist production. Levenson focuses on the emergence and consolidation of an explicitly *English* literary modernism which had at its London-based centre Ezra Pound, T.E. Hulme, Ford Madox Ford, Wyndham Lewis, and T.S. Eliot, and which evolved through the stages of Impressionism, Imagism, Vorticism, and, finally, Classicism (vii). He argues that the history of this *particular* formation of modernism – which was philosophically rooted in sceptical individualism, developed through egoism, and moved toward authoritarianism – was lost through the editorial misdating of Hulme's work in *Speculations* (1924), his posthumously published collected essays. The correct dating of these essays reveals a modernism that was not only far less homogeneous than literary history has led us to believe, but one which was marked by factionalism and, ultimately, by the critical hegemony of T.S. Eliot's *The Criterion* and all it stood for.

Levenson notes that "If we look for a mark of modernism's coming of age, the founding of *The Criterion* in 1922 may prove a better instance than *The Waste Land*, better even than *Ulysses*, because it exemplifies the institutionalization of the movement, the accession to cultural legitimacy" (213). Lawrence Rainey also focuses on 1922 but chooses instead the publication of Eliot's *The Waste Land* to mark the institutionalization of "modernism's unprecedented triumph" (Rainey 1989: 21). "The price of modernism" is a detailed examination of the financial negotiations which took place between Ezra Pound, T.S. Eliot, and various potential publishers of the poem, including Scofield Thayer of *The Dial*, John Peale Bishop for *Vanity Fair* and Horace Liveright of Boni & Liveright – all of whom entered a bidding war for the privilege of publishing the as-yet-unread poem. In these negotiations, which he led, Pound advanced the obviously successful argument that "the poem was important precisely for its representative quality" and that publishing it would indicate "an eagerness to position oneself as the spokesman of a field of cultural production, the voice for an array of institutions" (24). Rainey argues that the choice of publishing venue was almost purely strategic and was dictated by Pound's and Eliot's vision of a hegemonic modernism; *The Dial* enabled a "crucial moment in the transition of modernism from a minority culture to one supported by an important institutional and financial apparatus" (34). The highly self-conscious wheeling and dealing detailed by Rainey stands in marked contrast to the self-sacrificing and disinterested modernism celebrated by Harry Levin in his description of the modernists' "refusal to advertise themselves or to talk down to their audience in the hope of enlarging it" (Levin 1960: 628).

While Rainey details one skirmish in the "modernist" struggle over a discursive field, Bruce Robbins, in "Modernism in history, modernism in power" (1983), focuses less on the *construction* of "modernism" by its practitioners than on its *institutional legacy* (231). Levenson and Rainey differ from Robbins by charting the ways in which English literary "modernism," in its emphasis on movements and manifestos, borrowed certain strategies from the world of advertising and the mass media, while Robbins argues instead that modernist techniques have themselves been "incorporated into modernist commercials" (234) and that modernism now works "in the cause of consumption" (235).[11] Of greater interest, however, is his suggestion that English studies was shaped by modernism and "has remained a modernist discipline," valuing "the emotive over the rational; psychological and mythic universals over historical particulars; an idealized preindustrial past or highly selective tradition over a present that is judged, in the 'modern tradition,' to be sordid, chaotic, meaningless" (238). According to Robbins, one result of the institutional entwining of modernism and

English studies has been "a structural or procedural pessimism ... founded on the cultural despair of an elite" (241).

But again we must ask, how does raising the issue of gender affect such institutional analyses of modernism? While the modernist period saw the consolidation of English studies and art history as disciplines within the university – disciplines which consequently became increasingly "masculin-ized"[12] – it also saw women winning greater access to institutions of higher learning. Virginia Woolf's *A Room of One's Own* and *Three Guineas* attest to the enormous *hope* which women invested in their education. Did a humanistic training *mean* the same thing to women as to men? And what was the effect of the increasing collectivization (as witnessed by the proliferation of "movements") and professionalization of the arts upon women? Were they excluded from centres of modernist power and decision-making? Did they form collectives of their own? Did late nineteenth- and early twentieth-century social movements – most notably the universal manhood and women's suffrage movements – have any effect on the formation of "modernism"?

MATERIALIST CONFIGURATIONS

The marxist configuration of "modernism" has provided different ways of conceptualizing the link between "modernism" and elitism. (This is a question to which we shall return in Chapter 5 when we discuss, among other issues, the function of such low, or "applied", arts as journalism and illustration in the popularization of "modernism.") The marxist reformula-tion of the question of cultural value in modernism is perhaps most evident in Georg Lukács' defense of realism. While Greenberg argues that modernist avant-garde art is characterized by its difficulty and disciplinary purity – characteristics which protect it, and therefore "culture," from being absorbed by an ideology of mass production – Lukács argues, on the contrary, that a truly avant-garde art is one which is accessible to "the masses" and demonstrates "a vital relationship to the life of the people" (Lukács 1977: 57). Avant-garde art must be "anticipatory" or prophetic; only "great realism" is capable of penetrating the social surface to capture "tendencies which exist only incipiently and so have not yet had the opportunity to unfold their entire human and social potential. To discern and give shape to such underground trends is the great historical mission of the true literary avant-garde" (48).

As the editors of *Aesthetics and Politics* note, the late-1930s German debate around Expressionism and realism was "essentially a contest over the historical meaning of modernism in general" (Bloch *et al.* 1977: 12).[13] Lukács' later essay, "The ideology of modernism" (first published 1957), spells out more clearly his dissatisfactions with the world view or *Welt-anschauung* he saw revealed in the bourgeois-modernist "exaggerated concern with formal criteria, with questions of style and literary technique" (Lukács 1989: 597). As he does in "Realism in the balance," Lukács here takes Thomas Mann as his proto-realist and James Joyce as his proto-modernist, arguing that while the "traditional" Mann presents a view of the world as "dynamic and developmental" – hence capable of revolutionary change – the "modern" Joyce presents a view of the world as "static and sensational" (598). Lukács identifies several key components of the world-view of modernist literature: man "is by nature solitary, asocial, unable to enter into relationships with other human beings" (598), a condition Lukács calls "subjectivism"; man is an "ahistorical being" whose "examined reality is static" (599); modernist literature describes an "attenuation of reality and dissolution of personality" (601), an "ever-increasing part played by psycho-pathology" (603), and a lack of perspective (605). In short, modernist literature, taking an angst born out of the experience of the disintegration of *society*, "attains its effects by evoking the disintegration of the world of man" (608) thus robbing literature of its capacity to provide a unified vision of reality and to inspire social change.[14] "Modernism," Lukács concludes, "means not the enrichment, but the negation of art" (611).

Lukács' relatively unproblematized privileging of realism has, until very recently, led to critical dismissal of his work.[15] However, his iconoclastic refusal to, in his words, "systematically glorify the modernist movement" (Lukács 1989: 605) is a useful reminder that a formalist modernism did not always enjoy an almost universal critical hegemony. Similarly, Lukács' emphases on the importance of subject-matter and the transformative capacity of literature (and art) are useful tools for a feminist reassessment of "modernism." Some questions, however, which remain unanswered are: can Lukács' argument be extrapolated to include the visual arts? are the "attenuation of reality," the "dissolution of personality," and ahistoricism also qualities of women's modernist productions? and, if so, does this attenuation *mean* the same thing for modernist women as it does for men?

A more materialist account of modernity, one which may also be of some use to a feminist analysis although it is not itself informed by feminism, is Perry Anderson's "Modernity and revolution" (1988),[16] largely a review and critique of Marshall Berman's *All That Is Solid Melts Into Air* (1983). Anderson distinguishes between "modernity" and "modernism," borrowing Berman's definition of "modernity" as the *historical experience* linking modernization and modernism, or economic process and cultural vision (318); however, he departs from Berman in describing moder*nism* as a "cultural force field 'triangulated' by three decisive [historical] coordinates": the codification and institutionalization of a highly formalized academicism in the visual and other arts; the emergence of the key technologies of the second industrial revolution (telephone, radio, automobile, aircraft, etc.); and the imaginative proximity of social revolution (324–25). These three coordinates can be of enormous help and guidance to feminist scholars in tracing the conditions which enabled an unprecedented blossoming of women's literary and artistic production during the first four decades of this century. Among other things, Anderson's first coordinate points to the source not only of the wealth but of the cultural capital of such patrons of the arts as Natalie Clifford Barney, Peggy Guggenheim, and Nancy Cunard. His second coordinate helps to account for the growth in women's mobility, both economic, as women entered the increasing clerical work force, and geographical, as travel became easier and more widely accessible. Significantly, however, that "haze of social revolution drifting across the horizon" (325–26) which Anderson cites as an important aspect of the "overdetermined configuration" of modernism is nowhere in his article associated with the rise of women's suffrage movements or with the rise of modern feminism. (These are issues to which we shall return in Chapters 3 and 6.)

In his emphasis on imagined community, Raymond Williams shares Lukács' commitment to a unified social vision. Williams's essay on "The Bloomsbury fraction" (1980) – although drawing on a paradigmatic, even canonical modernist community – represents an attempt to reinvest "modernism" with hope.[17] In it he raises many of the same issues as Lukács, although Williams's focus is on cultural milieu rather than on cultural products; that is, he is more interested in examining the factors which enable a "fraction" of "an existing upper class" to make social interventions and the consequences of those interventions than in examining the texts, paintings, or social policies produced by the group. Bloomsbury is important as a group, argues Williams, "because so many significant *modern* cultural groups are formed and developed in [the same] way" (152, our emphasis). Unlike Lukács and Anderson, Williams does not completely ignore gender in his discussion of Bloomsbury; indeed, he argues that the Bloomsbury Group can be "separated out as a distinct formation on the basis of ... [its] social and intellectual critique, and the ambiguity of the position of women" or "the specific contradiction between the presence of highly intelligent and intellectual women, within these families, and their relative exclusion from the dominant and formative male institutions" (162). Similarly, Williams's discussion of the formation and place of the individual in Bloomsbury is more complex than Lukács' discussion of modernist subjectivity. Williams argues that while Bloomsbury had a highly evolved "social conscience," this must be distinguished from a "social consciousness" (156) and that, for Bloomsbury, "the social conscience, in the end, is to protect the private consciousness" (167). Williams looks to the novels of Virginia Woolf and E.M. Forster for evidence of the "sensibility ... of the substance of the civilized individual" (165–66), but by doing so overrides crucial differences between the two writers. This indicates a recognition of gender difference on the level of group formation but not on the level of text production, thus creating a problematic gap between social experience and artistic expression.

One question which must be directed at the Williams article is whether there is textual evidence, in Woolf's novels or Bell's paintings, which indicates whether or not "civilized individualism" and "social conscience" meant the same thing for the women of Bloomsbury as for the men.

FEMINIST CONFIGURATIONS

While male theorists of "modernism" have failed to adequately consider gender in their accounts either of the texts or the social formations of "modernism," feminist critics have been active in excavating and reconstructing women's contributions to the field, and evaluating the ways in which the field must be reconfigured as a result. Feminist critics have been at the forefront of the project which Williams described as that of "search[ing] out and counterpos[ing] an alternative tradition taken from the neglected works left in the wide margins of the century" (Williams 1989: 52). The last few years, in particular, have seen unprecedented research activity in the area of women's modernism, from important new studies of single authors and artists (like Diana Souhami's biography of Gluck, Sydney Janet Kaplan's monograph on Katherine Mansfield, and the volume on Djuna Barnes edited by Mary Lynn Broe) to synthetic reevaluations of the period. We will focus here on the period studies and suggest that they fall, very loosely, into three stages.

Like Raymond Williams, many feminist historians of "modernism" have emphasized community (an issue to which we shall return in more detail in Chapter 6). In *Writing for their Lives: The Modernist Women 1910–1940* (1987), Gillian Hanscombe and Virginia L. Smyers take the Bloomsbury Group as a paradigm of modernist community while at the same time arguing that there was "another 'group' or, more accurately, a loose network" of women writers, publishers, and booksellers (2). While more traditional critics of "modernism" emphasize *formal* experimentation and innovation, Hanscombe and Smyers emphasize instead women's experiments with *lifestyle*. Consequently, much of *Writing for their Lives* focuses on the relationships and sexual orientations of "modernist" women. However, Hanscombe and Smyers also differ from traditional critics in their emphasis on women publishers as well as women writers, in this way expanding our understanding of "modernism" as a cultural field. Shari Benstock's study of expatriate modernist women writers, *Women of the Left Bank: Paris, 1900–1940* (1986), similarly emphasizes women's communities; indeed, Benstock puts "the very definition of 'community' ... under examination" (34) in her book, whose three-part organization is governed by a spatial metaphor – discoveries, settlements, crossroads – and many of whose chapter titles invoke particular neighbourhoods and addresses. Like Hanscombe and Smyers, Benstock explores the wide variety of women's engagements with modernism, and the difference of women's *experience* of modernity, particularly in relation to the First World War, often regarded as modernism's crucible. She argues that feminist critical practice will reveal a modernism which will "be seen to be a far more eclectic and richly diverse movement than has previously been assumed" (6). In a slightly later article, "Expatriate modernism: writing on the cultural rim" (1989), she notes parallels between the projects of feminist critics of modernism and the writers they study: "In looking at female Modernists in exile . . . I am also looking at myself and at feminist colleagues whose 'writing on the rim' of modern culture is providing a powerful rewriting of female Modernism" (20).

While the projects of Hanscombe and Smyers and Benstock are largely recuperative, Sandra M. Gilbert and Susan Gubar's projected three-volume study, *No Man's Land: The Place of the Woman Writer in the Twentieth Century* (the first two volumes have been published as of this writing), is synthetic. They argue that literary modernism arose as a reaction to the "woman question" and in response to increasing numbers of women entering the literary marketplace: "Indeed, it is possible to hypothesize that a reaction-formation against the rise of literary women became not just a theme in modernist writing but a motive for modernism" (Gilbert and Gubar 1988: 156). While Benstock's book is organized around a careful and detailed reconstruction of expatriate women's communities in Paris during the first four decades of this century, and Hanscombe's and Smyers's approach is basically historical and biographical, Gilbert's and Gubar's methodology is essentially thematic. This has the advantage of enabling them to organize a huge mass of material, ranging historically from Tennyson's *The Princess* (1847–51) to Suzette Haden Elgin's *Native Tongue* (1984). However, in their often polemical strategy of "conflat[ing] and collat[ing] individual literary narratives, so that they constitute one possible metastory" (Gilbert and Gubar 1988: xiv) and in their emphasis on the "leitmotif" (Gilbert and Gubar 1989: xvi) they undermine the very important differences – economic, social, geographical, political – *between* women active in the field of modernism.

A third stage of feminist engagement in women's literary modernism is represented by Suzanne Clark's *Sentimental Modernism: Women Writers and the Revolution of the Word* (1991) and Marianne DeKoven's *Rich and Strange: Gender, History, Modernism* (1991). These studies differ from those of the first two stages by, firstly, limiting their approaches to issues *within* the field of women's modernism rather than trying to sketch the broad contours of the field, and, secondly, by discussing the ways in which women's modernism anticipates many of the issues and problems of post-modernism. Clark and DeKoven take up similar questions, but from quite different perspectives. Clark's book explores the ways in which American "modernism" marginalized a sentimental discourse typically associated with women; she "examines women's writing for the effects of the modernist revulsion against the sentimental, and their strategies for recovering bonds of emotional identity" (13). Her position is critical of the ways in which the modernist avant-garde accumulated symbolic capital by "gendering mass culture" (4) and, in so doing, separating literature from everyday life (41). DeKoven's study, on the other hand, re-examines the political implications of radical form which, she argues, is characterized by an "unsynthesized dialectic or unresolved contradiction" (25) between fear and desire for the kind of radical social change promised by socialism and feminism.

The fact that the texts discussed above are all feminist *literary* analyses of the field of women's modernism has to do with differences between the disciplines of literary criticism and art history. Art historical studies focus on more narrowly delimited periods and closely defined schools. Three recent examples of feminist art historical archaeology in the field of women's modernism are Whitney Chadwick's *Women Artists and the Surrealist Movement* (1985), *Women and Surrealism*, edited by Mary Ann Caws, Rudolf E. Kuenzli, and Gwen Raaberg (1991), and the collection edited by Teresa Grimes, Judith Collins, and Oriana Baddeley, *Five Women Painters* (1989). While Whitney Chadwick excavates and analyzes the involvement of women artists in the Surrealist movement – ranging from well-known figures like Frida Kahlo and Leonor Fini to lesser known individuals like Grace Pailthorpe and Valentine Hugo – the collection of essays in *Women and Surrealism* not only takes up the work of women artists, but also considers the ways in which women were constructed in visual and verbal discourses of surrealism. Both of these studies, which focus on women's participation in a major avant-garde movement, are thematically organized. In this respect, the studies of surrealism differ from the collection of essays in *Five Women Painters* which address five very diverse case studies of modernist women artists working in Britain: Laura Knight, Nina Hamnett, Dora Carrington, Winnifred Nicholson, and Eileen Agar. Each case study forms the nucleus of a chapter which is organized as a survey of the artist's life and career highlights. A general introductory chapter usefully draws comparisons between the various case studies by looking at the familial and institutional contexts which shaped the careers of British women artists during the first half of the twentieth century. In particular, such factors as educational opportunities, art networking, women's patronage of the arts, career opportunities, audiences, and the notions of a gendered style and imagery receive serious attention.

So far feminist literary and art historical accounts of women's modernism have largely concentrated on the still essential work of the excavation and recovery of lost women writers and artists. However, concurrent with the project of recovery we need detailed examinations – "thick descriptions" – of the conditions which made the blossoming of women's modernism possible *and* the ways in which women modernists either engaged or refused the normative discourses of "modernism." That is, we need both a materialist and a formalist fleshing out of women's modernism.

MODERNIST (IM)POSITIONINGS: THE CASE STUDIES

Modernist (Im)positionings is a feminist, cross-disciplinary, case-study inter-rogation of four key "modernist" terms: the avant-garde, professionalism, genius, and economic disinterestedness. It examines the ways in which women artists and writers within the field of "modernism" are positioned in relation both to male producers of "modernist" texts *and* each other. We are assuming here that "modernism" is not simply a series of discrete texts and images, but a discourse. This means that it is produced by various cultural agents – the writers and artists themselves, publishers, editors, gallery owners, patrons, and subsequent generations of intellectuals and academics – but also that *it is itself productive of meaning*. As a discourse, "modernism" has, in part, a disciplinary function. A hegemonic "modernism," such as that of New Criticism or Formalism which dominated the academy for four decades, privileges some texts and aesthetics, and renders others invisible; it makes some questions inevitable and others unthinkable. Radical experi-mentation with form, for example, is "modernist" while radical experimenta-tion with content is not. These disciplinary distinctions have obvious material effects which work to further reinforce a formalist hegemony by surrounding us with some images and texts while others simply become unavailable: Picasso's *Les Demoiselles d'Avignon* is reproduced in countless coffee-table and text books, Romaine Brooks's *Peter (A Young Girl)* is not; Joyce's *Ulysses* is reprinted, re-edited, re-authorized, Natalie Barney's poems are unread.

Given the authorizing power of such discourses, our decision to retain the term "modernism," in spite of its historical associations, is strategic, as is our decision to focus on the decades normally associated with "modernism" (or, in art history, with early modernism). In a sense, we want to *appropriate* the term and – by teasing out its aporias, its gender blindnesses, its *constructed-ness* – put it to feminist use.[18] Our choice of four key terms as the focus of our interrogation of "modernism" is not exactly arbitrary – they virtually emerged from the material during the four years in which we worked on this project – but neither is it exhaustive. We could as easily have focused on popular culture, cosmopolitanism, or specific literary and artistic move-ments. The same could be said for our choice of writers and artists who, in spite of their obvious differences from canonical male modernists and each other, nevertheless represent a rather narrow corridor of artistic production during the first four decades of this century. Our eight artists and writers are all white, English or American, living and working in three of the four metropolitan centres traditionally associated with "modernism" – New York, London, and Paris.[19] This means that we are unable to consider such crucial issues as the disciplinary function of "race" in constructions of "modernism" and modernist communities, or the cultural imperialism of centre/periphery models of "modernist" production; these are questions we hope to return to in future work. What we hope to accomplish here through our four case studies is, in part, to *trouble* or to "make messy" any easy narrative of literary or art history, whether traditional or feminist.

As our case studies will indicate, the ways in which women writers and artists were (and are) positioned within discourses of modernism vary considerably. Indeed, our notion of positioning is a complex and highly nuanced one which does not facilitate the creation of neat classification systems or totalizing theories. The different experiences of the women we examine – or at least, their textual and visual representations of those experiences – suggest that constructions of the artistic "self" varied widely even within a group of predominantly white middle- and upper-class women working in, or within easy access of, the metropolitan centres of London, Paris, and New York. Complicating assessment of these women's experiences is their precariously slippery place on the peripheries of predominantly masculinist avant-garde movements. Despite the fact that such marginalities have been strategically invested with greater value by late twentieth-century feminists, the women at the centre of this study clearly felt pressured by gender constraints. As a result, they experienced the familiar difficulties of being considered exceptional on the grounds that they failed to meet, exceeded, or ignored prevailing expectations. In terms of our group there was no single or consistent response to such pressures, which came from traditional and avant-garde circles alike (albeit often couched in different rhetorics). Instead, we will see these women adopting diverse social, political, sexual, and cultural stances both within the group and, on occasion, within an individual career.

In what follows, we will situate or *position* the women of our case studies in relation to four regulatory discourses of "modernism" – the avant-garde, professionalism, genius, and economic altruism – and show how these discourses are disrupted and complicated when they are re-examined in light not only of "gender" but of financial privilege. The women of this study inhabited all sorts of often contradictory subject-*positions* as women, creative artists, and professional wage-earners, and their representations of these experiences can help us to better understand the kinds of agency available to women cultural workers within particular social and historical contexts. As is evident from the first two sentences of this paragraph, the word "position" works both as a noun and a transitive verb. A position is "something posited," "a proposition or thesis laid down or stated;" to position is "the action of positing," "affirmation, affirmative assertion" (*OED*). We want to insist upon both parts of speech, both definitions, in our notion of "modernist (im)positionings." Our portmanteau word is intended to evoke the interpellation *but also* the agency of these artists and writers. The women of our case studies were and have continued to *be positioned*, to varying degrees, on the margins of cultural "modernism" but they also *imposed themselves*; they were frequently unwelcome but insistent gate-crashers at the (to impose upon Hemingway) moveable feast of "modernism." They were positioned as both objects and subjects of modernist networks, institutions, and discourses, negotiating (and occasionally acquiescing to) inherited positions and creating new ones. What we are suggesting by looking at the pattern of our case studies is *not* that women were consistently victimized, but rather that they developed diverse strategies for negotiating what were unequal, and thus frequently uneasy, relationships with their male modernist counterparts (and occasionally with each other). Because they occupied a precarious cultural position – outside of mainstream bourgeois culture but not fully within the recognized alternative/oppositional camps of the avant-garde – they needed to secure visibility in order to make their presence felt. In other words, they needed to impose themselves on a public which, for the most part, neither liked the sort of work they produced nor expected it from women writers and artists. Hence the (im)positionings of our title refers not only to the positions in which women writers and artists found themselves, but also to their stubborn negotiation and occasional refusal of those positions.

A position is a "situation, site, station" (*OED*) and thus the concept of (im)positioning is necessarily relational and contextual; it raises questions regarding cultural values and hierarchies – how they have operated in the past and how they might be restructured or even abolished. We will examine the work of women writers and artists who were for the most part, albeit often problematically, associated with the modernist avant-garde as opposed to more established cultural institutions. As we will argue in Chapters 2 and 5, the term "avant-garde" is inextricably bound to questions of positionality within bourgeois culture. Casting themselves as oppositional, various early twentieth-century avant-garde groups adopted innovative languages, values, and practices in order to criticize what they perceived as mainstream or philistine cultural ideals. While the politics of various avant-garde movements have been endlessly (and some would argue futilely[20]) debated, women have figured only peripherally in such discussions. Susan Suleiman has usefully conceptualized the problem by pointing to women's "double-marginality" as historical sexual and social outsiders. Something of women's paradoxical relationship to the avant-garde can be seen in our case studies where women were often initially attracted to ostensibly anti-bourgeois movements only to find them no more sexually tolerant than the patriarchal families they had escaped. The problem of how avant-garde the avant-garde wasn't when it came to questions of gender occasionally left the women of our case studies disillusioned and isolated. This was especially true of Vanessa Bell, Romaine Brooks and Djuna Barnes, who became more and more reclusive during the course of their careers.[21] As we will see, however, other women responded differently. Both Natalie Barney and Marie Laurencin developed circles of women that functioned as alternative support networks.

In Barney's case this involved organizing a lesbian salon, as well as initiating a lifelong relationship with the artist, Romaine Brooks, while Laurencin relied on several very close personal rather than professional friendships. Virginia Woolf was relatively protected within the confines of Bloomsbury, although, as we have argued, this also led to a certain isolation from other women in the avant-garde. Despite these circumstances, her feminist criticism was probably the most explicit and comprehensive of all the women in our study, and her co-ownership of The Hogarth Press, which gave her full control over the production and distribution of her work, enabled her to experiment freely in her creative and polemical writing. Gertrude Stein and Nina Hamnett seem to have negotiated their position in the avant-garde by flamboyantly adopting what were conventionally seen as male guises: genius in the case of the former, and bohemianism in the case of the latter. Although Stein and Hamnett clearly believed they possessed such qualities, they seem to have self-consciously emphasized them, perhaps to prove their avant-garde credentials. The women we consider sometimes also chose to work in styles, genres, media, and contexts which were seen as "in the feminine" and hence devalued as marginal, derivative, passé, or compromised. Rather than dismissing such work, or placing it in a separatist ghetto, we argue that it should be seen as an integral component of larger cultural patterns.

The notion of an "expanded cultural field," as elaborated by Pierre Bourdieu and others, helps us to understand what is at stake in adopting any particular cultural position or mode. From this perspective, cultural practitioners and consumers are neither disinterested nor transcendent, but are enmeshed in a messy material and ideological world with its systems of gender and sexual orientation, race and ethnicity, geography, money, and politics. This intersection of positionality and self-representation lies at the heart of our project. In the process of insisting upon their creative identities and inserting themselves into various "modernist" discourses, these women added new (and awkwardly fitting) layers of meaning to them. The word "position" has a further arithmetical meaning which is also relevant to our methodology as feminist critics excavating forgotten details of women's cultural production and reevaluating its place within more traditional constructions of "modernism": "A method of finding the value of an unknown quantity by positing or assuming one or more values for it, finding by how much the results differ from the actual data of the problem, and then adjusting the error. Also called *rule of (false) position, rule of falsehood, rule of trial and error*" (*OED*, italics in original). Our case-study approach is a kind of reverse enactment – an (im)positioning – of the rule of (false) position in that we evaluate various "actual data" of modernism (existing modernist discourses, canons, and institutions) by positing or assuming a value in the cultural work of various women artists and writers; we then add new layers of meaning to received "modernist" discourses. The case-study approach offers us a productive tension between, on the one hand, the detailed

18

re-creation of particular moments and terms of women's cultural production, and, on the other hand, the opportunity for speculation about "modernism" as a broad discursive field. Thus in addition to examining how the discursive field of modernism has been shaped, we also need to see how the women of our case studies were positioned within that field. In other words, we need to know how their material resources enabled or limited their cultural agency. It is hardly surprising that the issue of money seems to have been the most imposing factor in these women's literary, aesthetic, and personal lives. Although questions of money reappear throughout the book, it is crucial to preface our case studies with a description of the financial resources our subjects had at their disposal. In the remaining pages of this first chapter we explore how the financial positions of the women in our study affected their representations of themselves as writers and artists as well as the ways those self-representations circulated and were read by their modernist contemporaries and subsequent critics. In other words, we will examine how money (or the lack of it) related to their symbolic capital.[22]

In terms of cold, hard cash, Natalie Clifford Barney and Romaine Brooks were the wealthiest women of our study. Both received large inheritances which had been founded primarily on nineteenth-century expansionist enterprises.[23] Barney's wealth was derived on her father's side from mining and transportation, and on her mother's side from whisky. Her father, Albert Clifford Barney, inherited the Barney Car Works, a railroad car foundry which he sold to the Pullman Sleeping Car Company. He retired on the profits and, together with his wife, Alice Pike Barney, a painter, embarked on establishing a prominent social life in Washington D.C. (Wickes 1976: 18–20; Benstock 1986: 269). Upon her father's death in 1902, when she was 26 years old, Natalie Barney inherited $2.5 million; when her mother remarried in 1911, she inherited a further $1.5 million. As her biographers point out, Barney seldom alluded to the source of her wealth, preferring instead to reconstruct a family history that stressed her historical ties to France, her adopted country and one she associated with the cultural rather than the financial (Chalon 1979: 9; Wickes 1976: 16–18). Although we do not have the exact figures of her inheritance, Romaine Brooks was also enormously wealthy; unlike Barney, however, a break with her family meant that she experienced several years of extreme poverty before coming into her inheritance in 1902. Upon the deaths of her mother and brother, Brooks and her sister inherited the estate of Isaac Waterman, her maternal grandfather, who had amassed a fortune from coal mines in Salt Lake City and Kingston, Pennsylvania (Secrest 1974). Like Barney, Brooks claimed to be more interested in cultural rather than material circumstances. However, in spite of such disclaimers, both women used their wealth to experiment – Barney more publicly, Brooks more privately – with self-representation and lifestyle.

Barney's direct patronage of modernist enterprises – effected, as we will discuss in Chapter 5, largely through Ezra Pound (Wickes 1976: 160–65) – was less sustained than that of other women such as Peggy Guggenheim or Bryher (the chosen name of Winnifred Ellerman). Instead Barney channelled most of her resources and energy into creating an enclosed community of women writers, with its own systems of artistic production and distribution which allowed her an unusually high degree of control over her various visual and literary incarnations. Barney's home in the rue Jacob on the Left Bank was the site of the famous lesbian salon established by her in 1909; the salon, however, was Barney's second attempt to found a utopian lesbian community. In 1904 she and the poet Renée Vivien had travelled to the island of Lesbos with the intention of establishing a "Sapphic school of poetry;" while this school never materialized, in 1927 Barney did establish her *Académie des femmes*, "a counterpart to the Académie Française," which did not admit any women until 1980 (Jay 1988: 73, 33). In *Aventures de l'esprit* (1929) Barney provided detailed sketches and appreciations of many of the women writers associated with her academy including Colette, Mina Loy, Djuna Barnes, and Gertrude Stein. The *Académie des femmes*, designed in part to bring about an *"entente"* between English, American, and French women writers, also provided intellectual and social support for these writers and occasionally, as with Djuna Barnes's *Ladies Almanack*, raised donations and subscriptions toward the private publication of works.

While Barney used her wealth in part to create communities of women artists, it also enabled her to experiment with both visual and literary self-representations. As a young woman, Barney frequently adopted the persona and costume of "the page," both in her poetry and in her lesbian relationships. Wickes describes one evening in the spring of 1902 when "Disguised as street singers, [Barney] and the opera star Emma Calvé serenaded Renée [Vivien] … that is, Calvé sang the lament of Orpheus for his Eurydice, and when Renée opened her window, Natalie threw her a bouquet containing a sonnet in which she begged to see her" (Wickes 1976: 63–4). A photograph of Barney in a page costume with Vivien documents another such occasion (see frontispiece). Obviously, such elaborate stagings of one's fantasies and desires do not come cheaply. Somewhat later, Barney developed the persona of "the Amazon" as alluded to in the titles of two of her collections of pensées, *Pensées d'une amazone* (1920) and *Nouvelles pensées de l'amazone* (1939), and had herself photographed and painted in her riding habit as she had earlier been photographed in her page costume.[24] (See Brooks's portrait of Barney as *L'Amazone* in 1920 (Figure 2.2).) As Karla Jay points out, Barney's internalization of these personae is not unproblematic for they are "informed with the power relations that had given rise" to them (Jay 1988: 92). While Barney's wealth enabled her to live out a number of alternative identities, it also effectively protected her from having to think through the real implications of the power relations suggested by some of her costumes.

Chez Durand-Ruel, se révèle une artiste américaine de la plus profonde originalité: Mrs Brooks. Elle y expose des portraits et des tableaux de vu où s'atteste une recherche passionnée du caractère et qui sont peints dans des tona-lités harmonieuses. « L'art de Mrs Brooks, dit son préfacier, est un art de définition forte et d'expression exquise ». Nous donnons ici le portrait de Mrs Brooks dans son salon, à Paris, qui n'est pas moins original que sa peinture.

Figure 1.1 Photograph of Romaine Brooks at the piano (c. 1910–11). National Collection of Research Materials on Romaine Brooks, Archives of American Art, Smithsonian Institution.

Unlike Barney, who was always attracted to the *demi-monde*, Brooks entered the *haut monde* when she moved to a mansion in the fashionable avenue de Trocadero in 1908. Indeed, the earliest publicly circulated portrait photographs from the period show the artist as a society lady.[25] A typical example is one from around 1910–11 (Figure 1.1) which accompanied some of the press publicity surrounding her first exhibition at the Durand–Ruel Gallery. Here Brooks is shown demurely attired in a dark velvet dress and seated at the piano in her tastefully (and originally designed) black-and-white-and-grey drawing room.[26] By 1925, however, Brooks presented a very different image of herself as evidenced by another press photograph (Figure 1.2) where she stands in a gallery wearing a tailored man's suit. Significantly, the caption beneath the photograph describes her paintings as "remarkably forceful."[27] Evidently, as Brooks secured a certain degree of public recognition for her work, she felt more comfortable openly depicting her transvestite lesbian lifestyle in press photographs as well as in her publicly exhibited portraits of herself and friends. In 1923 she painted her famous *Self-Portrait* (Figure 2.1) which was widely exhibited in 1925 and received extensive press commentary. Clearly Brooks took great pleasure in the fact that as a woman and painter she had succeeded in the eyes of the world. Recalling her first exhibition in her unpublished autobiography, she noted:

> My exhibition had brought me into the limelights [sic] and I was now an easy target for all those who could not accept what seemed to them an unfair distribution of things. I remember meeting Boldini at a fete. Looking at me with ill-humour he said – "Que avoir des bras comme ceux-la et savoir peindre!" [sic] I sensed his antagonism and concluded that Boldini would naturally prefer surface values for women. Even his earliest paintings show that he could paint only these.
>
> (Brooks n.d.: 223)

Although Barney and Brooks were both extremely wealthy and had become lovers by the late 1910s, they pursued quite different strategies of self-representation which in turn underscore their different views of lesbian sexuality. While Barney fostered various circles of women (in particular her salon) and celebrated what she considered feminine values, Brooks adopted a somewhat stagey transvestite persona – perhaps in defence against what she saw as a hostile world. Evidently Brooks always viewed herself as something of a social outcast. Her increasingly reclusive tendencies – summed up by the Sartrean observation that "Hell is other people" (quoted in Secrest 1974: 204) – led her to largely abandon exhibiting her work by the late 1920s and, eventually, to withdraw from all but a close circle of friends. As her career progressed, she became increasingly fond of her paintings, refusing to sell or give them away. A photograph of her taken near the end of her life (Figure 1.3) shows the artist at home literally surrounded by her portraits. In this sense Brooks's wealth affected both her reputation as a "serious" artist and

Romaine Brooks whose remarkably forceful paintings aroused much favorable comment at her recent exposition in the Charpentier Gallery.

Figure 1.2 Photograph of Romaine Brooks in a man's suit (*c.* 1925). National Collection of Research Materials on Romaine Brooks, Archives of American Art, Smithsonian Institution.

Figure 1.3 Photograph of Romaine Brooks surrounded by her portraits (n.d.). National Collection of Research Materials on Romaine Brooks, Archives of American Art, Smithsonian Institution.

her market value, as Meryle Secrest explains: "The situation was complicated by the fact that her work had never had a market value. Because she never needed to sell, she never let her canvases be bought, never had a dealer, and never underwent the rough-and-ready competition of the marketplace" (Secrest 1974: 131). As Bourdieu's studies of cultural distinctions remind us, financial capital and symbolic capital are related but not necessarily coincidental and, by relying on her financial capital to underwrite her refusal to enter the cultural marketplace, Brooks's symbolic capital was significantly depleted.

If we have dealt at some length with the financial positioning of Natalie Barney and Romaine Brooks, this is because in possessing the sort of wealth that enabled them to create their own worlds, they differed considerably from the other women in this study. Despite the fact that Vanessa Bell, Virginia Woolf, and Gertrude Stein all had substantial middle-class inheritances that provided for such basic "necessities" as respectable accommodation and domestic help (and even the judicious purchase of relatively inexpensive avant-garde pictures), all three were very interested in the "extra" money they could earn from their creative work. For instance, as we discuss in Chapters 3 and 4, Woolf, Bell, and Stein clearly articulated their pleasure at receiving professional payment. In terms of financial resources, both Virginia and Vanessa Stephen were left enough money to support themselves by their father, Leslie Stephen, upon whose death they were able to take a house in Bloomsbury and maintain a middle-class, if slightly bohemian, lifestyle.[28] After her marriage to Clive Bell, whose family had considerable resources, Vanessa Bell was further provided with basic expenses for herself and her children.[29] Woolf was very conscious of the differences between herself and those women who had to find, rather than supplement, their living, discussing these differences at some length in such essays as her "Memories of a working women's guild." Even if they did not have to support themselves (and perhaps especially because of this), Woolf and Bell wanted to avoid being dismissed as amateurs or dilettantes, and receiving appropriate payment for their work was one of the ways in which they could assess whether it was being taken seriously. In the cases of Woolf and Bell, this need to be taken seriously precluded any elaborate self-styling or flamboyant displays of deviance beyond a tendency to dress and socialize informally (which was, in any case, the sort of eccentricity that was normally tolerated within all but the most rigid sectors of the English middle class).

Significantly, while Barney used her vast wealth to stage elaborate seductions, found a salon and an *Académie des femmes*, and to have her work privately published, Virginia and Leonard Woolf used their much more modest incomes to found The Hogarth Press in 1917. For the first six years, The Hogarth Press operated essentially as a small cottage industry with publications available solely by subscription; Leonard Woolf describes how "we printed in the larder, bound books in the dining-room, interviewed printers, binders, and authors in the sitting-room" (L. Woolf 1967: 77). The two objects of the Press were to provide Virginia with a hobby which would be "sufficiently absorbing to take her mind off her work" (L. Woolf 1964: 233) and "to produce and publish short works which commercial publishers could not or would not publish, like T.S. Eliot's poems, Virginia's *Kew Gardens*, and Katherine Mansfield's *Prelude*" (L. Woolf 1967: 66). The Hogarth Press authors list eventually comprised many of the leading writers and thinkers of the day, including, together with Eliot and Mansfield, E.M. Forster, Gertrude Stein, Laura Riding, Robert Graves, C. Day Lewis, Christopher Isherwood, John Maynard Keynes, and Herbert Read. Furthermore, the Press offered new translations of Rilke, Chekhov, and Freud (the complete standard edition of whose works they eventually published). Not only were Leonard and Virginia Woolf able to introduce new writers to the reading public, they were also able to experiment with forms of discourse and writing that were not profitable enough to interest the larger commercial publishers; these included not only short works like Mansfield's *Prelude*, but a series of pamphlets – conceived as commentaries on "contemporary political and social problems as well as on art and criticism" (L. Woolf 1967: 161) – which began as The Hogarth Essays and eventually branched out into four other series.[30] Through her co-ownership and operation of The Hogarth Press, Virginia Woolf was involved in the production of her books from inception to sale and was thus hugely aware not only of economies of cultural production, but of the market value of various authors. Moreover, as she noted in her diary of 1925, the Press freed her from what she clearly perceived as a male-dominated publishing industry: "I'm the only woman in England free to write what I like. The others must be thinking of series' & editors" (Woolf 1980a: 43).[31]

In many ways, Gertrude Stein's early career resembled that of the Stephen sisters although, as her career progressed, she adopted very different strategies of self-representation. Like Woolf and Bell, Stein lost both her parents at an early age – in her case in her teens. While Michael, her older brother (then aged 26), took over as head of the family and master of its assets, Gertrude and her younger brother, Leo, were sent off to continue their education. Eventually, after abandoning the possibility of a medical career, Gertrude settled with Leo in Paris where together they studied and collected the work of various Parisian avant-garde artists. It should be emphasized that their famous collection was built upon the fairly modest allowance that Michael gave them to live upon which, according to Leo, usually amounted to about $150 a month for pictures, books, and travel.[32] While Stein always had enough money to support herself (and was maintained in considerable domestic comfort during her long relationship with Alice Toklas), she was nevertheless delighted to start earning substantial sums of money when she published *The Autobiography of Alice B. Toklas* in 1933 at the age of 59. As we discuss in Chapter 4, Stein's sudden popular and financial success threw her into what we would now call an identity crisis: could she be rich and popular and still be a genius? However, her success also prompted her to write a series of articles on money – typically titled "Money," "All about money," "More about money," "Still more about money," and "My last about money" – for the 1936 *Saturday Evening Post*. These articles, which, as she acknowledges in *Everybody's Autobiography*, were perceived by "the young ones" as "reactionary" (Stein 1937: 310–11), call for government fiscal restraint in highly conservative, bourgeois, and even heterosexist terms: "So, now please, everybody, everybody everybody, please, is money money, and if it is, it ought to be the same whether it is what a father of a family earns and spends or a government, if it isn't sooner or later there is disaster" (Stein 1967: 333).

Marie Laurencin's case falls somewhere between the middle-class experiences of Bell, Woolf, and Stein and those of poorer women such as Barnes and Hamnett. As we discuss in our fourth chapter, Laurencin, the illegitimate daughter of a seamstress, started out with very meagre resources. Certainly she took quite a risk when she abandoned the financially safer option of a teaching career in favour of the considerably shakier one of avant-garde artist. Not surprisingly, during the early stages of her artistic career, Laurencin created something of a social stir as Apollinaire's young, unconventional companion. In some senses, one imagines she adopted a performative persona as some form of social compensation for the fact that, unlike most of her avant-garde contemporaries, she was not of bourgeois origin. Similarly it might be argued that the negative representations of Laurencin in the writings of Gertrude Stein and Fernande Olivier, for example, stemmed at least partly from class prejudice. Nevertheless, after a long and successful career, Laurencin eventually secured a thoroughly middle-class lifestyle as the owner of a modern Parisian flat as well as a house in the countryside. The fact that she attained such success entirely on her own (without the security of an inheritance or a husband's income) was clearly a source of pride. Although she can be criticized for producing formulaic work that catered to public expectations, she did not have the luxury of being too avant-garde or experimental to sell. While she always presented herself, in interviews as well as in her self-portraits, as a supremely feminine woman, she more often than not claimed a separate but equal status for feminine values and critiqued the social structures which denigrated them.

In contrast, Djuna Barnes and Nina Hamnett did not end up enjoying the sort of security that Laurencin worked so hard to achieve despite the fact that each was quite celebrated during her youth. Unlike the other women of this study, Barnes and Hamnett often lived in extreme poverty. As we discuss in Chapter 5, each had to work to support her writing or her art – Barnes as a journalist, writing and illustrating her own articles, and Hamnett as an artist's model. Each relied heavily on handouts and hand-me-downs, and each was forced to cultivate marketable social identities – Barnes as a great beauty with a cutting wit, and Hamnett as something of a Bohemian clown. The voyeuristic gaze to which these women subjected themselves in order to earn a living is perhaps nowhere more obvious than in Hamnett's autobiographies, *Laughing Torso* (1932) and *Is She A Lady?* (1955), which she admitted to writing for money. On both sides of the family, Nina Hamnett's relatives had been in the civil service. Her military officer father had been the son of an Indian civil servant and her mother the daughter of a naval officer. However, in 1904 (when Hamnett was 16) her father was court-martialled for accepting bribes and left the army in disgrace to drive a taxi-cab in London. After showing no aptitude for apprenticing in the post office, Hamnett was allowed to attend art school because it was free. Unable to buy paints and canvas and living at home, an uncle arranged for Hamnett to receive an advance of £50 from money left by her paternal grandfather. In addition to this some aunts gave her an allowance of two shillings and sixpence per week. Supplementing this income by giving private painting lessons, she managed to rent an independent studio for seven shillings and sixpence per week. The rent scarcely left her with enough money for food and other necessities (Hooker 1986: 28, 31) and her autobiographies are riddled with comments on money, difficult living conditions, and shortages of food together with long lists of those with whom she met to socialize and discuss art. Aside from her work, which she sold intermittently (especially at exhibitions, to friends, and to little magazines), her social connections were her lifeline for she depended on being such good company that she would be invited to visit, as well as offered cast-off clothing and the odd gift of money to support her painting and travel. She also modelled for such other artists as Roger Fry, Jacob Kramer, and Henri Gaudier-Brzeska. In many ways, her modelling was an extension of her public role as an exhibitionist bohemian clown – knowing and being known by everyone who frequented the avant-garde circles of London and Paris, performing endless introductions.[33] Hamnett seems to have had little interest in learning to manage her erratic income: when she had money she spent it freely and made no attempt to put anything away. Basil Bunting's comment on Nina in a letter to Alix Strachey sums up her situation: "Nina Hamnett subsists miraculously by rare falls of manna on the stormy coasts of Bohemia" (quoted in Collins 1989: 76).

Like Hamnett, Djuna Barnes was forced to support herself from an early age when she left her highly unconventional family in rural New York state to work as a freelance journalist in New York City. By 1913 she was earning $15 for an article or a picture, using this money to sustain herself and to contribute to the support of her mother, three brothers, and a grandmother (Field 1985: 13–14). As we shall see in Chapter 5, she wrote for most of the major New York newspapers before going to Paris sometime around 1920. There she soon acquired a reputation for elegance despite the fact her clothes were often borrowed and cobbled together from the cast-offs of richer friends such as Peggy Guggenheim. Recalling one such example, Peggy

Guggenheim recorded in her autobiography:

> Helen Fleishman told me to give Djuna some underwear. A disagreeable scandal ensued as the underwear I gave was Kayser silk and it was darned. I had three distinct sets of underwear: the best, which I had decorated with French lace and which I was saving for my trousseau; my second best that was new, but unadorned, and that which I sent to Djuna. After she complained, I sent her the second best sets.
>
> (Guggenheim 1979 (orig. pub. 1946): 28)

Clearly these incidents caused Barnes considerable resentment. Later, after giving up journalism to devote herself more fully to her writing, Barnes was still dependent upon the minimal patronage she continued to receive from Peggy Guggenheim, Natalie Barney, and, occasionally, Samuel Beckett. In 1939, when war broke out, Guggenheim paid for Barnes's passage back to New York where she rented the one-room apartment in Greenwich Village that would be her home for the next forty years. In 1942 she wrote to ask Robert McAlmon for twenty dollars to settle a dentist's bill: "I live on less than $20 a month for food – in fact $25 is all I have for *everything*" (quoted in Hanscombe and Smyers 1987: 103).

Judith Collins's observation about Nina Hamnett also applies to Djuna Barnes: "People responded to Nina because she was dashing and outrageous; she broke taboos of femininity and conventional morality and refused to be constrained by the limitations expected of a woman. But in placing her life and work before the public gaze she made herself vulnerable" (Collins 1989: 80). Indeed, one tentative conclusion that we can draw from our case studies is that the wealthier the woman artist or writer, the more control she was able to exert over the ways in which her representations (composed either by herself or by others) circulated. Thus representations *of* and *by* Hamnett – working as an artists' model or selling sketches for a train fare – circulated relatively freely while Brooks retained almost absolute possession of her own images. Ironically, however, although Barney and Brooks could create an effectively closed cultural economy of their own – and, it must be emphasized, to a large degree their lesbianism forced such an economy upon them – their art could suffer as a result.

In very different ways, our four case-study chapters act as gremlins in the machinery or technology of a "modernism" which is often characterized by its rejection of bourgeois materialism and the transcendence of regional, national, and factional differences in the quest for universal values. However, our case studies, which are organized around various couplings of the literary and the visual, also reveal alternative forms of cultural agency, from which we can learn today. Chapter 2 focuses on the writer Natalie Barney and the portraitist Romaine Brooks, lovers for half a century, and interrogates the degree to which theories of the avant-garde are unable to account for the strategic deployment of inherited images and genres by marginalized groups.

Chapter 3 focuses on the sisterly relationship of writer Virginia Woolf and painter Vanessa Bell, and examines the ways in which a rhetoric of professionalism differently inflected both their choice of genres and their self-representation. Chapter 4 centres on the writer Gertrude Stein and the painter Marie Laurencin, two women who moved in the same artistic circle but represented themselves and their abilities so differently that intimacy between them was impossible. This chapter contrasts Stein's identification with the notion of artistic genius with Laurencin's more ambivalent self-representation and self-positioning as an artist. Chapter 5 looks at two women – Djuna Barnes and Nina Hamnett – who needed to earn their livelihood as visual and literary artists, and examines the degree to which their work across two fields was often driven by financial necessity. It argues that serious critical assessment of their work has been impeded by the fact that both women frequently resorted to selling avant-garde culture to wider bourgeois publics by publishing popular magazine articles and sensational autobiographies. Chapter 6 examines the working strategies these women artists and writers used when negotiating the geographical spaces and political issues which shaped the modernist field.

2

FLEURS DU MAL OR SECOND-HAND ROSES?

Natalie Barney, Romaine Brooks, and the "originality of the avant-garde"

[W]hen at fifteen I read Oscar Wilde's short stories, my artistic vocation was decided.

Natalie Barney (quoted in Jullian 1969)

Perhaps [Lord Alfred Douglas] saw in me a dark edition of his own unquenchable youth hiding a like rebellion against the world and its censure. I certainly saw in him a "lapidé." How could it be otherwise ... a friend of Oscar Wilde. To me the attraction lay precisely in that direction.

Romaine Brooks, "No pleasant memories"

As the epigraphs to this chapter suggest, the figure of Oscar Wilde – together with those of other fin-de-siècle dandies and decadents – continued to resonate for Natalie Barney and Romaine Brooks (and for other modernist women writers and artists, like Djuna Barnes) long after he and his work had become passé within an emerging modernist avant-garde. Barney, in particular, seems to have felt a profound sympathetic identification with Wilde. A brief and accidental childhood meeting with him – recounted slightly differently in her 1929 memoir *Aventures de l'esprit* and a 1969 interview (see Jullian 1969: 231) – was later represented by her as formative, her "première aventure". Wilde apparently rescued the 5-year-old Barney from a group of teasing boys at a seaside resort, sat her on his knee, and told her a story. Barney claims that one immediate result of this encounter was her insistence on being dressed as Wilde's fairy-tale Happy Prince when she sat for her portrait by Carolus-Duran, a portrait which later served as the frontispiece to her first book of poetry, *Quelque portraits-sonnets de femmes* (1900). The inclusion of the Happy Prince portrait in this volume of explicitly lesbian love poems, published in the year of Wilde's death, may have been intended

31

Figure 2.1 Romaine Brooks, *Self-Portrait* (1923). Oil on canvas. 117.5 × 68.3 cm.
National Museum of American Art, Smithsonian Institution, gift of the artist.

as homage to a man who had contributed so hugely to her self-fashioning. Certainly Barney's biographers have called attention to the degree to which she seems – though perhaps largely retrospectively – to have modelled her personal and professional life on Wilde's. She was engaged for a few weeks to Lord Alfred Douglas, a match her father unsurprisingly declared unsuitable; she had an affair and a long friendship with Wilde's niece, Dolly Wilde, whose death inspired the series of anguished poems which concludes the volume *In Memory of Dorothy Ierne Wilde*, edited by Barney in 1951; and, as a writer, she saw herself primarily as a Wildean epigrammist (Wickes 1976: 11–12).[1] Romaine Brooks's identification with the decadent dandy is evident not only in her choice of costume in such self-representations as her 1923 *Self-Portrait* (Figure 2.1) and her choice of other cross-dressed sitters like Gluck (Figure 2.3) and Una, Lady Troubridge, but also in her sense of herself as one of "les lapidés," outcasts. As she claims in her unpublished memoir, "No pleasant memories": "In some dark corner of my inner consciousness these [early childhood] experiences had sown what would soon take the form of a secret craving for the negative exultation of those who are solitary and adrift" (Brooks n.d.: 22). Just as Brooks's visual aesthetics owe much to fin-de-siècle painters like Whistler, so the self-fashioning evident in her memoir – ripe with references to Baudelarian gardens whose "scent without sweetness might kill" (196) – owes much to late nineteenth-century literary decadence.

How can we understand the centrality of what appears to be a largely masculine decadent aesthetic in the lives and work of women like Barney and Brooks? Certainly fin-de-siècle decadence has proven problematic for many twentieth-century feminist critics such as Elaine Showalter who points out in *Sexual Anarchy* that the decadent aesthetic rejects all that is "natural" in favour of the artifical; anti-naturalism, according to Showalter, "inevitably leads to antifeminism; women were seen as closer to 'Nature,' to the body, and to a crude materialism, while men were aligned with 'Art,' to the intellect, and to spiritualism" (Showalter 1990: 170). Regenia Gagnier also notes an "antifeminist thread running through the polemical homosexual literature of the period" (Gagnier 1986: 41). And yet it should be stressed that late Victorian critics understood "the decadent and the New Woman [to be] twin apostles of social apocalypse" (Dowling 1979: 447) in their rejection of "normal" or "natural" social roles. However, even given this identification by the late Victorian public, why would Barney and Brooks have adopted the masculine form of the pairing? Although neither Barney nor Brooks practised a consistent politics – indeed, Brooks could be not only apolitical but fiercely antisocial – Barney nonetheless saw herself as a kind of *cultural* feminist, committed to furthering the work and associations of women writers. How did she reconcile her use of a decadent rhetoric, thematics, and pose with her support of women's cultural activity? And how did both Barney and Brooks understand their appeal to an aesthetic which was already "old-fashioned" by the time they began writing and painting, which had already been strategically "disavowed" by a largely masculine modernist avant-garde? For, as Linda Dowling argues, "by treating aestheticism and decadence as the last exotic pendants of a hopelessly frumpish Victorianism modernists made modernism newer, fathering themselves" (Dowling 1977: xvi). A closer scrutiny of the work of some *women* modernists, however, reveals a continuing appeal to the themes, images, and "poses" of late nineteenth-century decadence. This may help to account for the conspicuous shortage of women writers and artists who have been classified as avant-garde in the standard literary and art historical surveys of the early twentieth century. Instead of appearing as strikingly original and fashionably vanguard, the work of women writers and artists has, more often than not, been described as derivative, deviant, old-fashioned, and second-rate. Evidently mainstream bourgeois culture draws important distinctions between those privileged outsiders who are recognized as daringly advanced and a whole host of insignificant "others" whose differences are simply uninteresting.

Through our examination of the work of Barney and Brooks we want to address two issues. The first is the question of how differences are constituted as significant in the avant-garde discourses of twentieth-century culture. One of the most important mechanisms for differentiating between *and evaluating* various forms of deviance and marginality has been the binary opposition of original/copy. This opposition, more often than not, has marked the difference between masculine and feminine creative work in critical reconstructions of avant-garde modernism. However, the valorizing of "originality" in avant-garde discourse – neatly summed up in Ezra Pound's exhortation to "make it new" – is also conflated with a celebration of "the difficult," and little critical attention has been paid to the political and social effectiveness of such strategies.[2] One ironic consequence of this is that although the "margins" continue to be celebrated as feminine spaces, the women who inhabit them remain critically insignificant unless they accept an individualist ethos and produce recognizably "original" work.[3] The second issue we want to address is the question of why so many early modernist women resurrected the literary and visual styles of the decadents, symbolists, and aesthetes of the late nineteenth century. We will argue that while this "borrowing" or "echoing" of earlier styles has led to a critical devaluation of their work as derivative and second-rate, its strategic importance can only be understood within the context of an emerging discourse surrounding feminine, and especially lesbian, sexuality. Our focus on the work of writer and salonist Natalie Barney and painter Romaine Brooks will suggest that they have been constructed as "second-hand" artists in three overlapping areas: their work has been seen as of only secondary interest to their lives; they have been described as working in "old-fashioned" genres; and their lesbian sexuality (particularly that of cross-dresser Brooks), which formed the basis of much of their artistic production, was regarded as a pale copy of heterosexual norms. We are not interested here in evaluating their work or in arguing that it *should* be included in avant-garde literary or art historical canons. Rather, we want to reconstruct *their* reasons for making the artistic choices they did. The fact that both women were intrigued by representing themselves and their friends reveals much about how they imagined their positions – an imagining which sometimes bears little resemblance to their subsequent positioning in literary and art historical criticism.

THE "ORIGINALITY OF THE AVANT-GARDE"?

In keeping with the subject of this chapter, our subtitle is *borrowed* from a 1981 essay by Rosalind E. Krauss. In "The originality of the avant-garde," Krauss points to the fact that "[o]ne thing only seems to hold fairly constant in the vanguardist discourse and that is the theme of originality;" she then notes the ways in which the notion of "originality" is "bound together in a kind of aesthetic economy" with a notion of repetition; and, finally, she deconstructs the "originality/repetition" binary, concluding that both the avant-garde and modernism *"depend on"* (our emphasis) a repression of the second term of that binary code. While Krauss's essay grounds our own analysis of the critical reception of such artists as Barney and Brooks, we want to further her argument by considering two related issues which she does not discuss: the ways in which the second term of that binary has been feminized, and the ways in which the avant-garde – and especially the modernist avant-garde – has been consistently constructed in the masculine. In this model, men artists and writers are originators while women artists and writers are derivative, offering pale copies or translations of their colleagues' more "seminal" work. A recent article by Lori Chamberlain on the "sexualization" of translation metaphors traces the ways in which translation has itself been culturally constructed as "derivative" *and thus* feminine, as opposed to authorship which is "original" *and thus* masculine. Authorship is overdetermined as a relation of production and therefore of an engendering authority, while translation is a relation of re-production and therefore of a corresponding lack of authority. Chamberlain notes that "translation" is itself a metaphor which can cover a broad range of cultural activities:

> The cultural elaboration of this view suggests that in the original abides what is natural, truthful, and lawful, in the copy, what is artificial, false and treasonous. Translations can be, for example, echoes (in musical terms), copies or portraits (in painterly terms), or borrowed or ill-fitting clothes (in sartorial terms).
>
> (Chamberlain 1988: 455)

Chamberlain's elaboration of the translation metaphor helps us to understand why Brooks's portraits of cross-dressed lesbian artists, writers, and musicians – portraits whose *content* was clearly "original" in the sense that no one else was attending to these subjects – have been critically constructed as derivative and second-rate. In avant-garde terms her portraits represent mere copies of subjects who are themselves "copies" of a heterosexual "original" or "natural."[4]

The denigration of the copyist has been explored in the visual arts by Linda Nochlin who points out that realism is falsely perceived by its detractors as "a 'discovery' of preexisting objects out there or a simple 'translation' of ready-made reality into art" (Nochlin 1973: 25). Here the notion of copyist refers not only to the realist who directly transcribes nature but also to the practice of copying masterpieces, an activity that was especially important before the advent of photographic reproduction. Although copyists were often highly skilled specialists, their lack of originality meant that they were regarded as a lower order of artist (see Duro 1986 and 1988). This denigration of realism appears in Roger Fry's foundational modernist criticism where a dichotomy is set up between "fidelity to appearance" and the more highly valued "purely aesthetic criteria" (see Fry 1981: 8–9 and Nochlin 1973: 37–38). According to Fry, the purer art becomes, the less it can be related to the material world, which in turn leads to the increasing rarification of its audience. (Although Nochlin explores the class biases of a modernist position that rejects the mundane world of the masses, she does not consider its gender implications.) Clement Greenberg's 1939 essay, "Avant-garde and kitsch," heroized the avant-garde by ascribing to it a "superior consciousness of history" born out of "the first bold development of scientific revolutionary thought in Europe" (Greenberg 1961: 4). In "search of the absolute" the avant-garde owes "obedience" only to "some worthy constraint or original;" that is, to "the disciplines and process of art and literature themselves" (5–6). It is, however, significant that Greenberg's construction of the avant-garde depends upon his construction of "kitsch" as its binary opposite. Unlike Greenberg, Peter Bürger's definition of the avant-garde is not dependent upon the construction of a binary opposite. The avant-garde is distinguished from other art movements not by its style but by its project, the targeting of "art as an institution, and the course its development took in bourgeois society" (Bürger 1984: 22). This includes an attack upon the category of individual production and individual reception of works of art, together with an attack upon the idea of the work of art as "organic" and necessarily original. Bürger's *Theory of the Avant-Garde* obviously has much to offer a feminist analysis of the construction of the avant-garde; however, as with Krauss and Greenberg, his failure to consider the function of gender in the historical avant-gardes is revealing, for his theory cannot account for the ways in which art functioned for a social group which maintained an always tangential and often ironic relation to bourgeois rationality.

Susan Suleiman has noted the ways in which the word "avant-garde" evokes "a conceptual and terminological quagmire" and asks whether the term is "synonymous with, or to be subtly distinguished from, the experimental, the bohemian, the modern, the modern*ist*, the postmodern?" (Suleiman 1988: 148). This list is organized around such diverse issues as the form and content of the work, the lifestyle of the artist, and categories of artistic criticism. To qualify as avant-garde, is it necessary to be perceived as radical in all these respects? Or are some more important than others? And is it problematic to conceptualize these categories separately given their common strongly individualist bias which takes the form of a willingness to experiment with representational conventions and lifestyles? Moreover, it is clear from the history of the critical reception of Barney and Brooks that an unconventional lifestyle, particularly if it coincides with or is grounded in a lesbian identity, is no guarantee of an avant-garde reputation.

FLEURS DU MAL

One of the most significant aspects of the scanty literature on Barney and Brooks is the fact that their creative works have been virtually devoured by their lives. As Shari Benstock has noted, "to date, Natalie Barney's life has been rendered as gossip – lesbian gossip rather than literary gossip" and her writing has been read "as confirmation of her sexual and social exploits" (Benstock 1986: 271–72). Although Brooks's work has received more sustained attention, her life has also loomed disproportionately large in critical assessments of her significance. It could be argued that this is the negative side of having a life that "had the makings of legend."[5] We know the intricate details of Barney's and Brooks's fabulous fortunes, scandalous love affairs, outrageous dress, and even their interior furnishings, all of which figured prominently in a number of novels by their contemporaries. For instance, Barney appears in Liane de Pougy's *Idylle saphique* (1901), Radclyffe Hall's *The Well of Loneliness* (1928), Djuna Barnes's *Ladies Almanack* (1928), and Lucie Delarue-Mardrus's *L'Ange et les pervers* (1930), while Brooks appears in Radclyffe Hall's *Adam's Breed* (1926) and Compton Mackenzie's *Extraordinary Women* (1928). The same sort of sensational treatment continues in more recent biographies such as Jean Chalon's *Portrait of a Seductress: The World of Natalie Barney* (1979) and Meryle Secrest's *Between Me and Life: A Biography of Romaine Brooks* (1974) which at times exhibit an almost tabloid-style voyeurism. Repeatedly it is their lives (as opposed to their works) which are constructed as enduring artifacts – a tendency which is made clear in the following review of a 1962 special issue of *Adam* devoted to Natalie Barney:

> On the whole ... I am not inclined to think that we have neglected an
> important writer though I shall hurry to obtain "Souvenirs Indiscrets,"
> but I do feel that we are neglecting an important human being, trailing
> clouds of glory from the golden age of Les Années Dix, of the Mercure

and the N.R.F., of Proust and Apollinaire, Cubism and Les Six, and
with an exceptional gift of friendship.

(Connolly n.d.)

Ironically, the aestheticizing of Barney's and Brooks's lives – the cult of
personality which pervades their biographies – seems to have lowered rather
than raised the value of their creative work, perhaps because this conflation
of art and life runs counter to the "kind of Platonism" espoused by modernist
critics wherein "that which is removed from actuality is, by definition, the
most aesthetically valuable" (Nochlin 1973: 40). Clearly Barney's and
Brooks's work, rooted as it is in their social milieu and in autobiographical
experience, cannot be evaluated on the "purely aesthetic criteria" espoused
by formalist critics like Roger Fry. Instead, the social embeddedness of
Brooks's painting and Barney's writing has been seen as allowing *unproblematic* access to their personal histories and to their historical and cultural
milieus. While a cult of personality has to some degree arisen around many
male modernists – Ernest Hemingway and Pablo Picasso are obvious
examples – the individualism of the male artist, his tragic or heroic originality,
and, frequently, his self-sacrifice to his art are emphasized as salient features
of avant-gardism. This emphasis on male originality seems curiously
unwarranted given that the economically self-supporting, markedly heterosexual lifestyles of Hemingway and Picasso were more characteristic of the
dominant bourgeois culture of the period than Barney's or Brooks's
inherited fortunes and highly visible lesbianism. It would seem that Barney's
and Brooks's class privileges and frequently conservative politics have
disconcerted mainstream academics and feminist scholars alike – perhaps
because both groups have predominantly middle-class allegiances. To some
extent, lingering anti-aristocratic sentiments may have fostered the view that
Barney and Brooks were amateurish dilettantes as opposed to serious
professionals. However, critical refusal to consider the reasons why Barney
and Brooks *chose* to work within largely decadent paradigms has contributed
to a loss of historical nuance in understanding the function and meaning of
class privilege in their work. In any case, there is little evidence that their
work was any *more* autobiographical than that of, for example, Hemingway
or Picasso; the evidence suggests instead that Barney's and Brooks's work has
been interpreted as *merely* and *transparently* personal.

It is true that most of Barney's poetic and fictional texts contain strong
elements of autobiography, and that she is best remembered for her two
memoirs, *Aventures de l'esprit* (1929) and *Souvenirs indiscrets* (1960); it is
also true that the subjects of Brooks's portraits were herself and her friends.
(Because she did not need to earn her livelihood, Brooks was able to choose
her sitters, very carefully selecting only those whose physical appearance and
personality interested her (Breeskin 1986: 23).[6]) However, a closer examination of their autobiographies and other works reveals the degree to which

they consciously and consistently *fashioned themselves* out of a decadent philosophy and aesthetic.[7] They were not simply reflecting or reporting their lives and those of their friends, but *making* them visible – that is, making their lesbianism visible – by adapting literary and visual conventions which were already coded "homosexual," for, as Showalter notes, the term "decadence" was effectively a "fin-de-siècle euphemism for homosexuality" (Showalter 1990: 171).

That this was a fully conscious strategy is suggested in Barney's privately printed (only 560 copies were produced) English-language novel, *The One Who Is Legion, or A.D.'s After-Life* (1930). The novel is an at times frustratingly abstract, but also curiously compelling, first-person narrative told from the point of view of a genderless "shadow" who inhabits the body of a revivified suicide, "A.D." A.D. has no memory of her/his former life and must reconstruct it from such evidence as old love-letters and the books in A.D.'s library. The degree to which "A.D." – revealed as an always-already "composite" being – is a product of her reading is apparent in the following passage. The narrator reflects that

> What books produced you? might be asked as conclusively as – Who are your parents? ... Are we not each a circulating library spreading ideas, dreams, precepts, social and scientific prejudices – the first-hand work of some writer? That writer the writer of another; most inspiration merely unconscious plagiarism, and writing in general a moment of arrested development; for what is an opinion but a full-stop in our comprehension to be passed on through print without end?
>
> (Barney 1930: 95–96)

This scene – indeed, this chapter – is itself most obviously the "product" or the offspring of the library chapters of J.-K. Huysmans's *À Rebours* (1884), a novel which became known as the guidebook of decadence and which was popularized in the English-speaking world by Oscar Wilde's *The Picture of Dorian Gray* (1890).[8] Although Huysmans's hero, Des Esseintes, collects primarily literature of the Latin decadence, pride of place is given in his library to three poems by Baudelaire, copied, mounted, and exhibited in an elaborate triptych. Of these, "La Mort des amants" provides another possible source for the narrative and much of the imagery of Barney's novel. Baudelaire's sonnet describes the simultaneous death – presumably the suicide – of two lovers who anticipate their ultimate rebirth. The second and fourth stanzas read as follows:

> Approaching equally their final light,
> Our twin hearts will be two great flaming brands
> That will double in each other's sight –
> Our souls the mirrors where the image stands.
>
> . . .

And later, opening the doors, will be
An Angel, who will joyfully reglaze
The tarnished mirrors, and relight the blaze.

(Baudelaire 1993: 277)

Barney "borrows" the figure of the angel and elaborates on the figures of the two lovers who exist in the novel both as separate characters *and* as the composite being, A.D. *The One Who Is Legion* is, in part, an exploration of psychic "hermaphroditism" or doubleness – even multiplicity – of being; yet another of its literary sources is Balzac's *Séraphita*, as Barney makes explicit in the following passage (one of many extended poetic/epigrammatic passages in the novel):

A double being needs no other mate –
So seraphita-seraphitus lives:
Self-wedded angel, armed in self-delight,
Hermaphrodite of heaven, looking down
On the defeat of our divided love.

(Barney 1930: 100)[9]

Certainly the figure of the "hermaphrodite" was central to fin-de-siècle theorizing about sexuality and sexual orientation, though it could take forms ranging from the degenerative atavism feared by misogynist writers like Otto Weininger and Max Nordau to the more highly evolved "intermediate" or "third" sex postulated by social reformers and homosexual thinkers like Edward Carpenter.

From even these brief examples, it is obvious that *The One Who Is Legion* is a highly allusive novel which, like *À Rebours*, clearly acknowledges its literary, and especially decadent, borrowings. These "second-handed" qualities are characteristic of decadent writing. As one critic notes, "decadent texts flaunt their intertextuality, footnote themselves endlessly, self-consciously present their own literary genealogies," suggesting that it is futile to look "for depth when all is surface" (Spackman 1989: 34). However, the novel is also teasingly autobiographical: A.D.'s garden contains a four-columned temple (an obvious allusion to Barney's Temple à l'Amitié); she/he is a poet who has published a bilingual collection of poems, *Poèmes* (Barney's *Poems & Poèmes: autres alliances* was published in 1920); the reborn A.D. explores Paris on horseback (Barney was nicknamed l'Amazone by Remy de Gourmont in acknowledgment of her love of riding); A.D. has been spied upon and courted by a neighbour (Brooks's autobiographer records a similar incident in Barney's life (Secrest 1974: 333–34)); and, most significantly, A.D. has committed suicide out of guilt and grief at the suicide of a lover whose situation bears enormous resemblance to that of Barney's lover, the poet Renée Vivien (like Barney, A.D. finds out about her lover's death from a butler's terse comment that "Madame vient de mourir" (Barney 1930: 108;

Wickes 1976: 67)). Indeed, Renée Vivien's chosen name (she was born Pauline Tarn) is echoed or reflected in the novel's theme of rebirth. Clearly, *The One Who Is Legion* "flaunts" its own lack of originality, its dependence on literary and autobiographical sources. The novel also makes it clear that decadence is a chosen *alternative* to a more recognizably modernist aesthetic; within A.D.'s library "the mediums of modernism as mannequins of fashion, were also excluded, because an acquired speed can never represent a movement" (Barney 1930: 95). Just as *The One Who Is Legion* produces itself as a decadent novel thirty-five years after the trial of Oscar Wilde and after the "end" of decadence, so Barney's memoirs are at pains to (re)produce her as a decadent subject, so given over to fin-de-siècle languor that her books are no more than the accidental output of her writing-table: "Tous les dix ans, je me force à vider mes carnets, les tiroirs de ma table à écrire. Ce qu'ils contiennent devient des livres, presque à mon insu" (Barney 1929: 1). In her introduction to *Quelques portraits-sonnets de femmes* (1900) Barney suggests that she chooses to write primarily in French "parce qu'elle seule me fait penser poétiquement," and that she sometimes imagines "que mon âme est peut-être la tombe de quelques poètes francais" (vii). Certainly French was, for the late nineteenth- and early twentieth-century English-speaking world, the language *of* decadence, a movement which was represented in the 1895 English press as threatening "all the wholesome, manly, simple ideals of English life" (*Evening News*, quoted in Thornton 1979: 16). In *Aventures de l'esprit* (1929) Barney went one step farther and emphasized ancestral connections to France, including a French maternal great-great-grandmother and a paternal ancestor, Commodore Joshua Barney, who was presented at the French court and kissed by Queen Marie Antoinette as embodying in his person the New World (Barney 1929: 11); as one of Barney's biographers points out, many of her genealogical claims were likely "mythical" (Wickes 1976: 17).

A deliberate rhetoric of decadent self-fashioning is also evident in Romaine Brooks's still unpublished memoir, "No pleasant memories," which Brooks probably began at about the same time that Barney was writing *The One Who Is Legion*.[10] It should be noted that during this period Brooks also produced two drawings of emaciated and hermaphroditic figures for Barney's novel. Although the veracity of Brooks's often fantastic autobiography has been questioned by several writers (e.g. Sir Harold Acton, who knew her in Rome, Norman Holmes Pearson, Carl Van Vechten, and Meryle Secrest), and although critics have noted the degree to which Brooks altered key facts (eliminating her sister from the memoir, altering her own age, etc.) there has been little exploration of the ways in which Brooks borrowed liberally and self-consciously from decadent iconography to construct herself as an outcast or lapidé. In this way, Brooks refused the invisibility of the woman artist and aggressively adopted the coherent marginality of an already outmoded masculine avant-garde. Significantly, despite some reservations about the accuracy of the autobiography, the art historical literature on Brooks has largely accepted her written self-representation and has failed to note similarities between her verbal and visual strategies.[11]

"No pleasant memories" is organized into over 140 short "chapters," the majority of which detail Brooks's suffering at the hands of her mad and apparently sadistic mother, who seems to have resented the fact that Romaine was healthy while her preferred child, St. Mar (called St. Amar in the autobiography), was both ill and insane. There is some indication that Brooks intended her autobiography to be highly illustrated with photographs and line drawings, one of which depicts the mother about to whip her daughter with the son looking on. At the bottom of the drawing is the pencilled caption, "St. Amar 'placed himself between me & the whip. . . . Page 10."[12] The narrative is extraordinary – in an uncharacteristic understatement, Brooks describes her childhood as "unusual" (18) – and includes accounts of Romaine being abandoned by her mother who apparently left the young child for some months with her unsuspecting (and unpaid) washerwoman. Brooks concludes from this episode that "the effects of slum life were never effaced. In some dark corner of my inner consciousness these experiences had sown what would soon take the form of a secret craving for the negative exultation of those who are solitary and adrift" (22). After being discovered and rescued by her grandfather, the young Romaine was eventually placed in a convent by her mother who "accepted the possibility of my taking the veil" (60). The chapters which detail these experiences draw on a decadent preoccupation with a corrupt medieval Catholicism (Brooks recalls, for example, her fascination with her "most precious belonging ... nothing less than the photograph of a dead Sister" (68)), while those which describe the deaths of her brother and mother reveal a similar decadent fascination with death, decay, and physical corruption.

SECOND-HAND ROSES

A second recurring problem in critical evaluations of Barney and Brooks is the ways in which they are also seen, in their non-autobiographical work, as reviving conventional, even old-fashioned genres like the portrait and the courtly love poem. In taking up portraiture, Romaine Brooks was engaging a genre that was frequently perceived as derivative and commercially suspect. Throughout the eighteenth and nineteenth centuries portraiture was held in relatively low esteem by academicians who tended to regard it as less imaginative and morally instructive than the more complicated genre of history painting, and by the emerging avant-garde who criticized it for all too often catering to conventional wealthy tastes – for selling the bourgeois suitably smug self-images.[13] Although portraiture was to some extent being rehabilitated in certain avant-garde sectors by artists like Picasso, such works were not the mainstay of these artists' production.

And, in any case, unlike the bohemian Picasso, Brooks was an artist from the Right as opposed to the Left Bank. In other words, she was seen as part of an *haut monde* which preferred "old-fashioned" symbolist styles which invoked artists like Whistler, Condor, and Beardsley. For instance, the style of Brooks's *Self-Portrait* (1923) (Figure 2.1) bears a strong resemblance to such works as Charles Condor's *Portrait of Max Beerbohm* from the 1890s. The similarities extend well beyond the subdued tonalities and thinly painted surfaces of the background to include the presentation of stylishly poised figures in their immaculately tailored suits, identifying them as society dandies. Brooks's limited palette of greys, black, and white, her precise outlining and modelling, and her ethereally still atmospheric backgrounds deliberately resurrected a visual language of decadence, decay, and corruption which had been unfashionably passé (particularly in an English context) since the trial of Oscar Wilde. Brooks's preference for these forms (in contrast to more modernist Cubist fracturing, Fauve colouring, or Orphist celebrations of light and movement) has marked her out as imitative rather than innovative, an heir to old artistic wealth rather than the creator of new styles and schools.

The old-fashioned appearance of Brooks's portraits was not restricted to the style of her painting but also included her approach to composition and her use of conventions. For instance, in her painting of Natalie Barney as *L'Amazone* (1920) (Figure 2.2), the sitter is arranged in a time-honoured three-quarters pose and realistically rendered in terms of the details of her dress and her house, 20 rue Jacob, in the background, both of which indicate her wealthy status. Other accoutrements, such as the manuscript and miniature horse, make reference to Barney's passions for writing and riding. The horse additionally alludes to Barney's independence and to her famous and predominantly lesbian salon.[14] The fact that we are almost allegorically provided with so many insights into Barney's life establishes her as an independent entity who meets and returns the painter's gaze. Significantly, such autonomous sitters should be anathema to the modernist portrait painter, as Kirk Varnadoe indicates:

[T]he modern artist is the giver, rather than the captor or preserver, of identity. The artist assigns to his subjects a particular expressiveness and significance that originates in his own work rather than in the personality he treats.... The sitter is thus not simply placed in a referential system of accoutrements but more completely remade in terms of a system of artistic invention....

Since the modern portrait sitter acknowledges the artist's right to take liberties as he sees fit and accepts the artist's vision as valid on a level beyond comparable visual resemblance, the remaining *sine qua non* of the portrait, the indispensable element of identity, is the meaning conferred by the artist's stamp. Before being a banker or a critic or a

Figure 2.2 Romaine Brooks, *Natalie Barney "L'Amazone"* (1920). Oil on canvas.
86.5 × 65.5 cm. C Musées de la Ville de Paris, 1993/ Vis*Art Copyright Inc.

poet, the modern sitter expects to become a Dubuffet, a Pearlstein, a de Kooning.

(Varnadoe 1976: xiv–xv)

Clearly, Brooks did not assume the same sort of authority over her sitters as male modernist painters who were involved with projecting their perceptions onto a subject who was virtually "swallowed up" (Varnadoe 1976: xviii). While the implication of Brooks's "old-fashioned" approach will be considered in the next section, it is evident that it has disconcerted a number of modernist art historians, such as Joshua Taylor, who have resorted to special pleading for her recognition as a modernist:

> Romaine Brooks, in retaining contact with her own early preoccupation with character and the haunting loneliness of the individual was not being *retardataire*. By the 1920s her penetrating visual judgement could be seen as part of the new interest in psychology.... If she were less of an individual, less truly aware of her own aloneness and the personal role art played in her life, she might be counted a surrealist or be fitted with some other useful title. But her modernity lies not in a pictorial method or a school, but in her tenacious adherence to the right to be herself, to fight her own psychic battles ...
>
> (quoted in Breeskin 1986: 18)

Here Brooks's traditional pictorial conventions are excused on the grounds that her modernism resides in her quest to explore her own tortured individuality through her art. In other words, she imposes her own emotional state rather than her style on her sitters. Of course, this interpretation is based upon an earlier Romantic conception of the artist wherein authenticity and sincerity become the most important kinds of truth (Battersby 1990: 13).[15] As Adelyn Breeskin explains, "her own life was reflected in the people she depicted, and she has looked at both herself and her environment with a detachment that ill conceals the passion and imagination that were schooled in restraint by the cruelty of her early experience" (Breeskin 1986: 19). While this sort of special pleading argues that Brooks's portraits are not derivative in that she, the artist, is the real subject of the portrait, this viewing of Brooks through an older (i.e. pre-modernist) Romantic paradigm once again conflates her art and life and implies that Brooks was translating her lived experience rather than creatively imagining new forms. Even the tough rhetoric of individualism cannot gloss over the fact that Brooks cannot be significantly original on these terms. A more creative re-reading of the original/copy opposition is needed.

In this respect it is perhaps more interesting to consider the ways in which gender differences informed the practice of portraiture. While Brooks's psychological interests may have seemed "old-fashioned" as far as the

45

painting of male subjects was concerned, it was a relatively new issue for female sitters and artists. As Deborah Silverman points out, it was only in the 1890s with the emergence of debates around the *femme nouvelle* that a new conception of portraying women as psychological subjects first emerged. Whereas men had previously been rendered in terms of their inner life and character, women had largely been depicted as decorative surfaces and fashions. According to Silverman, art critics such as Camille Mauclair and Marius-Ary Leblond began to notice how new conceptions of femininity might erode the older conventions for representing gender in portraiture (Silverman 1989: 68–69). Since Mauclair's major essay on this subject was first published in 1899, it is evident that Brooks was involved with what was widely perceived as an experimental project as far as women were concerned. Clearly in this respect cultural agendas for men and women differed.

In much the same way that Brooks's portraiture drew upon an "old-fashioned" genre, Natalie Barney has been described as drawing upon the courtly love poem (as both Shari Benstock and Karla Jay have noted), adopting in many of her poems the voice of the male suitor: the page or the knight entreating the distant or cold lady. Certainly "the page" is one of the costumes and personae that Barney liked to adopt in photo-portraits of herself with various friends and lovers. The voice of the entreating male suitor is particularly evident in such poems as "A pilgrimage" in which the narrator, after asking "Is that your window with the moving shade / In pilgrimage I've come so far to see?", notes with regret that the wind can play about the loved one's neck and hair "While I must wait, as near as I may be" (Barney 1920: 27). The convention of the distant lady is represented even more explicitly in an earlier poem, "Une princesse lointaine" [A remote princess], whose claim that "Sapho revit sous l'extase de ton chant" [Sappho lives again in the rapture of your song] suggests that Renée Vivien (with whom Barney travelled to Lesbos to explore the possibilities of establishing a Sapphic school of poetry) was the poet's addressee. The last three lines of the sonnet are significantly ambiguous; it is unclear whether it is the lady's beauty or, in a radical departure from convention, her literary reputation (or both) which demands the sacrifice of her admirers: "Ton corps est une flamme où toutes tes prêtresses / Doivent jeter la fleur de leurs fraîches jeunesses / Afin d'entretenir ton immortalité" [Your body is a flame into which all your priestesses / Must toss the flower of their blooming youth / To maintain your immortality] (Barney 1900: n.p.). That Barney saw herself as not simply *adopting* but consciously *adapting* archaic forms is also evident from the dedicatory poem of her 1900 collection of lesbian love poems, *Quelques portraits-sonnets de femmes*. The sonnet, "Divagation" [Wandering], is dedicated to the memory of symbolist poet Stéphane Mallarmé, and its opening lines declare that "Ces vers sont dédiés / Aux Pétrarques sans Laure" ["These verses are dedicated / To all the Petrarchs without Laura;" the second line can also be read punningly as "To all the penniless [sans l'or]

Petrarchs"]. The fusion of the courtly love poem with a pose of decadent worldweariness is evident throughout the poem, but particularly in the last two stanzas which also dedicate the volume "Aux rêveurs sans espoirs, / Pales enfants d'Automne, / Aux rires dérisoires, // A leurs songes mort-nés / Voilés comme des nonnes / Pour rester parfumés" [To those who dream without hope, / The pale girls of autumn, / And their derisory laughter, // To their still-born dreams / Veiled like nuns / To keep them scented]. As noted earlier, this volume (which was illustrated with several portraits of women by Barney's mother, Alice Pike Barney) was published in 1900, the year of Wilde's death and therefore a year in which decadence was revived in the public imagination. Certainly the volume's explicitly lesbian content was noted by the American press – one review was titled "Sapho sings in Washington" – and by Barney's conservative father, who "bought up whatever copies he could find of the book and destroyed the plates" (Jay 1988: 4).

Benstock suggests that Barney's "use of traditional [poetic] forms consti- tuted an effort to summon literary authority, to place her poetry in a long and respected tradition" (Benstock 1986: 240), while Jay similarly suggests that Barney "sought to reclaim for women the whole of Western literary tradition from Sappho to the Symbolists" (Jay 1988: 92). Certainly, the need to summon authority by placing one's work in a recognized cultural tradition is a particularly pressing problem for women who have more often than not been exiled from prevailing literary and artistic canons. Frequently a conflict arises between wanting to be taken seriously and legitimized as a writer or artist (which usually means working in either conventional or *recognizably* avant-garde forms) and a need to explore alternative forms and issues that relate to one's position as a woman. In the late nineteenth and early twentieth centuries these contradictory aspirations generated a schizophrenic notion of the relationship between gender and culture, as Celeste Schenck has observed:

> [W]omen are always subjected to competing stereotypes: they are both "beneath" culture – too mired in nature to master the codes or poetic forms – and (notably in and after the Victorian period) "upholders of" culture – hence rigid, conservative, form-bound, repressive of sponta- neity and experimentation. The whole idea of the "genteel" against which Modernism defined itself seems to be inextricably bound to these contradictory, even schizophrenic, notions of femininity.
>
> (Schenck 1989: 228–29)

We are suggesting that Barney's use of archaic forms was more strategic than suggested by Benstock and Jay; nonetheless, an interesting demonstration of conflicting desires can be found in Natalie Barney's critical assessment, in her 1929 *Aventures de l'esprit*, of Romaine Brooks's painting. Throughout the text, Barney shifts uneasily between dismissing modernism, which she

47

realizes is a framework that Brooks does not fit into, and championing Brooks's individuality in order to prove that she is a great artist and equal, if not superior, to her modernist contemporaries. Significantly, however, Barney locates Brooks's originality in her evocation of decadent sentiments. This is made clear in Barney's somewhat extravagant assertion that,

> en effet, Romaine Brooks n'appartient à aucun temps, à aucun pays, à aucun milieu, à aucune école, à aucune tradition; elle n'est pas non plus en révolution contre ces institutions, mais plutôt, comme Walt Whitman, ni pour ni contre elles – elle ne sait pas ce qu'elles sont. Elle est le résumé, la "sommité fleurie" d'une civilisation à son déclin, dont elle a su recueillir la face.[16]
>
> (Barney 1929: 245)

Taken at face value, Barney's text could simply be read as a statement of middle-aged, outmoded avant-gardism, the nostalgia of someone who had not kept up with changing aesthetic tastes and was still rooted in the decadent movement of her youth. This was certainly a charge made against her by Ezra Pound whom she hired in 1919 to advise her on the poems which would become the *Poems & Poèmes: autres alliances* volume. In his response to the manuscript, Pound stated that "you are out of touch not only with editorial connections but with the best contemporary work" (Pound 1976: 282). However, it can also be argued that Barney and her circle deliberately revived decadent modes for strategic as well as sentimental reasons. As we shall see, the strategic nature of this revival – evident in her allusion to Walt Whitman who was, like Brooks, both American and homosexual, and who figured in the writings of such turn-of-the-century sexologists as Havelock Ellis and Edward Carpenter – becomes apparent only if it is understood as part of a desire to make a newly emerging lesbian identity publicly visible.

CONSTRUCTING VISIBILITY

The argument that Barney was simply summoning cultural authority by using the voice of, for example, the courtly love poet or the Wildean epigrammist assumes an aesthetics of coherence that is completely absent from her pensées, her poetry, and her memoirs; it also ignores the transgressive effect of speaking in the masculine. Moreover, in her poetry Barney was not speaking *as a man* but *in the literary voice of* a particular kind of male poet who was himself adopting a highly artificial or conventional mask or persona. In this way, Barney's poetic voice works in a way similar to, though by no means identical with, the transvestite costumes of Brooks and her sitters. The differences between literary and visual cross-dressing are, as we shall discuss below, significant.

Barney practised a kind of poetics of the fragment, as one of her pensées – "I never go to the end of an idea – it's too far" – suggests (Barney 1963: 54).

Furthermore, her most interesting collection of poetry is also her most duplicitous. *Poems & Poèmes: autres alliances* (1920) is a bilingual collection, published simultaneously in New York and Paris; the first twenty-six poems are in English, the last twenty-four in French, with the two halves (or "tongues") of the text separated by a transparent sheet of tissue paper on which is printed (within an oval) "A casement ope at night / To let the warm love in." The collection symbolizes, in part, Barney's commitment to effecting a rapprochement between two literatures.[17] However, many of the poems also (like her 1930 novel) explore doubleness and disguise, the masquerade, the layering of identity. In "Avertissement" [Warning or Notice], an English poem with a French title, Barney writes: "Leaving art to artists – we, love's lovers, / Keep for outworn Beauty a disguise. / ... So making everything seem otherwise: / Associations are our deities!" (Barney 1920: 20). In another poem from the collection, "Double being," the poet describes "A natural being, yet from nature freed, / Like a Shakespearian boy of fairy breed – / A sex perplexed into attractive seeming / – Both sex at best, the strangeness so redeeming! –" (Barney 1920: 15).

Almost all the poems in the *Poems & Poèmes* collection are written in the first person, whether singular or plural, and most of them in the "I-You" form of address that Ellen Moers has identified as a characteristic of women's love poetry. Thus the immediate sense of dissonance which is one effect of Romaine Brooks's portraits appears more coherently voiced in Barney's poems, in spite of the fact that the poems themselves describe and celebrate a fragmentary or doubled, but always *in*coherent identity. The strong dislocation the viewer feels when first encountering Brooks's portraits can be achieved, to a degree, in literature. In Radclyffe Hall's *The Well of Loneliness*, for example, the reader is jarred by references to Stephen Gordon as "she," the masculine proper noun disrupting the female pronoun. However, the historical consequences of assuming a masculine voice have been quite different from those of assuming the visible indicators of masculinity. There is historical evidence to suggest that patriarchal order is obsessed with the *visual* symbols of masculine power.[18] In *Surpassing the Love of Men* Lillian Faderman points out that throughout history lesbians were persecuted (often burned or drowned) for their sexual activities *if* they also cross-dressed as men, whereas if they engaged in the same activities in female dress, they were usually only reprimanded in the courts. She notes that the cross-dressing lesbian created more confusion about gendered roles, claimed male social privileges, and demonstrated her transgression publicly and deliberately in a manner that made her reform and return to conventional heterosexuality seem impossible.[19] In other words, cross-dressing took the "private" realm of the sexual into the "public" sphere (Faderman 1981: 47–61).

Perhaps Brooks's most direct use of a strategy of visual dissonance can be found in her portrait of *Peter (A Young English Girl)* (1923–1924) (Figure 2.3) where the title directs the viewer to look again and to look differently.

Figure 2.3 Romaine Brooks, *Peter (A Young English Girl)* (1923–1924). Oil on canvas. 91.9 × 62.3 cm. National Museum of American Art, Smithsonian Institution, gift of the artist.

The young English girl in this case is the artist Gluck (a rapidly rising star in the London arts world), who was to become well known for her cross-dressing in the extensive press coverage of her exhibitions from 1924 until the 1930s (see Souhami 1988). In Brooks's portrait, Gluck's immaculate suit jacket, starched white collar, and elegant green waistcoat echo the aristocratic male fashions Brooks had flaunted in her own self-portrait. The figure of the "mannish" lesbian, together with the reasons for her emergence at the turn of the century, has received useful critical attention from Esther Newton, Sonja Ruehl, and Katrina Rolley. Newton argues that "in the nineteenth century and before" women cross-dressers were primarily from the working class, and that "public, *partial* cross-dressing among bourgeois women was a late nineteenth-century development" (Newton 1984: 558). She attributes this shift to two related factors: one was the modernist identification with sexual freedom as a reaction against Victorian values; the other was the publication in 1895 of Havelock Ellis's "Sexual inversion in women."

> How could the New Woman lay claim to her full sexuality? For bourgeois women, there was no developed female sexual discourse; there [were] only male discourses – pornographic, literary, and medical – about female sexuality. To become avowedly sexual, the New Woman had to enter the male world, either as a heterosexual on male terms (a flapper) or as – or with – a lesbian in male body drag (a butch).
>
> (Newton 1984: 573)

Thus cross-dressing provided a visual code by which middle- and upper-class lesbians – released into sexuality from a nineteenth-century discourse of "romantic friendship" – could recognize each other. However, it is important to realize that the public construction of an identifiably lesbian sexuality postdated that of male homosexuality by approximately three decades. As Jeffrey Weeks points out, "by the end of the nineteenth century a recognisably 'modern' male homosexual identity was beginning to emerge, but it would be another generation before female homosexuality reached a corresponding level of articulacy;" moreover, "the lesbian identity was much less clearly defined, and the lesbian subculture was minimal in comparison with the male, and even more overwhelmingly upper class or literary" (Weeks 1981: 115).[20] The prior existence of a recognizably homosexual culture – especially as it was articulated by such decadent and symbolist poets as Baudelaire and given further visibility in the 1895 trial of Oscar Wilde – gave artists like Barney and Brooks a convention from which to draw in their construction of a specifically lesbian cultural identity. In adopting the voice of the Wildean epigrammist and decadent poet/novelist, or in assuming the costume of the dandy, Barney and Brooks deliberately invoked the cultural markers of a marginal, deviant, and illegal sexuality. Significantly, they did this at a time when lesbianism itself (at least in Britain) was increasingly being brought "into the scope of the Criminal Law" (Weeks 1981: 116).

Certainly, such lesbian cross-dressers as Radclyffe Hall, whose image was engrained in the popular imagination as the result of the 1928 obscenity trial of her novel, *The Well of Loneliness*, have been criticized for internalizing Havelock Ellis's categories of female inversion. However, Sonja Ruehl argues (borrowing from Foucault) that the very "process of categorization makes resistance to ... power possible" (Ruehl 1982: 17), and we would add that the flamboyant transvestism of Hall, Gluck, and Brooks was an effective and strategic "counter-discourse" (see Terdiman 1985). It is in the context of an evolving lesbian counter-discourse that the subversive nature of Brooks's self-portrait and her paintings of other lesbian women becomes apparent. Rather than being read as either literal transcriptions of her "reality" (i.e., projections of her suffering and emotional angst) or else as pastiches of Whistler or other decadent artists, her painting needs to be read as part of an ongoing attempt by lesbian women to publicly identify and verify their sexuality. Part of that process included culturally imag(in)ing themselves from a perspective that embodied their differences in a form that could be socially recognized.

The question of who was recognizing whom is taken up by Katerina Rolley in her analysis of the sartorial strategies of Radclyffe Hall and Una Troubridge. As Rolley suggests, there were different ways of interpreting the male cross-dressing of upper-class lesbians. While informed viewers recognized the lesbian implications of such attire, "for viewers who were unaware of their sexuality, especially those distanced by class, their appearance might be (mis)read as part of the aristocratic tradition of eccentricity, especially since Radclyffe Hall was also a writer" (Rolley 1990: 55). That they conformed to upper-class practices such as dressing for dinner and spending large sums on fashionable clothes sometimes overshadowed the lesbian implications of their dress. Furthermore, as Rolley points out, the fact that "masculine" styles, including short hair and tailored suits (albeit in less extreme forms), were in vogue during the 1920s led some people to conclude that Radclyffe Hall was simply adopting a form of "high-brow modernism."[21]

It should be emphasized that Barney and Brooks asserted their privileges of class in order to display a so-called deviant sexuality. Although both radically challenged prevailing social and sexual expectations that were placed upon women, neither was interested in a similar critique of the class structure. Both tended to view themselves as exceptional individuals. In Brooks's case this is perhaps best typified by her increasing withdrawal from society as well as her passionate friendship with the Italian decadent poet, Gabriele D'Annunzio whom she approvingly regarded as a sort of Nietzschean superman (unpublished and undated typescript: 255), while Barney's own elitism and conservative politics are evidenced by her Second World War support of Mussolini's Fascism (Jay 1988: 34). Given their socially conservative commitment to individualism, it is not surprising that Barney and Brooks took up the styles of Wilde and Whistler, both of whom posed as aristocratic dandies. Here it is important to acknowledge the contradictions that are raised when a radical critique of sexual orientation operates within a largely conservative view of the class hierarchy. Such political and aesthetic contradictions clearly resist easy classification as either conservative or radical.

The dilemma of appearances is familiar to feminists, lesbians, and other marginalized groups; how can one be identified *positively* as different when that difference is "always already" structurally denigrated? Here it is worth pursuing the dynamics of the categorization of dominance/deviance since they shed light on the ways in which the original and copy distinction has been applied to Barney and Brooks. It is also important to emphasize that while the *socially* "dominant" sexuality against which Barney and Brooks were defining themselves was not heterosexual femininity but heterosexual masculinity, the *culturally* dominant sexuality – that of the avant-garde – was in many ways that of masculine homosexuality, or at least masculine "homosociality" (Sedgwick 1985; see also Koestenbaum 1989).

In "The dominant and the deviant: a violent dialectic," Jonathan Dollimore (also borrowing from Foucault) describes how deviant groups become politically resistant through a series of negotiated stages. For instance, in the case of homosexuality, the group "begins to speak on its own behalf, to forge its own identity and culture, *often in the self-same categories by which it has been produced and marginalized*, and eventually challenges the very power structures responsible for its 'creation'" (Dollimore 1986: 180, emphasis in original). The resistance of any marginal group therefore necessarily moves through a number of stages during which different strategies are most effective. As Dollimore emphasizes, especially at the early stages,

> for the subordinate, at the level of cultural struggle ... [a] simple denunciation of dominant ideologies can be dangerous and counter-productive. Rather, they have instead, or also, to be negotiated. There are many strategies of negotiation; I am concerned here with two: the transformation of the dominant ideologies through (mis)appropriation, and their subversion through inversion.
>
> (Dollimore 1986: 181–82)

Radclyffe Hall's *The Well of Loneliness*, with its "conservative" portrait of an "authentic" yet "abject" lesbianism, is Dollimore's example of a strategy of transformation through (mis)appropriation, while Rita Mae Brown's *Rubyfruit Jungle* (1973) enacts a "subversion through inversion" of heterosexual norms. Dollimore suggests that "the complex changes of the intervening forty-five years" (185) enabled Brown's critique. However, the case of Barney and Brooks upsets any easy narrative of progress, for their constructions of lesbianism depended less on "images of authenticity taken from the established order" (185) than on the deliberate invocation and representation of *in*authenticity.[22]

In the case of Barney and Brooks, the second-hand need not be understood as second-rate but rather as a strategy of *recycling* images, voices, and costumes in the interest of creating a newly visible and deviant sexuality – albeit within the confines of an elitist and umproblematized social position. But to read Barney's and Brooks's work in its full complexity means calling into question our present rather narrow and discipline-bound notions of originality. Upsetting the signifying practices of the dominant social order entails not only finding new *forms* of writing and painting but the construction of new meanings, identities, and communities. In these terms, Brooks's *Self-Portrait* or *Peter (A Young English Girl)* are "original" in the ways they (mis)appropriate the sartorial style of the decadent dandy for the socially elite lesbian. This exploration of the visual confusions of cross-dressing upsets an essentialist understanding of gender and overturns the notions of "origin" and "imitation" as they are used to regulate gendered identity. Evidently Romaine Brooks was conscious of raising this problem in her painting when she noted in her autobiography that she was making great strides in her work and had "already painted a series of solitary figures that had of life only the camouflage of exaggerated attire" (unpublished and undated typescript: 210). Similarly, Barney's poem "Love's comrades" reads, in part, as a response to charges of poetic archaism and decadence:

> You say I've lived too long in France
> And wearied of the senses' dance?
>
> Like fresh air in an opium den
> You'll lead me out – to where? and when?
>
> ... I fear no country's ready yet
> For our complexities ...
>
> (Barney 1920: 18)

In addressing the visual construction of gender in her painting is Brooks being any less avant-garde than, for example, the Cubist painters who were interested in the interrogation of single-point perspective? Is it that issues of perspective and science have been seen as more properly belonging to the realm of painting than sexuality and sartorial codes? Or is it that moving towards abstraction is still considered a purer, more complicated form of painting – that painting which addresses the problem of painting, or the medium's internal system of representation, is necessarily of a higher order than painting which addresses systems of visual representation outside the world of art? These questions are disturbing because it seems that we have not fully dismantled the negative stigma attached to representational art, especially when it deals with such ostensibly mundane and "feminine" issues as fashion and sex-role stereotyping. Our inability to recognize such work as original rather than derivative perhaps reveals more about the limitations of our current critical apparatus than it does about Brooks's and Barney's work. In an article addressing the intersection of the feminist critique of patriarchy and the post-modern critique of representation, Craig Owens has suggested that all too often the former has been subsumed by the latter (Owens 1985). Has the possibility of writing the world differently through a form-breaking *écriture feminine* blinded us to the merits of alternative strategies that offer equally new ideas by reworking older forms? Ironically, according to Owens, in our post-modern period,

> In the visual arts we have witnessed the gradual dissolution of once fundamental distinctions – original/copy, authentic/inauthentic, function/ornament. Each term now seems to contain its opposite, and this indeterminacy brings with it an impossibility of choice or, rather, the absolute equivalence and hence interchangeability of choices. Or so it is said. The existence of feminism with its insistence on difference forces us to reconsider.
>
> (Owens 1985: 77)

The irony is that while we can celebrate the dismantling of the original/copy distinction by today's visual and literary artists, we have been less sceptical about the way these terms have been deployed in relation to the work of earlier periods.

3

PROFESSIONALISM, GENRE, AND THE SISTER(S') ARTS
Virginia Woolf and Vanessa Bell

I dont in the least want Mrs L's candid criticism; I want her cheque! I know all about my merits and failings better than she can from the sight of one article, but it would be a great relief to know that I could make a few pence easily in this way – as our passbooks came last night, and they are greatly overdrawn.

Virginia Woolf to Violet Dickinson, 11 November 1904
(Woolf 1975: 154–55)

I must tell you of my unexpected success. I have actually sold a picture to the Contemporary Art Society!! Ross & Aitken came to Gordon Sq. just before I left to see which of Duncan's works they would get. They liked the Queen of Sheba best, but that belongs to Roger & I dont know if he will let them have it. Then Ross saw a painting of a Spanish model by me & said he would buy it. I only asked £5.5.0 so it is not a great financial coup but I hope may help me to other commercial success. But I know really that nothing I can do will ever make money. Still I might make enough to pay for Asheham.

Vanessa Bell to Virginia Woolf, 23 August 1912[1]

Bruce Robbins has recently pointed out that recognition of modernism's link to an ideology of professionalism has achieved the status of a "commonplace narrative" (Robbins 1993: 64–65), a narrative which must be carefully nuanced to account for historical and gender-based differences. Certainly, as the above epigraphs indicate, the question of professionalism was experienced differently by Woolf and Bell, not only because of differences between writing and painting, but also because their involvement with the Bloomsbury Group positioned them differently from many of the other women of our study. While Barney's and Brooks's wealth freed them almost completely from considerations of the marketplace – allowing Barney to self-publish and allowing Brooks to choose her sitters and to refuse to sell her portraits –

56

Woolf and Bell needed to supplement the private incomes bequeathed them from their upper middle-class families.[2] Their financial positioning was less extravagant than that of Barney and Brooks, but also far more stable than that of Nina Hamnett and Djuna Barnes who were completely dependent upon the meagre wages their work commanded (or upon the charity of friends). In many ways, their upper middle-class status, combined with their attitudes to professionalism, marked Woolf and Bell as anomalous women modernists.

In this chapter we will explore Woolf's and Bell's representations of themselves and other women artists as a way of focusing on the ways in which an idea of "professionalism" mediates between gender, genre, and class within the discursive field of "modernism." More specifically, we will focus on Woolf's representations of the woman artist in her novels *To the Lighthouse* (1927) and *Between the Acts* (1941), and on Bell's self-portrait of 1915 together with her portraits of Virginia Woolf (1912) and Mary Hutchinson (1914); however, we will also allude to Woolf's and Bell's work in less privileged genres like the polemical essay and domestic genre painting. We will be assuming Jameson's argument that "Genres are essentially literary [or visual] *institutions*, or social contracts between a writer [or artist] and a specific public, whose function is to specify the proper use of a particular cultural artifact" (Jameson 1981: 106); however, unlike Jameson, we will deploy gender as a key term in our analysis. The questions underlying our case study in this chapter are: how did women work within and modify inherited genres? how were genres "gendered," that is, hierarchized? what was the intended audience of the various genres within which Woolf and Bell worked? and how did they imagine themselves and other women as artists working within a financial and cultural marketplace?

BLOOMSBURY AND (WOMEN'S) MODERNISM

In order to ground these questions both historically and within a discourse of "modernism," it is important not only to locate Woolf and Bell *as women* within the context of the Bloomsbury Group – that is, to locate the ways in which Bloomsbury enabled some kinds of work and identifications while limiting others – but also to understand the continuing instability of the Bloomsbury Group's critical reputation.[3] Unlike other "modernist" cultural formations or associations, of which the Imagists and the Futurists are only two examples, the degree of Bloomsbury's "modernism" has always divided critical opinion. In a talk given to the Memoir Club in 1951 Vanessa Bell drew a distinction between pre- and post-First World War Bloomsbury and between Bloomsbury and the high modernists: "I was among those who left London in 1916 and when I came back three years later I realized very clearly how all had changed. Nothing happens twice and Bloomsbury had had its day. It dissolved in the newer world and the younger generation, now known as the Twenties" (V. Bell 1975: 83). Many years later Hugh Kenner dismissively claimed that Virginia Woolf is "not part of International Modernism; she is an English novelist of manners, writing village gossip from a village called Bloomsbury" (Kenner 1984: 57). Perry Meisel, on the other hand, argues that the Bloomsbury novel provides "the middle, saving ground" of reflexive realism together with a "genuinely collective and evolutionary sensibility" (Meisel 1987: 7, 161).

We will suggest (and our debt here to Raymond Williams is large) that it was Bloomsbury's commitment to a public sphere and to some degree of social action which distinguished it from what has since been constructed as a "high modernism." This commitment, though inherited from a potent Victorian mixture which combined Puritan, Quaker, and Clapham Sect influences (see Rosenbaum 1983a and 1983b), was reformulated by Bloomsbury – and especially by Virginia Woolf – as a professional ethics. It is perhaps its "evolutionary sensibility" – together with the commitment to friendship which S.P. Rosenbaum has called the "original and enduring basis of the Group" (Rosenbaum 1975: x) – which has made the Bloomsbury Group a kind of touchstone of humanistic modernism for many feminist critics. Gillian Hanscombe and Virginia L. Smyers, for example, call the first chapter of their 1987 book, *Writing for their Lives: The Modernist Women 1910–1940*, "Another Bloomsbury?" They argue that while the myth of the Bloomsbury Group ("in whose atmosphere a great number of feminists and literati unusually co-mingled") suggests a unique exchange between feminism and modernism, this group was not the only one in which such exchanges took place. Hanscombe and Smyers note that there was another "group" or "network" of women writers – H.D., Dorothy Richardson, Djuna Barnes, Mina Loy, Gertrude Stein, etc. – most of whom lived and worked in the metropolitan centres of London, Paris, and New York. (Although Hanscombe and Smyers concentrate on modernist women writers, artists like Romaine Brooks, Gluck, and Marie Laurencin were also part of that international community.) What is interesting about the comparison which Hanscombe and Smyers draw between the Bloomsbury Group and that other "network" is the degree to which the Bloomsbury Group is assumed as a model of feminism and modernism. We will argue here, however, that while Bloomsbury provided Virginia Woolf and Vanessa Bell the space and freedom to work as individual modernist artists, this was nonetheless a relatively private space and an often confining freedom; consequently, their experience of women's modernism was in some ways isolated and anomalous. Indeed, and in spite of Hanscombe and Smyers's evocation of "another Bloomsbury," there has been little attempt to locate Woolf and Bell within the larger context of a specifically *women's* modernism, nor has there been much consideration of how they were positioned as upper middle-class women in the context of the Bloomsbury Group.

In his 1980 article, "The Bloomsbury fraction," Raymond Williams focuses on how the Bloomsbury Group was positioned in relation to the British cultural establishment, emphasizing Bloomsbury's role as a class fraction, an anomalous group within the English intelligentsia. According to Williams, Bloomsbury's anomalies consisted of its social and intellectual critique of the status quo and its sexual tolerance (despite the ambiguous position of women within the group). Rather than seeing Bloomsbury as a deviant class fraction, Williams argues that its attitudes were instrumental in reshaping British ruling ideology during a period of social, intellectual, and cultural crisis. In effect, Williams suggests that the group facilitated a progress towards liberalization and modernization "within the professional and highly educated sector" (163). While Williams leaves the notion of the kind of social progress achieved by such fractions ungendered – that is, Bloomsbury represents a broadly humanistic and bourgeois ideal of the "civilized individual" – he does mention the contradictory presence of gender relations *within* Bloomsbury, "the specific contradiction between the presence of highly intelligent and intellectual women ... and their relative exclusion from the dominant and formative male institutions" (162) such as Cambridge University and the professions of colonial administration. Williams's analysis of Bloomsbury's commitment to an ideology of individualism makes it clear how and why members of Bloomsbury could only partially take account of gender and class in their social vision, and why – for Bloomsbury – social *conscience* remained quite distinct from social *consciousness*.

We are not denying that Bloomsbury provided an important critical space for reimagining social and sexual relationships, nor that this was a space from which Woolf and Bell clearly benefited. Indeed, as Christopher Reed has pointed out, the fact that Bloomsbury was less sexually repressed than most other sectors of British society has contributed to the group's denigration and continued marginality within a heterosexist modernist canon. Our objectives are not to extricate Woolf and Bell from this context, nor to claim (as have some critics) that the homosexuality of certain male members of the group made Bloomsbury a particularly misogynist sphere for women.[4] Rather, we are interested in examining how the specific context of working within Bloomsbury was both enabling and limiting for Woolf and Bell, hence our somewhat paradoxical characterization of Bloomsbury as a sphere of confined freedom. In other words, while Woolf and Bell's involvement with non-traditional and, in some cases, homosexual men facilitated a critique of Victorian gender hierarchies, the relative comfort of that space (a material as well as a psychological comfort) removed the necessity for them to seek alliances with other female avant-garde practitioners.

This relative isolation might partially account for Woolf's and Bell's inability (or perhaps unwillingness) to recognize and critique the limitations of their own position within Bloomsbury when gender differences did come into play. This is something that Reed does not adequately stress in his otherwise useful reassessment of the group's critical fate. His premise that Bloomsbury has come to represent the transgression of patriarchy's ultimate prohibition through its celebration of feminized men (Reed 1991: 59) needs to be questioned. Of equal importance to Bloomsbury's critique of gender is the notion of the masculinized woman (in this case the woman who claimed an equal cultural status for her writing or painting). Furthermore, it should be pointed out that during the 1920s and 1930s a relatively covert male homosexuality was less limiting for artists and writers than being female. For instance, whether or not Duncan Grant's and Vanessa Bell's personal relationship was based on a sense of creative and domestic equality (and there are suggestions that Bell occasionally wondered about this), there is extensive evidence indicating that during their lifetimes the British artistic establishment took the work of Grant more seriously – giving Grant more press coverage, often casting Bell's work as a pale imitation of his, and confusing their work at her expense. Such differentials in professional status outside Bloomsbury need to be accounted for when discussing power relations within the group.

Understanding Bloomsbury's relationship to the institutions of British culture is especially important given that the group's members largely saw themselves as part of an oppositional movement. Again, and as Nina Miller observes in a different context, this is an instance where gender must be carefully considered: "As outsiders to the public sphere of cultural value, women had neither the investment in nor the sense of direct pressure to perpetuate the status quo that men had; hence neither could their opposition-ality to it have the same defined cast" (Miller 1991: 54). Miller argues that women writers (and artists) identified themselves vicariously with their male counterparts in order to see themselves as artistic subjects. While Miller is writing about women in heterosexual relationships in the bohemian Green-wich Village circles of New York City, we will suggest that her model can usefully be applied to the case of Vanessa Bell, whose involvement with Duncan Grant must be considered on a number of intersecting fronts – from the domestic and personal to the professional and public.

The relationship of women to the larger field of cultural traditions and institutions was a central preoccupation of Virginia Woolf, who developed a highly theorized and materialist feminist analysis of women's exclusion from literary history in *A Room of One's Own* (1929) in addition to a feminist analysis of the causes of war in *Three Guineas* (1938). Both works exhibit sensitivity to nuances of privilege and class as does her 1930 essay, "Memories of a working women's guild." In this essay, Woolf anticipates Williams's distinction between social *conscience* and social *consciousness* by noting how the political support and sympathy of middle and upper middle-class women for working women's concerns is based on conviction rather than experience or feeling:

All these questions ... which matter so intensely to the people here, questions of sanitation and education and wages, this demand for an extra shilling, or another year at school, for eight hours instead of nine behind a counter or in a mill, leave me, in my own blood and bones, untouched. If every reform they demand was granted this very instant it would not matter to me a single jot. Hence my interest is merely altruistic.

(Woolf 1967: 136)

While avoiding a too easy conflation of gender and class, Woolf nonetheless suggests a *kind* of class identification based on gender; this is most obvious, perhaps, in the lack of formal education shared by the "daughters of educated men" and working-class women (see also Rosenbaum 1983a: 32).

Although with less political and social self-consciousness, Vanessa Bell also dealt with the representation of women in a number of portraits, self-portraits, and genre scenes produced throughout her career. Here we are especially interested in a series of early portraits of women executed between 1912 and 1919 (including paintings of Virginia Woolf, writers Iris Tree and Mary Hutchinson, and physician Marie Moralt) because their curiously unindividuated nature seems to foreground many of the tensions underlying the notion of female professional identity during this period. Unlike Brooks, whose friends were usually celebrities (e.g. Ida Rubenstein) and who exhibited her portraits in mainstream as opposed to avant-garde or alternative venues, Bell largely painted her portraits for the enjoyment of friends.[5] Such informality combined with the fact that England (in contrast to Paris) was perceived as a cultural backwater where the making of reputations was not taken as seriously, meant that unlike Brooks and Laurencin, Bell had more room to experiment with the genre without being negatively stereotyped as a fashionable portrait painter. Critics have observed that in these portraits Bell repeatedly portrays the women with curiously featureless and dissolving faces (see, for example, Casteras 1984 and Gillespie 1988). One of the most conspicuous examples is her image of *Mary Hutchinson* (1915) (Figure 3.1) where the brush work of the face blends into a flesh-toned background which is bordered on the left and right edges by an abstract pattern of stripes that gestures to Vanessa Bell's own abstract paintings from the period. While undoubtedly the stress on the surfaces and the self-conscious reference to her own art take up the formalist concerns of Post-Impressionism, such pictures also emphasize (whether intentionally or not) the painter's problematic role in the representation of femininity, which in turn raises questions about the stability of sexual categories and gendered identities. Such recurring, dissolving images of women in Bell's work should be seen in the wider context of the much negotiated imagery of women in the suffrage campaigns of this period as well as in relation to the anomalous position of women in the Bloomsbury Group.[6] Rather than reading the

61

Figure 3.1 Vanessa Bell, *Portrait of Mary Hutchinson* (1915). Oil on board. 73.2 × 57.7 cm. The Tate Gallery, London.

visual language of these paintings as a simple metaphor of female "experience," it is more useful to consider the ways in which Vanessa Bell's pictures of women and Virginia Woolf's writing provide insights into the particular creative working conditions of the Bloomsbury women.

Although Woolf and Bell saw a lot of their Bloomsbury friends, both women were surprisingly isolated from other modernist women writers and painters, particularly those who experimented with lifestyle. Katherine Mansfield was perhaps the only other gifted and committed woman writer with whom Woolf had sustained personal contact (although she was intimate with the novelist and travel-writer Vita Sackville-West there was never any question in their relationship of who was the more gifted writer – Woolf rather unkindly characterizing Sackville-West as writing "with a pen of brass" (Woolf 1977: 150)); and, although The Hogarth Press published works by Gertrude Stein and Laura Riding, Woolf makes only fleeting reference to them in her diaries and letters.[7] Furthermore, despite a childhood acquaintance with Una, Lady Troubridge and despite her willingness to testify at the 1928 obscenity trial of Radclyffe Hall's *The Well of Loneliness*, Woolf seems not to have been aware of such communities of women as Natalie Barney's lesbian salon in Paris (Rosenman 1989: 641, fn. 31). Nor did she publish in the "little magazines" – many of which were edited by women such as Dora Marsden, Harriet Monroe, Margaret Anderson, and Jane Heap – which were a characteristic of literary modernism.[8]

In many ways, however, Bell was even more isolated from women's modernism than Woolf. Much of her painting took place in the rural surroundings of her farmhouse, Charleston, near Lewes in Sussex.[9] At Charleston her closest painting companions were Duncan Grant, with whom she shared many models and still life arrangements, and sometimes Roger Fry. Furthermore, Roger Fry and Clive Bell were probably her most influential critics in terms of pointing out old masterpieces and current trends, providing aesthetic theories, and assessing her work both informally and in published reviews. Bell's move to Charleston in 1916 – a way of providing the farm work which exempted Duncan Grant and David Garnett from conscription – marked a shift in her relationship to the contemporary art scene, for in London she had been more involved with organized groups. In 1905, for example, she had founded the Friday Club, an exhibiting society comprised mainly of fellow artists from the Slade School. The club included a lively group of women, several of whom – Margery Snowden, Sylvia Milman, and Mary Creighton – were Bell's friends. By 1913, however, Vanessa Bell had withdrawn from the Friday Club, finding its members somewhat "amateurish" as she became more interested in the type of modernist work exhibited at the Post-Impressionist exhibitions held in London in 1910 and 1912 (Shone 1975). And, as we have already noted, the move to Charleston represented to Bell, in part, the end of an era marked by innocence and experimentation: "All the world was hostile close round one and Bloomsbury had no changing atmosphere in which to move and expand and grow. So when the young men were finally forced to take some share in what was going on for the most part they chose to work on farms, and this meant a dispersal and general scattering" (V. Bell 1975: 83). And, in spite of the fact that Virginia Woolf drew clear parallels in *Three Guineas* between the "tyrannies" of the public and the private worlds, she nonetheless insisted – through her call for an "Outsiders Society" – on a private solution to that most public of problems, war. The "Outsiders Society," supported by "the psychology of private life," would "maintain an attitude of complete indifference" in response to a masculine call-to-arms and would thus effectively disarm unthinking patriotism (Woolf 1938: 194).

Although it is tempting to speculate, it is impossible to know how greater exchanges with other modernist women writers and painters might have affected Virginia Woolf and Vanessa Bell. Their relative isolation from such networks may be partly explained by the prevailing Bloomsbury ethos of individualism and its concomitant distinction between the public and the private. The emphasis Bloomsbury placed on protecting private life markedly contrasts with the slippage between public and private, performative and personal, which characterized many other modernist women of our study. While Vanessa Bell was painting in relative seclusion at Charleston, artists such as Gluck and Romaine Brooks deliberately displayed their lifestyles and their work in the pages of the popular press and glossy magazines of the period.[10] In their very public adoption of masculine attire, Gluck and Brooks staged a transgression which contrasts sharply with Bloomsbury's reluctance to be publicly scrutinized, a reluctance which is noted in a letter Virginia Woolf wrote to her nephew Quentin Bell during the obscenity trial of Radclyffe Hall's *The Well of Loneliness*:

> At this moment our thoughts centre upon Sapphism – we have to uphold the morality of that Well of all that's stagnant and lukewarm and neither one thing or the other; The Well of Loneliness. I'm just off to a tea party to discuss our evidence. Leonard and Nessa say I mustn't go into the box, because I should cast a shadow over Bloomsbury. Forgetting where I was I should speak the truth.
>
> (Woolf 1977: 555)

For Woolf and Bell the Bloomsbury Group's distinction between the private and the public life was further complicated, on the one hand, by the weight of a Victorian and familial discourse of separate spheres and, on the other, by an emerging discourse of women's professionalism.

PROFESSIONALISM, FEMINISM, AND MODERNISM

> If you succeed in your professions the words "For God and Empire" will very likely be written, like the address on a dog-collar, round your neck.
>
> (Woolf 1938: 127)

Virginia Woolf addresses these remarks in warning to women who aspire to join "the procession of the sons of educated men" and to enter the "preaching, teaching, administering justice, practising medicine, making money" professions. As she notes in the second part of *Three Guineas*, published in 1938, women had been allowed access to professional life in Great Britain for approximately twenty years and, although they had not yet achieved significant power or salaries, they *were* "trapesing along at the tail end of the procession" (112). Women were at a historical point of transition, "on the bridge" between the private house and the public world. The moment had arrived, argued Woolf, to ask serious questions about what we might today call professional deformation and its social consequences. She noted that "the professions have a certain undeniable effect upon the professors. They make the people who practise them possessive, jealous of any infringement of their rights, and highly combative if anyone dares dispute them," and asked whether "in another century or so if we practise the professions in the same way, shall we not be just as possessive, just as jealous, just as pugnacious, just as positive as to the verdict of God, Nature, Law and Property as these gentlemen are now?" (121). If women were not only to enter but to *better* the professions (and, as a result, to reduce the chances of war) they must "help all properly qualified people, of whatever sex, class or colour," to enter professional life. In the practice of their professions, women must refuse to give up the lessons learned by the uneducated "daughers of educated men": poverty, chastity, derision, and freedom from unreal loyalties. That is, women must earn only enough money to be financially independent and to satisfy their physical and intellectual needs; they must refuse to "sell [their] brain[s] for the sake of money;" they must refuse (and poke fun at the desire for) fame and praise; and they must rid themselves of the kinds of unreal loyalties (national, religious, family) which divide communities and lead to war (145–46).

By the time Woolf published *Three Guineas* in 1938, she had been worrying at the question of women and the professions for over a decade. In October 1928 she delivered the two papers on "Women and fiction" at Newnham and Girton Colleges, Cambridge, which would evolve into *A Room of One's Own* (1929), and in January 1931 she gave a speech on "Professions for women" to the National Society for Women's Service. It was this speech which became *The Years* (1937) and *Three Guineas*.[11] Throughout these texts there is a clear and absolutely consistent identification between professionalism and earning one's living. This identification manifests itself in Woolf's rhetorical appeal to precise sums of money – the £500 a year of *A Room of One's Own* and the three guineas of her book by that name[12] – and to material conditions of work. Indeed, she claims throughout these polemical texts that one of the reasons the profession of writing appeals to women is, in marked contrast to music and painting, the cheapness of its materials: "For ten and sixpence one can buy paper enough to write all the plays of Shakespeare – if one has a mind that way" (Woolf 1942: 149).

Woolf was certainly not alone among feminists of the period in emphasizing the primary importance of financial independence. *The Freewoman*, for example, consistently argued that the ability to earn a living wage was more crucial to women's independence than the vote.[13] The following entry appeared in the 7 December 1911 issue, a full eighteen years before the publication of *A Room of One's Own*:

> the feature of the week which we consider of greatest importance to Feminists is the fact that a woman has been appointed Insurance Commissioner at a salary of £1,000 a year, no diminution of salary being made on account of sex. This is a landmark.... We shall claim a share of titles and places of consideration, but, above all, we shall endeavour to rouse women's ambition in the attainment of high wages. One thing women lack above all others, and that thing is money.
>
> (Gawthorpe 1911: 42)

In 1919 the *Fortnightly Review* published Gertrude M. Tuckwell's "Equal pay for equal work" (the title must give sad pause to feminists today) which documented continuing as well as new inequities in pay rates for men and women in industry and the professions. Tuckwell's article serves as a useful and sobering companion piece to *Three Guineas*. Published the year following women's partial enfranchisement in Great Britain, it was written while much of the legislation which would allow women access to the professions was before the courts and before Parliament. The vote and access to professional life were, of course, granted "as a recognition of the part women [bore] during the war in the service of the State" (Tuckwell 1919: 72).[14] This gives added ironic force to Woolf's argument since gains won as a result of one war were to be used to prevent another.

The fact that arguments about the significance of financial independence for women, and about the necessity for women to break into those professions which were still dominated by men, had been made repeatedly and forcefully since the early years of the century suggests that, in this area, Woolf's great contribution was less as an originator than as a popularizer. Comments in several letters to friends and admirers after the publication of *A Room of One's Own* suggest that she saw the function of that book as largely pedagogical and its audience as comprised primarily of young women. In a letter to Dorothy Brett, for example, she remarks, "I am very glad you like A Room. It was rather popularised for the young and should have had more in it. But I wanted them to swallow certain ideas with a view to setting their brains to work" (Woolf 1978b: 167). A much later draft letter to Benedict Nicolson (the art historian and son of Vita Sackville-West) passionately defends Bloomsbury's commitment to social change against his charge that Roger Fry (and, by implication, the rest of Bloomsbury) occupied "an intensely private world" and "allowed the spirit of Nazism to grow without taking any steps to check it" (Woolf 1980b: 413–14). In response, Woolf cites her own non-fictional texts – *The Common Reader, A Room of One's Own*, and *Three Guineas* – in the same breath as Leonard Woolf's *Empire and Commerce in Africa: A Study in Economic Imperialism* (1928) and John Maynard Keynes's *The Economic Consequences of the Peace* (1919), in this way emphasizing what she saw as the primarily social function of these texts as opposed to her novels, which she expected to perform a different kind of work and which were consequently intended for a different audience (Woolf 1980b: 419–21). It might also be argued that Vanessa Bell's participation in directing the Omega Workshops along with Roger Fry and Duncan Grant was an example of Bloomsbury's social commitment, in terms both of providing work for unemployed avant-garde artists and introducing affordable Post-Impressionist designs to the broader English public in the form of relatively inexpensive decorative objects, ranging from furniture and textiles to pottery and needlework.[15]

Woolf's commitment to a materialist cultural politics is well known, as is her commitment to a more balanced gender and class representation in the professions. In this, too, she was neither alone nor original. As Nancy F. Cott points out in *The Grounding of Modern Feminism*, "Since the mid-nineteenth century, women's rights activists had made access to the professions part and parcel of their demands for balancing the sexual power in society" (Cott 1987: 215). However, less fully explored has been the question of the relationship between professionalism and the experience and self-representation of women writers or artists, particularly in the "modernist" period. For although a discourse of "professionalism" had been forming around the arts and letters since the later nineteenth century, it manifested itself in different ways for men and women, and amongst women of different classes. We will locate some of these differences through a discussion of the effect of professionalization on the writer's or artist's choice of genre; however, we will first turn to Nancy Cott and Louis Menand to sketch in a little of the history of the relationship between, on the one hand, professionalism and feminism, and, on the other, professionalism and the arts.

Although Nancy Cott's chapter on "Professionalism and feminism" focuses almost exclusively on the experience of *American* women in the first decades of this century, some of her arguments can be extrapolated to help explain part of the appeal of a newly conceived or "feminized" professionalism to Englishwomen like Virginia Woolf. As Cott points out, "Unlike business or politics, careers in the professions were not easily reducible to the profit motive or the naked drive for power; the hallmarks of the professions were training and service, open to idealization by aspiring women" (216). The appeal of professionalism was, in part, the appeal of being judged on one's merits and individual talents – according to "empirical, rational, and objective standards" (234) – rather than on the basis of one's gender or class affiliation. Significantly, this appeal could also create a conflict between individual and collective identity. By the later 1920s and 1930s most women professionals had abandoned a collective feminist identity and had invested heavily in "the professional credo, that individual merit would be judged according to objective and verifiable standards" (234).

The danger of women adopting a professional credo was foreseen by Woolf, who worried that women would either be appropriated by the establishment (as her comments in *Three Guineas* suggest) or that they would abandon their larger quest for social equity in an increasingly individualistic and competitive professional sphere. Although Woolf and Bell felt that they should be fairly rewarded for their cultural labour (and, as our epigraphs to this chapter indicate, delighted in being paid), both were curiously ambivalent about their own professional status. Many factors seem to have contributed to their ambivalence: the lack of a women's tradition, the somewhat isolated and individualist ethos of Bloomsbury, and the absence of clearly defined criteria for measuring success within the avant-garde. For women, the last issue was particularly complicated. Too much favourable recognition from the establishment inferred that one's work was not breaking new ground. Indeed, it was better to be criticized or ignored by the mainstream press. All too often, however, women were ignored and criticized on account of their gender rather than on the basis of a serious evaluation of their work. The same sorts of gender bias were equally operative in alternative critical circles with the result that women were cast as marginal for all the wrong reasons. In Bell's case, there was the further complication that the practice of painting rarely followed the usual career trajectory as she explained in a letter to Roger Fry:

> You know it's utter nonsense for you to talk of having done everything at the wrong time of life. Really intelligent people with something in them like you and me, always are old and sedate when they are young. . . . You know painters especially don't do anything very good till they're nearly 50. Isn't that true?
>
> (Spalding 1983: 102.)

In part, too, Woolf's and Bell's ambivalence about their professional identity stemmed from the fact that the ideology of professionalism during this period was not monolithic. As Louis Menand points out in *Discovering Modernism*, although "it clearly belongs to the movement toward a democratic social system and a free-market economy," professionalism also "threatens to replace class elitism with elitism of another kind" through the principles of professional training, self-government, and self-policing; the professional association comes to represent the collective authority of the group (Menand 1987: 112–13, 118). Menand charts the effect of the rise of an ideology of professionalism on literature but many of his insights can be extrapolated to the visual arts. He argues, in part, that "the emergence of the values associated with professionalism influenced to some degree the way literature was perceived by its audience" and, more specifically, that "the critical vocabulary used to distinguish good literature from other kinds of writing, and to justify the social importance of the literary vocation, adapted itself to meet the standard of a set of altered occupational standards" (100). The professionalization of the arts and of the artist – underway since the later nineteenth century – had a number of effects, many of which reached their apogee in the modernist period: the professional was distinguished from the dilettante or the amateur;[16] the "professional association" became a distin- guishing feature of modernism, taking the form of various "isms" – Imagism, Futurism, etc. – and of group publishing and exhibition (118–22); the notion of a tradition became central to modernist criticism (this corresponded, of course, with the establishment of English and art history as disciplines within the university), coinciding paradoxically with a disparagement of the arts and literature of the nineteenth century (100); and, finally, professionalism meant the entrenchment of formalism (129).

However, each of these effects coincides with the experience of the woman artist or writer in different ways. For instance, would the professional association mean the same thing to male and female writers? This question becomes especially pertinent in light of, for example, Ezra Pound's disparag- ing comments about the decline of Imagism into "Amygism." His remarks were made after Amy Lowell arranged – following the publication of Pound's 1914 anthology *Des Imagistes* and independently of him – for the publication of three subsequent volumes of Imagist poetry,[17] and they suggest that the inclusion (or worse, the predominance) of women writers in such ventures as Imagist group publishing meant the sure decline of the movement or the association. Furthermore, would professionalism be similarly understood by women writers and women artists, given that women entered the literary profession earlier and in greater numbers than they entered the visual arts? Gertrude Stein and Marie Laurencin, for example, had very different professional self-images; Stein was more inter- ested in disciplinary autonomy and invention, Laurencin in making money from her art. Would the notion of a tradition mean the same thing to women writers, most of whose literary foremothers consisted of now disparaged nineteenth-century novelists and poets, and women painters who had comparatively few foremothers to evoke? Were amateurism and dilettantism labels that could be used against the self-publishing and patronage efforts of very wealthy women like Natalie Barney, Romaine Brooks, and Peggy

Guggenheim? We will attempt to address at least some of these questions by examining more closely the ways in which Woolf and Bell, as two women artists of the professional class, represented themselves and other women artists.

REPRESENTING PROFESSIONALISM, OR, "WOMEN ARTISTS ARE ALL AMATEURS"

Women in the educated classes are almost universally taught more or less of some branch or other of the fine arts, but not that they may gain their living or their social consequence by it. Women artists are all amateurs.

This quotation from John Stuart Mill's *The Subjection of Women* precedes Norman Feltes's discussion, in *Modes of Production of Victorian Novels*, of George Eliot's mid-nineteenth century engagement with a newly coalescing discourse of literary professionalism (Feltes 1986: 41). Feltes argues that it is important "to see professionalization historically as ... a project of occupational organization for control of the relations of production *and to the exclusion of women*" (50, emphasis added); furthermore, he proposes to read "in the details of George Eliot's publishing practice ... the struggle between her vocation, her will to be a professional, and the dominant, patriarchal structures of professional authorship and publishing" (45). Our strategy is slightly different. In this section and the next, we will examine not only the publishing and exhibition practices of Woolf and Bell but also their representational practices; in this way we hope to expose some of the tensions for modernist women between, on the one hand, a "feminist" ideology of professionalism which demanded the right to a fair, living wage for one's cultural labour and, on the other hand, an individualist and "modernist" ideology of artistic (and financial) disinterestedness. This tension was expressed, by men and women of the period, in a sometimes contested and much-defended hierarchization and gendering of literary and visual genres. This hierarchization was reinforced by the increasing numbers of women in the artistic professions and the consequent devaluing of genres – such as the portrait and, to a lesser degree, the novel – which expressed a more overt association with women and with professionalism (writing for money); this devaluation coincided with the privileging of more seemingly disinterested genres, such as abstract painting and avant-garde poetry.[18]

Mill's 1869 observation that "Women artists are all amateurs" would seem ironically to be borne out by an examination of the representation of the woman artist in Virginia Woolf's novels and in Vanessa Bell's portraits. Although critics have pointed out that many of Woolf's heroines, such as Mrs. Ramsay in *To the Lighthouse* and Clarissa Dalloway in *Mrs. Dalloway*, are "life artists" – using such media as personal relationships and parties to express their sensibilities – only two of her ten novels contain detailed portrayals of women engaged in more recognized forms of artistic expression.[19] Lily Briscoe in *To the Lighthouse* (1927) is a painter and Miss La Trobe in *Between the Acts* (1941) is a playwright. They are also amateurs and spinsters, "outsiders" who are tolerated by the communities on whose edges they live, and who seem to regard their unmarried status and their financial disinterestedness as essential to their art. In this way they would appear to represent the "daughters of educated men" to whom Woolf appeals in *Three Guineas*, members of the Society of Outsiders, practising the traditional women's virtues of chastity and poverty. However, given Woolf's emphasis on the importance of women's accession to the professions, combined with her explicit description of the arts *as* a profession, Lily Briscoe's and Miss La Trobe's *lack* of professional status indicates a deeper ambivalence on Woolf's part. This ambivalence regarding the value and desirability of "professionalism" is articulated by Woolf on two different fronts – journalism and novel-writing – with two different results. As Andrew McNeillie, editor of the newly collected *Essays of Virginia Woolf*, points out, as a result of her forty-year career as a literary journalist, much of Woolf's achievement was "traditional in nature;" he notes that this gives her a "unique position among modernist writers as a woman of letters" (McNeillie in Woolf 1986: ix).

The fact that much of Woolf's literary journalism was "traditional" in nature, albeit brilliant, may be ascribed to the demands and conventions of the magazines and newspapers where she placed her work. Her insistence on making a living *as* a "woman of letters" meant that whenever possible she sought out publication venues which would pay her adequately for her labour. Consequently she published very little in the "little magazines" which have been so closely identified with literary avant-garde modernism. Even a cursory glance at B.J. Kirkpatrick's invaluable *Bibliography of Virginia Woolf* indicates that over a period of almost forty years – a period representing literally hundreds of reviews and essays – Woolf published perhaps fewer than a dozen pieces in what we would today call "alternative" journals. Her primary outlets were such mainstream liberal and left-of-centre publications as the *Times Literary Supplement*, the *Nation and Athenaeum*, the *New Republic*, *The Criterion*, and the *New Statesman and Nation*, with occasional appearances in mass circulation women's magazines like *Good Housekeeping* and *Vogue*.[20] It is significant that Bruce Richmond, the editor of the *Times Literary Supplement* had originally approached Woolf's illustrious father, Leslie Stephen, as a potential reviewer in 1902; it is also significant that Roger Fry became art critic for *The Athenaeum* in 1901 (before going on to edit the *Burlington Magazine* in 1909), fellow Bloomsbury Group member Desmond MacCarthy became the drama critic for the *New Statesman* in 1913 and its literary editor in 1920 (until 1927), Leonard

Woolf took over the literary editorship of the *Nation and Athenaeum* in 1923 (after Maynard Keynes assumed the chairmanship of the new Board of Directors), a post he held until 1930, and close friend T.S. Eliot took on the full-time editorship of *The Criterion* in 1925. Like Vanessa Bell, Woolf tended to work within her circle of close friends and extended family. On the very few occasions when she did place her work in less familiar or non-traditional venues, her motivation seems to have been either political conviction and sympathy (though again publication was usually also prompted by personal friendships) or literary prestige. Thus, for example, in 1920 she published "The plumage bill" in the *Woman's Leader and the Common Cause* (edited by Ray Strachey), in 1929 she published two excerpts from *A Room of One's Own* in the feminist journal *Time and Tide* (founded by Lady Rhonnda), and in 1936 she published "Why art today follows politics" in the *Daily Worker*. Interestingly, she placed two pieces in *The Dial* – "Mrs Dalloway in Bond Street" in 1923 and "Miss Ormerod" in 1924 – the only small literary magazine whose good opinion she seemed to regard as the imprimatur of modernist success, as a 1920 diary entry indicates: "I have read 4 pages of sneer & condescending praise of me in the Dial the other day [in a review by Kenneth Burke of *Night and Day* and *The Voyage Out*].... The Dial is everything honest vigorous & advanced; so I ought to feel crushed" (Woolf 1978a: 118).

In 1921 Woolf pondered the relationship between "popularity" and literary reputation and drew an implicit distinction between the writing she did for money (her articles) and the writing which expressed "my own point of view" (her novels).

> Well, this question of praise & fame must be faced.... How much difference does popularity make? ... One wants, as Roger said very truly yesterday, to be kept up to the mark.... One does *not* want an established reputation, such as I think I was getting, as one of our leading female novelists. I have still, of course, to gather in all the private criticism, which is the real test. When I have weighed this I shall be able to say whether I am "interesting" or obsolete. Anyhow, I feel quite alert enough to stop, if I'm obsolete. I shan't become a machine, unless a machine for grinding articles. As I write, there rises somewhere in my head that queer, & very pleasant sense, of something which I want to write; my own point of view.
>
> (Woolf 1978a: 106–7)

It is significant that Woolf here associates – in a gesture typical of avant-garde modernism – "popularity" both with the feminine and the marketplace; it is only outside of market considerations, with the help of her own press and the "private criticism" of friends, that she can aspire to genuine literary substance. Given that Woolf's first novel, *The Voyage Out*, was published by her half-brother Gerald Duckworth (associated at least metonymically with the sexual abuse she suffered from her other half-brother, George Duck-worth), it is important to stress here that Woolf's co-ownership of The Hogarth Press represented for her freedom from what she saw as two interrelated markets: that of the exchange of women in a patriarchal sexual economy, and that of the exchange of commodities in a capitalist economy. Her sense that women were victimized by both is clear in a 1938 comment to Shena, Lady Simon: "But who are the capitalists? not women. Every day I'm having that proved to me" (Woolf 1980b: 303). Thus in Woolf's case the financial disinterestedness to which avant-garde rhetoric and self-presentation aspired was complicated by the sexual politics of the market-place; "popularity," which enabled one to make a living wage by writing, could be a sign of professionalism or of a more ambivalently inscribed femininity.[21]

Just as Woolf's commitment to an ethos of women's professionalism resulted in her decision to publish in periodicals which would pay a fair wage, and thus also resulted in her absence from the more avant-garde "little magazines," so her ambivalence about that same professionalism is expressed formally in those novels which explore the condition of the woman artist. Not only are Lily Briscoe and Miss La Trobe amateurs, but the novels in which they appear have both been described as generic hybrids: *To the Lighthouse* as a novel/elegy and *Between the Acts* as a novel/drama. As Woolf notes in her 1925 diary, "I am making up 'To the Lighthouse' – the sea is to be heard all through it. I have an idea that I will invent a new name for my books to supplant 'novel.' A new —— by Virginia Woolf. But what? Elegy?" (Woolf 1980a: 34).[22]

In fact, any consideration of the woman artist or writer suggested to Woolf a crisis in genre, as her discussion of the "tools" of the writer's craft in *A Room of One's Own* indicates. The following passage elaborates the effects upon the woman writer of the lack of a women's literary tradition, but it also raises questions about the gendering and the hierarchization of genre:

> such a lack of tradition, such a scarcity and inadequacy of tools, must have told enormously upon the writing of women. Moreover, a book is not made of sentences laid end to end, but of sentences built, if an image helps, into arcades or domes. And this shape too has been made by men out of their own needs for their own uses. There is no reason to think that the form of the epic or of the poetic play suit a woman any more than the sentence suits her. But all the older forms of literature were hardened and set by the time she became a writer. The novel alone was young enough to be soft in her hands – another reason, perhaps, why she wrote novels. Yet who shall say that even now "the novel" (I give it inverted commas to mark my sense of the words' inadequacy), who shall say that even this most pliable of all forms is rightly shaped for her use? No doubt we shall find her knocking that into shape for

herself when she has the free use of her limbs; and providing some new vehicle, not necessarily in verse, for the poetry in her. For it is the poetry that is still denied outlet.

(Woolf 1929: 115–16)

Just as Woolf concludes this passage with an appeal to "the poetry that is still denied outlet," so she concludes the book with an appeal to "the dead poet who was Shakespeare's sister" in the hope that she will "put on the body which she has so often laid down" (172). Indeed, the underlying logic of *A Room of One's Own* suggests that poetry is a higher literary form than the novel, and much of the book is devoted to answering the question of why there have been so few women poets and playwrights while there have been so many gifted and successful women novelists. Woolf's conclusion is primarily a materialist one; poetry and plays demand a degree of concentration and freedom from domestic distraction that is still denied women (99–100). However, the question which is *not* asked is why poetry, a genre in which, according to Woolf, women did not historically excel, is privileged above the novel, a genre in which women obviously excelled.

As Celeste Schenck points out, this is a political question. While traditional genre theory, "the law of genre," suggests "the enforcement of generic purity, the policing of borders" – without making too much of the similarities, we want to point out that these are functions which are shared by the professional association – Schenck argues that genres "might be more usefully conceived as overdetermined loci of contention and conflict than as ideal literary types that transcendentally precede and predetermine a literary work" (Schenck 1989: 281, 282). If we accept this premise, which is certainly borne out in Woolf's case, and if we also accept Fredric Jameson's premises – that first, "the production of aesthetic or narrative form is to be seen as an ideological act in its own right, with the function of inventing imaginary or formal 'solutions' to unresolvable social contradictions" (Jameson 1981: 79), and that second, "Genres are essentially literary *institutions*, or social contracts between a writer and a specific public, whose function is to specify the proper use of a particular artifact" (106) – it is possible to begin to understand the complicated ways in which an ideology of professionalism is intertwined with a crisis of genre in Woolf's and Bell's work.

Michael Levenson has argued that the highly poetic lyricism of *To the Lighthouse* "positions [Woolf's] work within an unstated but active play of opposing genres. Specifically, it represents an attempt to escape from the prestige of epic, the very shape of which, she suggests in *A Room of One's Own*, fails to conform to the sensibility of women." Moreover, "the effort to write a novel that achieves the self-containment of a lyric poem ... is in this case entirely congruent with the problem of personal integrity" (Levenson 1991: 171, 205). Levenson's reading of what we are calling a crisis of genre – a reading which is fully cognizant of Woolf's sense of "contending modernisms" (174) – is useful and convincing. However, while it accounts for the class positioning of Lily Briscoe,[23] it does not account for her amateur status. Significantly, her amateurism is implied rather than described; it is represented almost entirely by the *absence* of references to, for example, the apparatus of professional associations, exhibition, and connoisseurship. Indeed, the few direct references to the probable fate of Lily's painting reinforce the degree to which both her professional *and* her social status are marginal, redundant: "It was then too, in that chill and windy way, as she began to paint, that there forced themselves upon her other things, her own inadequacy, her insignificance, keeping house for her father off the Brompton Road" (Woolf 1927: 34–35); "only a few random marks scrawled upon the canvas remained. And it would never be seen; never be hung even, and there was Mr. Tansley whispering in her ear, 'Women can't paint, women can't write'" (78); "There it was – her picture. Yes, with all its green and blues, its lines running up and across, its attempt at something. It would be hung in the attics, she thought; it would be destroyed. But what did that matter?" (319–20). Lily is clearly positioned outside of the two economies which marked, for Woolf, the space in which she negotiated her professional identity: the sexual (represented here by marriage – "With her little Chinese eyes and her puckered-up face she would never marry; one could not take her painting very seriously" (31)) and the economic (represented by professionalism).

Critics have commented on the fact that, at the novel's conclusion, Lily Briscoe is the same age as her author; this is obviously significant in a novel that was, from its inception, so openly autobiographical.[24] However, it is also important because it locates Lily (who would have been born, like Woolf, in 1882) very explicitly as a product of late Victorian England, as the daughter of an educated man, who was herself denied formal education or training, and as "redundant" in a marriage market. Lily's vocation is unrecognized and her social, like her professional, identity is constituted by lack. Miss La Trobe, on the other hand, is an outsider by reason of her sexual orientation; snubbed by the villagers whose pageant she has written and staged, she sits alone at the Inn, nodding over her drink and dreaming of "words without meaning – wonderful words" (Woolf 1941: 248).

Miss La Trobe is, together with Doris Kilman of *Mrs. Dalloway*, one of the most unreadable of Woolf's characters and critics have been divided on their interpretations of her. Judith L. Johnston has noted parallels between La Trobe's directorial and dramatic style and that of the rising Hitler and Mussolini (Johnston 1987: 264, 266–67); B.H. Fussell, on the other hand, argues that Miss La Trobe is a "caricature of the artist," a satiric self-portrait: "here is a Portrait of the Artist as old Bossy, a squat spinster" (Fussell 1980: 263). However, Miss La Trobe is not simply a spinster but a lesbian, and her lesbianism is important to an understanding of the implications of the differences between her artistic practice and that of Lily Briscoe. Unlike painting, playwriting and directing are public performances; as Miss La Trobe scribbles in the margin of her manuscript, "I am the slave of my audience" (Woolf 1941: 247). Although she is an amateur, her work and consequently her life are in the public eye; being outside a capitalist and a patriarchal sexual economy has protected neither her privacy nor the consolations of her artistic vision. A figure of fun to the villagers, who wonder if "perhaps, then, she wasn't altogether a lady?" (72), her willingness to engage in public display combined with her lack of professional status position her uncomfortably in their eyes between the masculine and the feminine, between the public and the private, the social and the domestic. Her polemics – which are perhaps intended to evoke Woolf's own *Three Guineas* ("She wanted to expose them, as it were, to douche them, with present-time reality" (209)) – isolate her almost completely from the community which resents the mirrors she has trained upon them. Both *To the Lighthouse* and *Between the Acts* enact the difficulty of holding in suspension, much less reconciling, the competing claims of professionalism and artistry, the public life and the private life, the polemical and the visionary; however, it is Miss La Trobe who most clearly marks an uncomfortable transition, positioned as she is "between the acts" of women's social and cultural history.

"ALL THIS FATAL PRETTINESS": A DOUBLE MARGINALITY

Vanessa Bell's portraits of male artists and writers frequently depict them either at work – as in *The Studio: Duncan Grant and Henri Doucet Painting at Asheham* (1912), or *Portrait of Duncan Grant Painting* (c. 1915), or in her 1933 portrait of *Roger Fry* with a brush and palette, or 1940 portrait of *Leonard Woolf* at his desk – or with allegorical emblems of their vocations, as in her 1911 portrait of *Lytton Strachey* in which he is depicted seated in an armchair with a number of books displayed above his head. Interestingly, in instances where she depicted both male and female artists, as in *Frederick and Jessie Etchells Painting* (1912) (Figure 3.2), Frederick is shown upright painting at an easel while Jessie crouches seated on the floor working in a more confined space. Moreover, many of her portraits of female professionals such as the poet *Iris Tree* (1915) or the writer *Mary Hutchinson* (1915; this portrait is also called *Mrs. St. John Hutchinson*) (Figure 3.1) contain no visual references to their work. Only the 1912 and 1934 portraits of Virginia Woolf refer, and then usually obliquely as through the presence of an open though unread book, to the woman sitter's profession.[25] More typically Bell omitted professional references in portraits of her sister (see Figure 3.3).

Significantly, a large number of Bell's representations of women fall instead into the category of the domestic genre painting, a traditionally undervalued genre. Among the best known of these are *A Conversation*

Figure 3.2 Vanessa Bell, *Frederick and Jessie Etchells Painting* (1912). Oil on board. 51.1 × 52.9 cm. The Tate Gallery, London.

Figure 3.3 Vanessa Bell, *Virginia Woolf* (1912). Oil on board. 15¾ × 12 inches. Monks House, Rodmell, Sussex (The National Trust). Reproduced by permission of Angelica Garnett.

(1913–16), *The Tub* (1917), *The Nursery* (1930–32), and *Interior with Housemaid* (1939). While the usually anonymous women in these paintings are engaged in some form of identifiable activity, the women of her portraits are either lost in revery (as in the Virginia Woolf portraits) or more formally composed and more obviously sitting *for* the artist (as in the Iris Tree and Mary Hutchinson portraits). It is possible to read against the grain of these two genres some indication of the tensions Bell experienced in the divided sense of herself as, on the one hand, a serious and professional artist and, on the other hand, a wife, mother, lover. Although space limitations preclude analyzing these various roles at length, it should be emphasized that after painting, Bell found her three children one of the most absorbing aspects of her life (Spalding 1983: 77). Her creative organization of domestic surround-ings (much admired by members of Bloomsbury including her sister) was, to a large extent, to accommodate the needs of her children and her lovers, as well as her painting. Attaining a domestic environment that could encompass all these elements clearly afforded Bell great pleasure which was expressed in many paintings of maternal and domestic subjects, as well as in eleven photographic albums containing snapshots of family life taken between 1907 and 1946.[26]

It was through portraiture that Bell first began to realize herself as a professional artist. As Frances Spalding notes:

> Throughout this period [c. 1905] she was attempting to place her painting on a more professional basis. She began to take an interest in portraiture and early in 1905 had gone down to the home of Lord Robert Cecil at Chelwood Gate in Sussex in order to paint a portrait of his wife Nelly, who had been introduced to the Stephens by Violet Dickinson.... [T]his was the first painting Vanessa exhibited. When shown at the New Gallery in April 1905 it brought the artist her first portrait commission from a stranger. (55)

Furthermore, during the summer and autumn of 1905 Bell founded the Friday Club which provided not only a community of artists but also the promise of regular exhibitions. Over the next several years she sporadically exhibited a few works (primarily still lives and portraits) at venues such as the Friday Club, the Allied Artists' Association and the New English Art Club. Significantly, Bell's first uncommissioned sale, *The Spanish Model* (referred to in the second of the two epigraphs with which we opened this chapter), occurred in 1912 when Robert Ross and Charles Aitken were visiting Duncan Grant's studio. Unable to acquire Grant's *Queen of Sheba* because it had already been purchased by Roger Fry, they settled on Bell's *Spanish Model* which, as the artist pointed out, was modestly priced (Spalding 1983: 105).

This incident is telling because it reveals not only Bell's deep-seated professional anxieties and insecurities but also her tendency to see her own work as second-rate, especially in comparison with the painting of Duncan Grant. While she clearly enjoyed working with Grant, often finding him inspirational, supportive, and good company, their close working relationship caused her many professional anxieties, both in terms of public recognition and, possibly more damagingly, in terms of self-esteem. Perhaps because Bell needed only to *supplement* her income by selling paintings – unlike Grant, who had no professional income until John Maynard Keynes established one for him in 1937 (Turnbaugh 1987: note, plate 16) – she exhibited less frequently, sending fewer works to exhibitions such as the Grafton and London Groups. It is significant that her first solo show (other than a small exhibition at the Omega Workshops in 1916) was not until June 1922 when she was featured by the Independent Gallery. In contrast, although he was six years younger than Bell, Grant held his first solo show in 1920. For many years, Bell was overshadowed by Grant, who received more extensive press coverage, even from Clive Bell and Roger Fry (Twitchell 1987: 177–78). Furthermore, critics nearly always assumed that Vanessa Bell's work was influenced by Grant, whom they believed the stronger artist. The gender bias of such assumptions is revealed in the warning that Roger Fry issued to Vanessa Bell in a 1920 letter. Anxious to stress that Bell should avoid exhibiting works based on models she had shared with Grant, Fry described how Henry Tonks, a Slade professor of painting, had responded to Bell's and Grant's work:

> Your *Visit* (no. 19) occupies the centre of the wall facing one entering... it was Tonks, not me who did it.... The amusing thing is that [he] doesn't to this day know whom it is by. He's got you and D[uncan] exactly inverted and gave me a little lecture on what a pity it is that women always imitate men. For all that you and D[uncan] must work, I don't say apart, but not on such similar themes. It's bad for both of you.
>
> (quoted in McNamara 1983: 7)

Such differential assessments of their professional worth evidently persisted over the next few decades. For example, in 1940 a typical assessment of their working relationship was provided by Alan Clutton-Brock in an article on Vanessa Bell published in *Studio*. After positively asserting that neither artist imitated the other, he went on to point out that the "main distinction between the work of Duncan Grant and Vanessa Bell is that she was the less ambitious artist of the two, and this was in some ways her advantage." While he felt that this assisted her sense of design, since she was less tempted to explore the third dimension, his conclusion nonetheless implies that he found her lack of ambition appropriate to a female artist who, for the most part, specialized in domestic genre painting: "At her best Vanessa Bell was a very easy and quite unaffected artist, painting what pleased her in her immediate surroundings and content with an agreeable, fluent and allusive idiom of design" (Clutton-Brock 1940: 90).

Evidence suggests that Bell internalized prevailing public attitudes about the weaknesses of female painters and saw her own talent as secondary. Expressions of such insecurity appear throughout her career. Recalling her initial meeting with Roger Fry around 1902 or 1903, Bell, only partially ironically, described herself as a "terrible low creature, a female painter" in relation to Fry, "the newest and most learned of young critics" (quoted in Collins 1984: 7). Far more frequently, however, Bell used Duncan Grant as a standard of comparison. Her choice was hardly surprising given that the two artists worked together on an almost daily basis. The following excerpt from a 1912 letter to Roger Fry is a typical example of her many self-disparaging comparisons: "I have been doing designs with Duncan all day, and his are much better than mine and I'm rather depressed. His are so gay and lively – mine rather dull and stupid. I want you to tell me if they have any good in them after all … and then Duncan's colour – oh, it's long since I've been so depressed by working with him" (quoted in Spalding 1983: 116). Yet, in spite of the fact she often believed that Grant was the superior artist, she was not blind to the weaknesses of his work. A typical case in point was Grant's *Queen of Sheba* which she forthrightly described as "too sweet, too pretty and too small" with the "usual English sweetness coming in and spoiling all" (Spalding 1983: 112). Clearly, such independent judgement testifies to Bell's strength of character as well as the potential for mutual criticism in her working relationship with Grant. While the existence of such criticism indicates a certain degree of security on Bell's part, her choice of language is revealing. The fact that she unproblematically used the gender-biased terms of art criticism of the period suggests that Bell largely internalized the binary configurations of value that operated within modernist aesthetic discourses – casting England as provincial in relation to Paris, and the work of women as inferior to that of men. Within this binary, femininity and Englishness were often conflated as Bell revealed in her discussion of the aesthetic sensibilities of Nan Hudson and Ethel Sands, two women artists whom Bell did not want included in the Omega Workshops. Writing to Fry in 1912 she observed:

> I was a little alarmed at their excessive elegance and eighteenth century stamp. It isn't what we want even for the minor arts, is it? Won't they import too much of that? Of course I know they're useful, but I do think we shall have to be careful especially in England where it seems to me one can never get away from all this fatal prettiness. Can't we paint stuffs etc. which *won't* be gay and pretty?
>
> (quoted in Collins 1984: 26)

This sense of what we are calling a double marginality – Englishness in a modernist art world which looked to Paris, and femininity in a patriarchal avant-garde – operated throughout Bell's painting, particular in her self-representations as an artist during the period from 1910 to 1920, the period in which Bell was engaged in her most experimentally avant-garde work. In comparison to her portraits of Duncan Grant, which usually showed the artist at work, Bell seldom depicted herself in the act of painting.[27] As Richard Shone suggests, her reasons for painting Grant at work were partly practical in that Grant disliked sitting (Shone 1980: 25). In contrast, Bell sat for numerous portraits by Grant, most of which (like her own self-portraits) portray her as a woman rather than as a painter. Interestingly, when Grant did portray her at work, as in his *Vanessa Bell Painting* (1913) (Figure 3.4), the artist is shown seated before her easel with her back toward the viewer.[28] Much like Jessie Etchells (Figure 3.2), Bell is shown quietly working in a confined space rather than making large painterly gestures.

There are more than merely practical issues at stake in this gendering of gestures, and it is useful to compare Grant's relatively understated presentation of Bell in her role as artist with examples of male portraiture which have been more highly valued within the modernist canon. Significantly, such representations of male artists usually depict the artist standing and defiantly wielding his brush. One of the best-known examples of this genre, Ernst Ludwig Kirchner's 1910 *Self-Portrait with Model* (Figure 3.5), displays the artist in a brightly coloured, loosely open dressing-gown, standing before his canvas in the left foreground of the picture, and holding a red-tipped brush at groin level. The identity of the artist is clearly revealed as he turns full face to meet the eyes of the viewer. In contrast, his model sits in the background gazing obliquely at the artist. As feminist art historians Irit Rogoff and Carol Duncan have argued, these poses – typically utilized by male artists such as Kirchner, Matisse, Vlaminck, and Derain (to name only a few) – inscribe and display their cultural mastery and authority (Rogoff 1990; Duncan 1973).[29] Indeed, when Marie Laurencin was interviewed in the 1920s, she turned conventional wisdom upside down by announcing that painting was an especially appropriate job for a woman since it required both natural sensibility in addition to the ability to sit quietly on a chair all day long manipulating small brushes. When Laurencin added that the painting profession thus seemed an *inappropriate* activity for strong men, the interviewer felt obliged to intervene and stress that, while Laurencin always sat down to paint, most men painters preferred to stand (Todd 1928: 92). Thus Grant was adhering to a well-established convention when he chose to portray Bell sitting in a traditionally "feminine" position.

If Bell's identity remains something of a mystery in Grant's 1913 portrait of her (since the viewer sees only her back), the precise identity of the picture she is working on is equally obscure. In spite of its size (the painting is almost as big as the painter), the canvas is not readily recognizable as one of Bell's masterpieces. Instead it is a simple still life. Again it is tempting to compare the Bloomsbury painters with their more famous continental modernist counterparts, particularly Matisse, whom Bell and Grant both admired. For example, in his *Red Studio* of 1911 (Museum of Modern Art, New York),

Figure 3.4 Duncan Grant, *Vanessa Bell Painting* (1913). Oil on canvas. 30 ×
22 inches. Scottish National Gallery of Modern Art, Edinburgh.

Figure 3.5 Ernst Ludwig Kirchner, *Self-Portrait with Model* (1910/26). Oil on canvas. 58 × 39 inches. Hamburger Kunsthalle.

despite the non-specificity of the title, Matisse precisely identifies several of his well-known canvases which function as surrogates for or signatures of the painter. Thus the viewer is visually informed that this is the studio of Matisse, even though the painter himself is absent. Unlike Matisse, Grant does not portray Bell as a distinctive individual despite the fact that both she and her work are physically present. Even the specificity of Grant's title seems to dissolve upon a closer examination of this curiously anonymous image.

In contrast to Grant's more traditional gendering of painterly gestures, Bell occasionally broke with convention by showing him working from a chair. In one of her better-known examples, *Portrait of Duncan Grant Painting* (c. 1915)[30], Bell portrays Grant sitting next to an easel which is just beyond the left edge of the frame. Although Grant's body faces the viewer, his head is shown in profile as he twists (somewhat awkwardly) to reach the canvas. Presumably Bell resorted to this unusual pose to avoid obscuring Grant's body with the easel. Although Grant is shown seated, Bell's portrait of him still endows the artist with the same sort of cultural authority that we saw in Kirchner's *Self-Portrait*. Like Kirchner, Bell emphasizes the sitter's individualism and physical activity.

At this point it is worth pausing to consider the fact that Bell's *Portrait of Duncan Grant Painting* was executed during the same period as Grant's *At Eleanor: Vanessa Bell* (Figure 3.6). Both works were painted at Eleanor House, a cottage on the Sussex coast where Bell, Grant, and Grant's lover, David (Bunny) Garnett stayed together during the spring of 1915. Despite the awkwardness of the situation for Bell – who was determined to maintain her relationship with Grant at all costs, even though (as she admitted in a letter to Roger Fry) she "couldn't help minding some things and feeling out of it and in the way" (quoted in Spalding 1983: 144) – she completed a number of canvases. While she depicted Grant painting, he portrayed her at leisure, leaning back in a yellow and white striped armchair. Grant's painting of Bell is a curious combination of modernism and conventionality. The bold red of Bell's dress with its complementary green outlining, the striking green shadows on her face and neck, the enlargement of her hands, and the emphasis on the flat decorative patterning of the wall behind the chair all reveal Grant's knowledge of French Post-Impressionism. At the same time, however, the picture displays qualities more reminiscent of Victorian academic painting; these qualities include the illusion of three-dimensional space (suggested by Bell's three-quarter pose as well as the volume of the winged armchair), the sitter's languid pose, and the beautifully delicate rendering of her facial features. It is tempting to read the stylistic dualities in this work as symptomatic of Grant's unconscious ambivalences toward Bell as an older woman, painter and equal, friend and lover. The slippage between these categories perhaps prevented Grant from fixing an image of her.

As we have already pointed out, it was not only Duncan Grant who sometimes had difficulty *seeing* Bell as an artist. On occasion critics and

Figure 3.6 Duncan Grant, *At Eleanor: Vanessa Bell* (1915). Oil on canvas. 65.9 × 55.5 cm. Yale Center for British Art, New Haven, Paul Mellon Fund.

Figure 3.7 Vanessa Bell, *Self-Portrait* (*c.* 1915). Oil on canvas. 63.7 × 46.2 cm. Yale Center for British Art, New Haven, Paul Mellon Fund.

friends mistook her work for Grant's while Bell frequently questioned her own artistic ability. Perhaps revealingly, Bell portrayed herself with unfocused eyes (actually devoid of pupils), staring mistily into space in her own *Self-Portrait* dated circa 1915 (Figure 3.7). On the one hand, it must be acknowledged that this image of Bell conveys great strength in terms of her large physical size, foreground position, and pyramidal stability. The sense of Bell's power is reinforced by her confident handling of modernist devices, ranging from the bold patterning of her dress and abstract background (both of which flatten the picture plane) to the thin painterly application of large blocks of colour that reveal the sketchy pencil underdrawing and reserve ground of the primed canvas. And yet, on the other hand, this demonstration of technical bravado is hardly echoed in the pose of the painter who is offered to the viewer as a woman at leisure without brushes, palette, or easel. Instead, Bell makes only the most indirect reference to her work by adding a few vertical stripes to the background which recall the style of her abstract painting from the previous year.[31] It should be stressed that only Bell's friends would have recognized this reference since her abstract paintings were not widely exhibited during this period. Otherwise, she provides no indication of her profession.

The fact that Bell did not overtly refer to her artistic status in this self-portrait provides an interesting point of comparison with the other modernist women artists of this study. Although she was perhaps closest to Nina Hamnett in terms of their mutual friendship with Roger Fry and their contact through the Omega Workshops, Bell's *Self-Portrait* seems almost reticent when compared with Hamnett's rather more flamboyant *Self-Portrait* of 1913 (Figure 5.3, page 144), which shows Hamnett in the guise of bohemian rebel with bobbed hair and smock. Indeed, Hamnett's self-representation is closer to that of Romaine Brooks's *Self Portrait* of 1923 (Figure 2.1) in which the artist openly lays claim to male privilege and dress. Instead, Bell portrays herself as an attractively dressed woman. On closer scrutiny, however, Bell's attractiveness is a curiously elusive phenomenon rendered in a modernist style that draws our attention to the composition's formal values (i.e. its patterning, geometric simplification, and brushwork) rather than its illusionistic details. As Susan Casteras has observed,

> an obvious likeness is evident, yet the artist has underplayed her considerable personal beauty ... and instead employs strong color and outline to animate the figure and the surface. The colored hatching on the side of the nose again derives from Picasso, while the variegated patches defining her hair and the background space project a decided boldness.
>
> (Casteras 1984: 14)

In this respect, Bell's *Self-Portrait* is perhaps closest in spirit to a self-portrait by Djuna Barnes (Figure 5.2, page 134) which was published in a *Pearson's*

Magazine interview of the artist by Guido Bruno in 1919. Significantly, Bell and Barnes, both well known for their beauty, opted to portray themselves using simplified, highly stylized and masklike forms.

For the most part, this aspect of Bell's work has been understood as an outgrowth of her interest in the "significant form" of modernist painting (in Clive Bell's famous phrase), which led her to capture expression through shape and colour rather than narrative detail. Nevertheless, from a feminist perspective there is more to Bell's choices than a purely formalist inclination. As we have already noted, her portraits of women between 1912 and 1919 (see, for example, Figures 3.1 and 3.3) are characterized by their curiously featureless and dissolving faces. Although a tendency towards increasing simplification is evident in her other subjects from this period, both the frequency of her female subjects and the extremity of their simplification suggest that Bell may have been drawn to such experimental modernist forms because they seemed especially appropriate for female subjects whom she found increasingly difficult to visualize in more concrete terms.[32] It should be remembered that it was precisely during these years that women's traditional social roles were being challenged and intensely scrutinized, particularly in relation to the suffrage campaigns and the political and industrial mobilization of women during the First World War. To some extent, the hotly contested debates over how women should be appropriately represented – whether in imagery, in parliament, or in the work force – must have complicated Bell's perception of her own position as a professional female artist, even though (unlike other women in the Bloomsbury Group such as her sister and Pippa Strachey), Bell was not overtly involved with the women's movement.

In contrast to Woolf, who articulately discussed the problem of women adapting or making a genre for the expression of their experience, Bell (whether consciously or not) explored these issues visually by creating a new fluid working space somewhere between the traditional categories of portraiture, domestic genre, and still life. Her intense interest in the private, the personal, and the mundane appeared in the subjects she chose to paint, the undervalued genres that gave her most pleasure, and her preference for a quietly secluded country life over a more publicly flamboyant professional career. Although Bell clearly found these choices personally enabling, the fact that for the most part they ran counter to the trends established by more publicly recognized male modernists contributed to waves of self-doubt on Bell's part as well as her own initial devaluation in the modernist canon. As Janet Wolff has reminded us, the experience of women (which often revolved around the personal and domestic) needs to be considered in a modernism which is all too often seen through the gaze of the male flâneur (Wolff 1985).

4

THE MAKING OF GENIUS
Gertrude Stein and Marie Laurencin

and there at her house I met Gertrude Stein. I was impressed by her coral brooch and by her voice. I may say that only three times in my life have I met a genius and each time a bell within me rang and I was not mistaken, and I may say in each case it was before there was any general recognition of the quality of genius in them. The three geniuses of whom I wish to speak are Gertrude Stein, Pablo Picasso and Alfred Whitehead.

> (Stein 1960; first pub. 1933: 5)

If I feel so far removed from painters, it is because they are men, and in my view men are difficult problems to solve. Their discussions, their researches, their genius, have always been too much for me.... But if the genius of men intimidates me, I feel perfectly at ease with everything that is feminine...[1]

> (Laurencin 1956: 16)

The odour of genius seems to have permeated the air of those Parisian cafés, salons, and ateliers that were frequented by early twentieth-century writers, painters, critics, and patrons of the arts. What exactly genius was, when it was worth something, how one fostered it, and whether one had any were crucial questions. For instance, in his 1907 review of the Salon d'Automne, Apollinaire described how Cézanne recounted giving one of his paintings to a local family on the occasion of their daughter's first communion. The rather conventional family was horrified by such an avant-garde picture and barely thanked the highly amused painter. According to Apollinaire, the family subsequently discovered the value of genius:

> A few days later, he [Cézanne] went back to see the same people. The whole family surrounded him, thanked him, and spoke of his genius.
>   Since they had last seen him, those fine people had done a bit of investigating and found that the painting was worth money.
>
> (Apollinaire 1972: 24)

Apollinaire was not the only writer to dwell on this issue. Half seriously, half ironically, Robert McAlmon entitled his memoirs of the period's personalities *Being Geniuses Together* to acknowledge not only their achievement but also their somewhat extravagant posing. Significantly, McAlmon's acknowledgement of his father-in-law's (the wealthy Sir John Ellerman, Bryher's father) giftedness was less ambivalent: "As regards finance, Sir John had that thing which need not be looked upon with awe, *genius*" (McAlmon 1968: 4). In 1917 Djuna Barnes interviewed the editor and writer Frank Harris and recorded his fears that not enough was being done to nurture genius in literature and the visual arts. Harris warned:

> The men of genius are always there . . . but if you do not help them, they will not be able to produce the great works. Shakespeare would never have done his best work, never have written *Hamlet* or *Othello* or *Anthony and Cleopatra*, if Lord Southampton had not given him the one thousand pounds which made his high achievement possible.
>
> (Barnes 1985: 209)

While Harris worried about supporting genius, Janet Flanner (who took the pen-name of Genêt when writing her famous "Letters from Paris" for the *New Yorker* from 1925 onwards) avidly described it in the case of Picasso:

> Pablo Ruiz Picasso began being an artist at the age of prodigy – at about seven. . . . The excesses of his artistic endowments, of his will, of his life appetites and his character appear to have been idiosyncratic from earliest childhood, so that becoming prodigious and phenomenal was, for him, the only form of being natural. . . . From the first, even among artistic geniuses, Picasso was clearly hatched as the white blackbird, the *rara avis*.
>
> (Flanner 1990; orig. pub. 1947: 174–75)

As Flanner's remarks illustrate, references to the man of genius emphasize his rarity, precocity, and vulnerability, but also his *naturalness*; men of genius are born (or, in the case of Flanner's Picasso, hatched) not made.

Modernist references to women of genius, on the other hand, are more often comic or ironic and are intended to deflate both the possessor and the pursuer of feminine genius by pointing to its artifice or constructedness. For example, the well-known New York lawyer and collector of avant-garde painting, John Quinn, was reportedly "mad to mix with genius," and became so fascinated by Marie Laurencin's eccentric personality that he was willing to rush around Paris in search of a singing canary to indulge her passion for animals (Hyland and McPherson 1989: 64). Significantly, however, although Quinn admired and collected the works of Marie Laurencin, when he attempted in 1922 to order genius hierarchically he placed Laurencin not in the first category (which included Picasso, Matisse, Braque, and Derain), nor in the second (which included Brancusi, Rouault, Dufy, and de Segonzac), but rather in the third (with Gris, Villon, Metzinger, de la Fresnaye, and Chabaud) (Reid 1968: 542). Similarly, Vanessa Bell's early letters to Virginia Woolf are full of gently ironic references to her sister's genius, as the following extract from a 1908 letter indicates: "Did Lytton [Strachey] propose to you this afternoon? & did he say I could send you his poems? I would rather you married him than anyone else, but perhaps on the whole your genius requires all your attention" (30 July 1908, Berg Collection).

The above anecdotes raise a number of questions, among them: why did "modernism" revive a predominantly Romantic discourse of genius, and how did women writers and artists position themselves in relation to that discourse? how did women further position themselves in relation to the obviously vexed issue of the relationship between genius and money (as expressed in concerns over patronage and the market value of works of art)? how did a discourse of creative genius affect women's career patterns in terms of selecting the genres in which they would work, securing reputations, interacting with colleagues, and organizing their working lives? what is the significance of women's claims to or refusals of "genius"? how have contemporary and subsequent critics gendered genius, and what role has this gendering played in positioning women within literary and art historical canons? To answer these questions, we will focus on the work and self-representations of Gertrude Stein and Marie Laurencin. Not only did Stein and Laurencin tackle the problematic question of women's genius in very different ways, but they also provide an important and neglected case study of modernist women's cultural patronage and, at least partly, professional friendship, a friendship which has been overshadowed in subsequent reconstructions of the period through an almost exclusive critical focus on Stein's relationship with Toklas. As Marjorie Perloff has noted, in many ways Marie Laurencin – "an artist but not a literary artist and hence not a direct threat to Gertrude Stein" – served as one of Stein's alter egos (Perloff 1988: 66). Indeed, Stein became Laurencin's first buyer when she acquired her *Group of Artists* (Figure 4.1) in 1908. After this purchase Laurencin maintained friendly relations with both Stein and Alice B. Toklas. She continued to correspond with Toklas after Stein's death in 1946.

As the epigraphs to this chapter seem to suggest, Gertrude Stein and Marie Laurencin saw themselves as occupying opposite ends of a creative spectrum, almost as if they parodically conformed to stale stereotypes of masculine genius and feminine sensibility. Stein insisted upon her own genius; speaking for and as Toklas at the end of the "autobiography," she notes that Gertrude had often urged Alice to write her autobiography, even going so far as suggesting several possible titles: "My life with the great, wives of geniuses I have sat with, my twenty-five years with Gertrude Stein" (Stein 1960: 251). In contrast, Laurencin expressed her alienation from male constructions of genius in a tone that ranged from defensive and apologetic to irate. Refusing to be measured by the prevailing male models of success, Laurencin

Figure 4.1 Marie Laurencin, *Group of Artists* or *Les Invités* (1908). Oil on canvas. 64.87 × 81 cm. The Baltimore Museum of Art: The Cone Collection formed by Dr. Claribel Cone and Miss Etta Cone of Baltimore, Maryland.

presented herself as a painter of supremely feminine sensibility located outside the male-dominated circles of the Fauves, Orphists, and Cubists. Stein's self-constructions as and exploration of "genius" are most evident in her "open and public" books, her "audience writing" (see Dydo 1985a: 4): her two popular autobiographies, *The Autobiography of Alice B. Toklas* (1933) and *Everybody's Autobiography* (1937), and her lectures, "Portraits and repetition" (1930), "How writing is written" (1935), and "What are masterpieces and why are there so few of them" (1940). As far as Marie Laurencin is concerned, these issues are treated most directly in interviews with the artist and in her pictures of herself and her friends, including *Portrait of Picasso* (1908), *Group of Artists* (1908), and *Apollinaire and His Friends* (1909), and again in such later self-portraits as *Femme Peintre and Her Model* (1921).

TASTE IS THE FEMININE OF GENIUS

Before we can understand the significance of Stein's and Laurencin's self-representations and meditations on "genius," however, we need to understand the ambivalence with which the term was regarded during the period. As Louis Menand has pointed out, and as we touched upon in the previous chapter, a Romantic discourse of artistic "genius" was *in part* displaced in the early twentieth century by a discourse of artistic professionalism ("genius, that which is given and cannot be earned, is not the basis for the professional's claim to superiority" (Menand 1987: 115)). Nonetheless, the term retained its Romantic appeal. In his thumbnail history of "genius," Donald Pease has argued that the term became a crucially important component of authorship – or cultural authority – in the late eighteenth century when feudal governments based on the divine right of kings gave way to bourgeois republics based on property. No longer the spokespersons for critical emancipatory movements (since the new bourgeois order had assumed power), authors increasingly separated themselves and their cultural productions from political life and, in the process, became more and more preoccupied with the intricacies of professionalism. Pease outlines the social consequences of this shift, which is traditionally described as the emergence of Romanticism. He notes that it was the term "genius" that "enabled this separation of the cultural from the political realm" by establishing a Republic of Letters which, becoming increasingly self-referential, produced "a cultural alternative to the world of politics" (Pease 1990: 110). The separation of culture from other, especially material, spheres of human activity reached its height in the twentieth century (when "the economic, political, psychological, and historical conditions that provided the material environment for an author's work were denied any determining relationship with it" (Pease 1990: 111)). At this point, a discourse of artistic professionalism began to emerge from a discourse of artistic genius.

While Pease's thumbnail sketch needs to be viewed cautiously and modified when it comes to particular case studies, it offers some enabling generalizations about the genealogy and social configuration of "genius," especially as this concept related to different notions of professionalism in the cultural sphere. First, Pease's sketch helps to account for the increasingly apolitical and professional claims of the avant-garde during this period. Instead of seeing themselves as politically oppositional and attached to a community, a growing number of authors and artists saw themselves as a socially alienated caste within a larger professional group.

Nonetheless, "modernist" recourse to the privileges of "genius" was frequent and was prompted largely by the need to obtain patronage, to justify certain excesses or extravagances, or to disqualify and marginalize the cultural productions of women. For, as Christine Battersby has pointed out in *Gender and Genius*, the twentieth century also inherited from the Romantics a notion of genius predicated on "a logic of exclusion" (6) which worked to reinforce man/animal, civilized/savage, and male/female divisions. This had enormous repercussions for the woman artist who was faced with the choice of surrendering her sexuality and becoming a surrogate "male" or retaining her "femininity"/"femaleness" and failing to "count as a genius" (Battersby 1989: 3). The correlation between virility and genius is carried to extravagant ends by, for example, Ezra Pound in his "Postscript to *The Natural Philosophy of Love* by Remy de Gourmont" (1958) in which he quotes Gourmont's speculation that "Il y aurait peut-être une certaine corrélation entre la copulation complète et profonde et la développement cérébral." Pound not only agrees that this is both possible and probable, but advances as a hypothetical elaboration the proposal that the brain itself is "in origin and development only a sort of great clot of genital fluid held in suspense or reserve." This would explain, says Pound, "the enormous content of the brain as a maker or presenter of forms" (Pound 1958: 203). Although Pound insists in his "Postscript" that he is not writing an "anti-feminist tract" and that he does not want to engage in a "journalistic sex-squabble," and although he emphasizes that he is speaking of two *principles* that are not necessarily peculiar to either sex, the implications of his rhetoric are clear.

Modernist attitudes toward creativity remained largely shaped by, on the one hand, the sort of nineteenth-century Romantic sentiment which is neatly summarized by Edward Fitzgerald's comment to a friend in 1877 that "Taste is the feminine of genius,"[2] and, on the other, by the influence of such turn-of-the-century tracts as Otto Weininger's *Sex and Character*, originally published in German in 1903 and translated into English in 1907. The implication of Fitzgerald's comment is, of course, that women could acquire the lesser attribute of taste but only men could possess the superior attribute of genius. In addition to invoking a Victorian ideology of "separate spheres" in which the feminine is associated with the domestic, this gendered division also echoes the avant-garde distinction between "copy" and "original" which we looked at in connection with Natalie Barney and Romaine Brooks. In effect, the person of taste learns that which is familiar or already coded while the genius explores uncharted territory or new codes. As with the craft of the copyist, the acquisition of taste requires a form of apprenticeship which differs from the supposedly natural gift of genius.

The influence of Weininger's misogynist and anti-semitic *Sex and Character* was especially pernicious and reflected, in its preoccupation with degeneracy, "modernism's" continuing decadent legacy (see Karl 1988: 86–90; Battersby 1989: 113–23). At the time of its publication, it was only the latest in a series of works which attempted to situate "genius" within a discourse of physiology; others included Nisbet's *The Insanity of Genius* (1891), Max Nordau's *Degeneration* (1892), and Cesare Lombroso's *The Man of Genius* (1863) (Menand 1987: 184–85, fn. 25).[3] Attaining instant notoriety, Weininger's central premise was that "the man of genius possesses, like everything else, the complete female in himself; but the woman herself is only a part of the Universe, and the part can never be the whole; femaleness can never include genius;" furthermore, "A female genius is a contradiction in terms, for genius is simply intensified, perfectly developed, universally conscious maleness" (Weininger 1907: 189). While there was nothing new in Weininger's misogynist theorizing, the book captured the public imagination and initiated extensive commentary in the press of the period. Indeed, the book's currency was not confined to antifeminist circles; in April and May of 1912 the feminist periodical *The New Freewoman* published extracts from *Sex and Character* to which readers responded in the June issue. And, as is now well known, Gertrude Stein's early work – and, to a degree, her self-styling as a "male genius" – was influenced by Weininger's theories; as she commented in a notebook of the period: "Pablo & Matisse have a maleness that belongs to genius. Moi aussi perhaps."[4]

EVERYONE CALLED GERTRUDE STEIN GERTRUDE...

I want to say frankly that I think you have written a very peculiar book [*Three Lives*] and it will be a hard thing to make people take it seriously.

F.H. Hitchcock, Grafton Press ("a firm that specialized in private printings"), 1909 (Gallup 1953: 44)

Dear Madam, I really cannot publish these curious Studies.
Austin Harrison, Editor, *English Review*, 1913 (Gallup 1953: 73)

Here there is no group of *literati* or *illuminati* or *cognoscenti* or *illustrissimi* of any kind, who could agree upon interpretations of your poetry. More than this, you could not find a handful even of careful readers who would think that it was a serious effort.

Ellery Sedgwick, *Atlantic Monthly*, 1919 (Gallup 1953: 130)

The little rhythms which ripple through your picture [*Portrait of Cézanne*] do not, to my heavy wit, call up the faintest suggestion of the exciting impression of a Cézanne.

Ellery Sedgwick, *Atlantic Monthly*, 1927 (Gallup 1953: 210)

We live in different worlds. Yours may hold the good, the beautiful, and the true, but if it does their guise is not for us to recognize.

Ellery Sedgwick, *Atlantic Monthly*, 1932 (Gallup 1953: 256)

There has been a lot of pother about this book of yours [*The Autobiography of Alice B. Toklas*], but what a delightful book it is, and how glad I am to publish four installments of it! During our long correspondence, I think you felt my constant hope that the time would come when the real Miss Stein would pierce the smoke-screen with which she has always so mischievously surrounded herself.... Anything we can do to help the success of the book, as well as the serial, will certainly be done.

Hail Gertrude Stein about to arrive!

Ellery Sedgwick, *Atlantic Monthly*, 1933 (Gallup 1953: 260–61)

With the 1933 publication of *The Autobiography of Alice B. Toklas* Gertrude Stein *did* "arrive," but where? This series of quotations, tracing her journey from self-published author to best-seller, suggests a number of possible debarkations: she had, in writing Toklas's "autobiography," arrived at the "real Miss Stein;" she had, after years of rejection and misunderstanding, arrived to well-earned public acclamation and recognition of her genius; she had "arrived" in America, as evidenced by her highly popular and well-publicized lecture tour of 1934–35; and – with the four-part serialization of *The Autobiography* – she had arrived at her life-long dream of publication in *Atlantic Monthly*. She had also achieved a modest wealth.[5] Significantly, however, Stein's popular success provoked a crisis of identity which eventually articulated itself as an epistemological and ontological crisis around "genius." She wrote about the causes and effects of this crisis most explicitly in "And now," a 1934 *Vanity Fair* article which later formed the basis of *Everybody's Autobiography*:

What happened to me was this. When the success began and it was a success I got lost completely lost. You know the nursery rhyme, I am I because my little dog knows me. Well you see I did not know myself, I lost my personality.... So many people knowing me I was I no longer and for the first time since I had begun to write I could not write and what was worse I could not worry about not writing and what was also worse I began to think about how my writing would sound to others, how could I make them understand, I who had always lived within myself and my writing.

(Stein 1934: 280)

In *Everybody's Autobiography*, published three years later, Stein explicitly related her crisis of identity and writer's block to the effect both of celebrity and of financial success ("Just at present my passion is avarice" (Stein 1937: 128)). However, immediately following its description of this crisis, *Everybody's Autobiography* articulated a series of meditations on the meaning, recognition, and rarity of "genius" together with a description of the conditions which make "genius" possible. The coincidence of these three thematic preoccupations – money, celebrity, genius – makes it clear that Stein's conception of "genius" had been, at least initially, a Romantic one and that if she was to retain the term, she had to rethink and redefine it. As Christine Battersby points out, "For the Romantics the figure of the genius was used to distinguish between the world of Art (appreciated by an elite group of critics) and works produced for popular consumption by the masses" (Battersby 1989: 6). Could one be a genius and a best-seller?

One way in which Stein attempted to resolve this dilemma was to distinguish between her "open and public" books, or her "audience writing", and her "real kind" of books (Dydo 1985a: 4) and to attempt to *use* her new popularity to find publishers for her more esoteric works. She was, for example, able to persuade Harcourt to publish an abridged edition of *The Making of Americans* (parts of which had, at Hemingway's instigation, been published in Ford Madox Ford's *Transatlantic Review* in 1924, and which Robert McAlmon had, seemingly to his regret, published through his Contact Publishing Company two years later[6]), and Bennet Cerf published *Three Lives* (originally self-published through the Grafton Press) and *Portraits and Prayers* in his Modern Library edition in 1933 and 1934 respectively (Mellow 1974: 425; Stein 1937: 98–100). Until the massive success of *The Autobiography*, Stein had published primarily in the small literary presses of the period (*Transatlantic Review*, *The Dial*, *The Criterion*) and through Plain Editions, the publishing house she and Toklas founded in 1929 and financed through the sale of Picasso's *Woman With a Fan* (1905). Stein's efforts to achieve a wide, even a mass, readership indicate not only her desire for fame but the degree to which, for her, a discourse of "genius" conflicted with a discourse of "professionalism;" her status as a writer and a self-proclaimed genius was seemingly not secure unless it was validated by the major publishing houses and mass circulation periodicals.[7] As seems clear from *Everybody's Autobiography*, professional validation for Stein, as for Woolf, required that she be paid for her work.

However, Stein also used *Everybody's Autobiography* as a forum in which to rethink and reground the notion of genius. Her only half-ironic fascination with her own genius had been evident from the 1933 publication of *The Autobiography of Alice B. Toklas*. Throughout that work she makes detailed observations about her literary concerns, writing techniques, and habits of work, constructing herself in ways that corresponded to prevailing myths of masculine genius. The reader is told, for example, that she usually wrote all night from eleven until dawn and never threw away any scrap of paper on which she had written (Stein 1960: 41, 52). Such anecdotes reinforce her image as inspired, eccentric (writing while ordinary people slept), and in a constant state of creativity – her merest doodle worthy of preservation. With respect to her place in literary history, Stein has Alice remark: "The young often when they have learnt all they can learn accuse her of inordinate pride. She says yes of course. She realises that in english literature in her time she is the only one. She has always known it and now she says it" (77).

For Stein the notion of genius was closely connected to formal and conceptual innovation. This often meant portraying people and objects in exploratory ways which the public found unfamiliar and therefore "ugly," as her approving quotation of Picasso indicates: "As Pablo once remarked, when you make a thing, it is so complicated making it that it is bound to be ugly, but those that do it after you they don't have to worry about making it and they can make it pretty, and so everybody can like it when the others make it" (Stein 1960: 23). This would suggest that for Stein at this period, "genius" was at odds with public acclaim. Furthermore, the great writers and artists – the geniuses – live fully in the continuous present rather than in memory or imagination. This was a point Stein took pains to stress in her lecture "How writing is written," delivered at the Choate School during the 1934–35 academic year:

> [E]very contemporary writer has to find out what is the inner time-sense of his contemporariness. The writer or painter, or what not, feels this thing more vibrantly, and he has a passionate need of putting it down; and that is what creativeness does. He spends his life in putting down this thing which he doesn't know is a contemporary thing. If he doesn't put down the contemporary thing, he isn't a great writer, for he has to live in the past. That is what I mean by "everything is contemporary." The minor poets of the period, or the precious poets of the period, are all people who are under the shadow of the past. A man who is making a revolution has to be contemporary. A minor person can live in the imagination. That tells the story pretty completely.
>
> (Stein 1974: 158)

Stein followed up on this argument in "What are master-pieces and why are there so few of them," her 1936 lecture to Oxford and Cambridge. She used this lecture as the occasion to tease out some of the implications of what we have called her earlier "identity crisis," and to reinforce the division between her "audience" writing and her "real" writing. Genius – and thus the creation of masterpieces – requires a radical self-forgetting; it is, in this sense, deeply impersonal. Self-forgetting is the result of the artist's ability to immerse him/herself in the moment of creation, that is, in the continuous present. "Identity" implies "memory" or "recognition;" thus, "one has no identity . . . when one is in the act of doing anything" (Stein 1967: 148). Stein further makes it clear that her audience writing – her autobiographies and her lectures – are not masterpieces, a category reserved for her "real" writing.

> At any moment when you are you you are you without the memory of yourself because if you remember yourself while you are you you are not for the purposes of creating you. This is so important because it has so much to do with the question of a writer to his audience. One of the things that I discovered in lecturing was that gradually one ceased to hear what one said one heard what the audience hears one say, that is the reason that oratory is practically never a master-piece very rarely and very rarely history, because history deals with people who are orators who hear not what they are not what they say but what their audience hears them say.
>
> (Stein 1967: 149–50)

Given Stein's emphasis on the abandonment of identity in the act of creation, it is not surprising that it is only in her public writing that she can meditate on the meaning of "genius;" such a meditation obviously requires enormous self-consciousness. What *is* surprising is her evident need to do so. Significantly, her construction and advertisement of herself as a "genius" is founded on a logic both of difference and identity: she is *different* from her brother Leo because she is a genius; she is the *same* as Picasso and Einstein because she is a genius. In both cases she measures herself against a dominant and/or significant male. Indeed, much of her self-construction as genius in *The Autobiography of Alice B. Toklas* is predicated on her difference from the women, "the wives," who attend her salon.[8] Biographers and critics have frequently noted the degree to which Stein constructed herself in the masculine, and this has created problems for many feminist critics. Shari Benstock's judgement is typical: "Stein . . . was unconventional in her choice of sexual partner, in her dress, and in her writings, but the coincidence of these oddities did not constitute a subversive feminism" (Benstock 1986: 176–77). Stein's explanation, to her feminist friend Marion Walker, that she does not at all mind "the cause of women or any other cause but it does not happen to be her business" (Stein 1960: 83) has also been problematic.

However, Stein's self-construction as a male genius is not seamless and her identity crisis of 1933–34 provoked her to reposition herself – albeit very slightly – in relation both to other women artists and to the discourse of genius. This is most evident in *Everybody's Autobiography* which is prefaced by an anecdote relating the author's meeting with Dashiell Hammett (a meeting which was clearly seen by Stein as one of the "perks" of celebrity). Stein relates a dinner conversation; the following passage is long but worth quoting in full:

> I said to Hammett there is something that is puzzling. In the nineteenth century the men when they were writing did invent all kinds and a great number of men. The women on the other hand never could invent women they always made the women be themselves seen splendidly or sadly or heroically or beautifully or desparingly [sic] or gently, and they never could make any other kind of woman. From Charlotte Bronte to George Eliot and many years later this was true. Now in the twentieth century it is the men who do it. The men all write about themselves, they are always themselves as strong or weak or mysterious or passionate or drunk or controlled but always themselves as the women used to do in the nineteenth century. Now you yourself always do it now why is it. He said it's simple. In the nineteenth century the men were confident, the women were not but in the twentieth century the men have no confidence and so they have to make themselves as you say more beautiful more intriguing more everything and they cannot make any other man because they have to hold on to themselves not having any confidence.... That's interesting I said.
>
> (Stein 1937: 5)

Indeed, this passage *is* interesting and not least because it echoes Virginia Woolf's description, in *A Room of One's Own*, of the "shadow shaped something like the letter 'I'" which falls across the page of Mr. A's writing (Woolf 1929: 150). Stein's implication is clear: male writers of the twentieth century are unable to abandon identity in the act of creation; consequently, it falls to the "self-confident" woman to be the century's literary genius. It is also significant that it is only self-confidence which enables the abandonment of identity, and this gives us a clue to Stein's endless self-aggrandizement and self-publication as a "genius." By the time of *Everybody's Autobiography* it becomes clear that her emphasis on her own genius is less monomaniacal (or, at least, not *only* monomaniacal) than strategic.

Also by the time of *Everybody's Autobiography* it becomes clear that for Stein "genius" is grandly impersonal and, at least in part, attributable to historical accident: "After all a genius has to be made in a country which is forming itself to be what it is but is not yet that is what it is is not yet common property" (Stein 1937: 92). As an American and a woman, Stein was ideally situated to assume the role of the literary genius of the twentieth century. Interestingly, once she had worked through more thoroughly her own stake in a discourse of genius, she was able to represent the struggles and insights of at least one other woman artist more sympathetically and generously than she had in *The Autobiography of Alice B. Toklas*. In *Everybody's Autobiography* it is only Marie Laurencin who has the courage to tell Stein why the painters had been offended by her earlier book:

> It was interesting, she stated what they felt they the men could not say this thing because as they said it it would have sounded foolish to them but that is the way they did feel, I imagine Marie Laurencin was right painters feel that way ... Marie Laurencin said it and she saw it and it has to be seen.
>
> (Stein 1937: 34–35)

BUT EVERYONE CALLED MARIE LAURENCIN MARIE LAURENCIN

> Everyone called Gertrude Stein Gertrude, or at most Mademoiselle Gertrude, everyone called Picasso Pablo and Fernande Fernande and everybody called Guillaume Apollinaire Guillaume and Max Jacob Max but everyone called Marie Laurencin Marie Laurencin.
>
> (Stein 1960: 60)

As Stein suggests in the above passage, a politics of *naming* can work both obviously – as with the patronym, which Lacan has punningly labelled the *non/ nom du père* and which confers identity and subjectivity in patriarchy – and subtly, to position women within a complicated network of cultural relations and cultural capital. Marjorie Perloff draws out the distinctions suggested by Laurencin's naming as it is described by Stein, concluding that "the Picasso–Apollinaire cenacle did not quite know how to assimilate the woman painter in their midst. To call her 'Marie' would be to equate her with Fernande the mistress or Gertrude the hostess, and so she is called Marie Laurencin even as it is still customary today to talk of Joyce, Lawrence, and Virginia Woolf, or, for that matter, of Hemingway and Gertrude Stein" (Perloff 1988: 68).

Like Nina Hamnett and Djuna Barnes, the subjects of our next chapter, Marie Laurencin appears frequently in memoirs of the period. However, these appearances tell the reader less about Laurencin than about cultural resistance to the idea of the serious woman artist, especially if the woman insists upon her femininity. Sadly, in her own 1933 memoir, Fernande Olivier contributed rather venomously to the derogation of "the woman painter" (the choice of "painter" rather than "artist" is significant), as the following passages illustrate:

> It was at [Sagot's] house that Picasso and Apollinaire met Marie Laurencin for the first time. An innocent abroad, she tumbled (goodness knows how) into Clovis Sagot's gallery on the Rue Laffitte. She looked like a little girl, and had a little girl's mixture of naiveté and viciousness, a good deal too naive to be true. Marie Laurencin, a pupil

at an art school on the Boulevard de Clichy, was to become "*the* woman painter of the gang."

(Olivier 1964: 43)

In spite of Apollinaire, who was extremely taken with her and wanted to impose her on us, she was not accepted into our little group straight away. She was incapable of being natural and she seemed affected to us, a bit silly, very contrived and self-conscious and chiefly interested in the effect she produced on other people. She would listen to herself talking, watching her carefully childish gestures in the mirror as she spoke.

(Olivier 1964: 85)

Given such constructions, it is therefore significant that Stein purchased Laurencin's *Group of Artists*, also known as *Les Invités* (Figure 4.1), painted in 1908. According to Stein, "It was the first picture of hers anyone had ever bought" (Stein 1960: 62). Although Stein recalled that Fernande Olivier had told her about the picture, Olivier observed instead that: "It was mainly for fun, and due to Picasso's encouragement that the Steins bought a picture by her: quite a large composition, consisting of a seated group of some of the artists she knew" (Olivier 1964: 109). Given Olivier's obvious dislike of Laurencin, it seems likely that she wished to imply that Stein's purchase was more an act of generosity than connoisseurship. However, more important than Stein's motives was the fact that Laurencin's painting joined Stein's widely viewed and highly regarded avant-garde collection which included works by Cézanne, Matisse, Braque, and Picasso. Such prestigious company did much to enhance the reputation of so young an artist. Marie Laurencin herself later acknowledged the importance of this purchase when she claimed, inaccurately, that: "My first picture was a portrait of Guillaume Apollinaire in which Picasso and Gertrude Stein also figured" (Todd 1928: 92). Her inaccuracies are revealing: this was not her first picture, but rather the first one which she sold; furthermore, she confused this picture with a subsequent verison of it which did include Gertrude Stein but which she gave to Apollinaire. These memory lapses (which make both Stein and the sale of the picture loom larger than life) indicate the importance she attached to the purchase of this picture as launching her career.

Her much discussed *Group of Artists* depicts Apollinaire seated reading a golden book, Laurencin next to him holding a faded rose, Picasso and his dog, Frika, and Olivier beneath a bouquet of flowers. The work is roughly painted in the artist's primitive style which has variously been likened to Persian miniatures, the painting of Henri Rousseau, and eighteenth-century paintings and engravings (Gray 1958: 10–11; Olivier 1964: 108–9; Hyland and McPherson 1989: 61). The figures consist of outlined colour blocks with stylized, masklike faces. A curvilinear rhythm of interlacing limbs and

Figure 4.2 Marie Laurencin, *Réunion à la campagne* or *Apollinaire et ses amis* (1909). Oil on canvas. 130 × 194 cm. Musée National d'Art Moderne, Centre Georges Pompidou, Paris.

repeating oval-shaped faces draws the composition together. Some accounts of the picture have seen it as Laurencin's relatively straightforward view of her friends: her conflicted emotions for Apollinaire (her face in shadow and the faded flower she holds towards the poet), her sense that Picasso was unapproachable (with a frontal neck and torso and a profile head), and her satirical view of Fernande Olivier who has alternatively been described as "simpering a little foolishly beneath the bouquet" (Gray 1958: 12) or "playful and flirtatious" (Sandell 1980: 25). Other accounts have interpreted the picture as more deeply symbolic. For instance, Julia Fagen-King has described the picture as a Rosicrucian representation of the birth of a new epoch with "Apollinaire–Christ, Marie–Madonna and Picasso–Baptist as its heralds" (Fagen-King 1988: 94).

While there is some debate over Laurencin's intended level of meaning in *Group of Artists*, critics have generally agreed upon the symbolic nature of her second and more ambitious rendition of the same theme titled *Réunion à la campagne* or *Apollinaire et ses amis* (Figure 4.2) which was painted in 1909 and owned by Apollinaire until his death in 1918. Here the friends have been rearranged and placed outside: Apollinaire (now with a cat) still occupies the central position; on his left, and representing the Three Graces, are (from left to right) Gertrude Stein, Fernande Olivier, and a blonde woman who might be Marguerite Gillot, mistress of Paul Fort (Fagen-King 1988: 97–98); on his right are Picasso, an unidentified woman who might be Marie Laurencin's mother, the poet Maurice Chevrier (also known as Cremnitz), and the seated figure of Laurencin. In a recent article, Renée Sandell has argued that Apollinaire (complete with halo), Laurencin, and the cat appear as a holy family group surrounded by their disciples (Sandell 1980: 26). In a similar vein, Julia Fagen-King proposes that Laurencin was commenting on her own creative practice as well as that of Apollinaire: "The three admired personages, Picasso, Pauline Laurencin and Cremnitz, are placed against a backdrop of a canvas on an easel, perhaps Laurencin's way of acknowledging the sources of inspiration for her own artwork – Picasso's style, her mother's support, and the poetic qualities of the literary world" (Fagen-King 1988: 100). Just as these three figures are linked to Laurencin, the Three Graces represent the sources of Apollinaire's poetry. Again, according to Fagen-King: "In Laurencin's painting, it would seem that the senses (represented by Olivier), linked to the mind (represented by Stein), produce the fruits of the artistic ideal within a framework of love (represented by Gillot)" (Fagen-King 1988: 98).

In terms of their use of such "literary" tropes as the Three Graces and the attributes of the rose and book, both of these group portraits seem to be based on a retrospective symbolist aesthetic. (It might be recalled that such attributes were also favoured by Romaine Brooks, as noted in our first chapter.) Indeed, Laurencin often asserted her interest in the work of past painters: in a 1923 interview she cited Goya and Titian as her favourite painters; these were later changed to Botticelli and Ghirlandaio in the 1942 edition of her *Carnet des nuits* (Buffet 1923: 394; Laurencin 1956: 18).[9] Significantly, Apollinaire argued that this link to past tradition was something which characterized what he called "female painting." His point is developed at some length in his essay "The decorative arts and female painting:"

> It seems to me that it would obviously be in the decorators' interests to study carefully the works of today's female artists, who alone possess the charming secret of the gracefulness that is one of the most original traits of French painting. This is true both of the works of the so-called French primitives and of the delightful and tasteful marvels that could have been only produced in France and that were painted by Watteau, Fragonard, Corot, Berthe Morisot, and Seurat.... This new delicacy, which is like an innate sense of Hellenism possessed by the French woman, can be found to a high degree in the works that Mlle Laurencin is currently exhibiting at the Barbazanges Gallery.
>
> (Apollinaire 1972: 210)[10]

While Apollinaire saw Marie Laurencin's relation to the tradition of French painting as an indication that women artists had something to offer the modernist movement, the majority of critics regarded her use of past styles and fantastic scenery as decidedly anti-modernist. A typical case in point was the anonymous critic of the *Art Digest*:

> She [Laurencin] stands among the moderns as vaguely distant as the elfish maidens she paints in their elusive surroundings.... Fearful perhaps that the titans would submerge her entirely, convinced that her own personality was essentially feminine and exquisite rather than intellectual and dynamic, she swept clear of their sphere of influence, and developed what she considered her true character as an artist. The results are extremely well known. Everywhere today one sees her blue and gray rose confections, flat decorations of fluttering wraith-like women whose ancestors are the ladies in Persian miniatures, 18th century prints, and even the profile pastels of Manet.
>
> (anon 1937: 10)

Here Laurencin's aesthetic was seen to be at odds with that of the modernist titans of Cubism: hers was feminine, elusive, exquisite, and nostalgic while theirs was intellectual, dynamic, and modern.

It is surprising, then, that Gertrude Stein bought Laurencin's *Group of Artists*, especially given that her own theories of portraiture were much closer to Cubist aesthetics. For instance, in her lecture "Portraits and repetition" she made it clear that neither description nor memory should play any role in portraiture. Instead, she was interested in capturing the rhythm of a person's existence through a continuous succession of sensual observations gained by listening and looking both inside herself and inside the person under scrutiny (Stein 1967: 119). For Stein the process of writing a portrait involved an interactive exchange between writer and "sitter." Throughout the lecture, Stein defends herself against the charge that she was endlessly repetitive by drawing attention to the Bergsonian notion that the continuous movement of time made exact repetition impossible. Her series of slightly shifting observations is clearly illustrated in the opening of her portrait "Picasso:"

> One whom some were certainly following was one who was completely charming. One whom some were certainly following was one who was charming. One whom some were following was one who was completely charming. One whom some were following was one who was certainly completely charming.
>
> (Stein 1967: 213)

These slight variations on a theme draw the reader's attention to the passage of time within the text in much the same way that a Cubist portrait demonstrates the movement of the painter around the subject and through time. Stein's ordering principle is one of accretion by succession, rather than an ordering by relation or association. It is for this reason that her portraits contain no overt description or even narrative, for these imply association or relation, which in turn implies memory, which takes one out of the continuous present.[11]

While Laurencin shared Stein's interest in the interaction between the artist and model, she remained interested in description, memory, and the transcendence of time. In fact, she explicitly likened her pictures to stories:

> I love portraits. To me a portrait is like a voyage: it has to me the attraction of a new experience. When I make a portrait I feel as though I were travelling through another person. I do not like to paint men. I don't know if I am capable of painting a man's portrait. My ambition is that men should have a voluptuous feeling when they look at the portraits I paint of women. Love interests me more than painting. My pictures are the love stories I tell myself and which I want to tell others.
>
> (Buffet 1923: 396)

Thus, while Stein drew on the avant-garde visual aesthetics of Cubism in constructing her portraits, Laurencin drew on more conventional – even sentimental – literary aesthetics in her emphasis on visual narrative. But is it possible to "read" Laurencin's "love stories" against the grain?

Recent scholarship on Laurencin has noted that several of her early works humorously parody the work of her famous male counterparts. For instance, Julia Fagen-King has convincingly argued that Laurencin's etching, *Le Pont de Passy* of 1908 (Figure 4.3), mockingly reinterprets Edouard Manet's well-

known *Le Déjeuner sur l'herbe* of 1863 (Musée d'Orsay, Paris). Substituting herself for the nude woman, Laurencin has turned the two male figures into a cat (Apollinaire) and a monkey (Picasso) seated around a basket of fruit very similar to the type which Picasso used in his paintings of this period. Furthermore, as Fagen-King points out, these substitutions were Laurencin's way of humorously responding to the joke in Bateau Lavoir circles that she and Olivier were represented as prostitutes in Picasso's 1907 *Les Demoiselles d'Avignon* (Museum of Modern Art, New York). Picasso is thought to have drawn inspiration for *Les Demoiselles* from the brothel scene in his copy of Apollinaire's pornographic manuscript *Les Onze milles verges*. Evidently he used Apollinaire's coded description of Laurencin as a prostitute in an "open book" position (who has, like the other prostitutes in the story, been blown apart and anatomically fractured by the sudden explosion of a shell) as the basis for his female figure in the lower right. Fagen-King susepcts that as Picasso rendered Laurencin as a prostitute, she turned him into a monkey (Fagen-King 1988: 103–8).

Similarly, her 1909 *Réunion à la campagne* has been read as a further parody of Picasso's *Les Demoiselles*. If one compares the studies for both paintings,[12] it is evident that Laurencin (Figure 4.4) utilized Picasso's composition by incorporating his Three Graces on the left, placing Apollinaire in the original position Picasso used for the sailor (who was subsequently omitted from the final version), and inserting herself in the lower right. As Hyland and McPherson note, Laurencin gentrified Picasso's brutal composition by showing herself demurely seated in a pale blue dress (Hyland and McPherson 1989: 25; Pierre 1988: 47–51). This evidence of Laurencin's humour suggests that some of her "stories" were subversively up-to-date rather than "merely" sentimental, and that she irreverently addressed the latest concerns of the French avant-garde by making fun of Picasso's *Les Demoiselles*, a painting which was probably then (and certainly now) considered to be the most important modernist masterpiece of the period.

Thus while Stein positioned herself in possessive and hyperbolic relation to "male genius," Laurencin's positioning was quietly (and parodically) adversary. Indeed, the evidence suggests that Laurencin was as interested in questions of genius as was Stein; however, unlike Stein's, Laurencin's reflections on her own practice come to us mediated by the voices of others who interviewed the artist. This difference between the lecture and the interview format says something not only about the prestige of these two individual women, but also about the relative intellectual status of their two disciplines. It should be noted that being a visual artist placed Laurencin in an especially difficult double-bind since neither artists nor women were expected to be articulate – they needed others to speak on their behalf.

In contrast to Stein's split between a masculine creative self and a feminine body of work, Laurencin saw herself, her subject matter, her style, and her media as quintessentially feminine. In a 1923 interview with Gabrielle Buffet

Figure 4.4 Marie Laurencin, study for *Réunion à la campagne* (1909). Black-lead and brown wash on paper. 20.3 × 26.6 cm. Musée National d'Art Moderne, Centre Georges Pompidou, Paris.

published in *Arts*, Laurencin described her favourite subject matter: "I love the details of life. I attach great importance to costumes, to hats, to all that is suitable to woman and beautifies her. A fashionable woman is to me the greatest work of art. I love feminine appearance. The hands of women, their feet are my great preoccupation" (Buffet 1923: 394, 396). In the interview Laurencin argues that delight in dressing her dolls as a child led her to the profession of portrait painting. As a youth, she first started painting her cat, Poussiquette (who she felt had the face of a woman). It was an experience which in turn led her to self-portraiture: "After I began to paint myself my own portrait has always kept me busy" (391).

For the most part, art critics have tended to see Laurencin's interest in her own portrait as a typical form of feminine self-obsession. Commenting on the artist's mature style in the 1920s, Roger Allard presented a point of view that other critics have subsequently repeated time and again in the Laurencin literature. After observing that all of nature was nothing but a cabinet of mirrors in which Laurencin saw her own reflections, Allard continued:

> C'est, comme je l'ai dit ailleurs, que son art égoïste rapporte tout à soi, qu'elle n'eût guère d'autre sujet qu'elle-même, et d'autre souci que de se retrouver. N'ayant d'inclination que pour les objets ou les formes naturelles qui lui ressemblent, pour les animaux ou les plantes qui ont sa flexibilité vigoureuse, elle découvre partout des reflets de son propre visage et des raisons plus pressantes et plus imprévues de s'aimer elle-même. C'est Narcisse, mais décent et sans trouble, mais capable de donner la vie et la durée à ses images fugitives.
>
> (Allard 1925: 50)[13]

According to Allard, there was no distance between Marie Laurencin and her art: they were one and the same. Here we can draw parallels with the case of Romaine Brooks who, in a similar fashion, was seen as projecting her own tortured psyche onto her sitters.

While the artistic genius is expected to be closely identified with *his* work, when it comes to women such a relationship is differently interpreted and used as evidence of women's limited ability to imaginatively manipulate their subject-matter. This double standard of critical evaluation is hardly surprising in patriarchal culture where representations of the male self are viewed as positive acts of creation, while representations of the female self are cast as derivative. In other words, the modernist female artist was caught in an impossible bind since representing herself as a woman meant renouncing her claim to originality. It is only very recently that feminist art historians have started dismantling such limited models of creativity. For instance, Hyland and McPherson suggest that Laurencin's self-portraits stemmed from an impetus that her male colleagues likely would have found baffling. Discussing her *Femme Peintre et son Modèle* (Figure 4.5) they note:

Figure 4.5 Marie Laurencin, *Femme Peintre et Son Modèle* (1921). Oil on canvas. 81 × 65 cm. Collection Hervé Odermatt, Paris.

The subject of the artist in her studio, so often portrayed by Picasso, is here given a specifically feminine twist. The model (the double of the artist) is in this case a woman. The creative process, which for Picasso remained integrally linked to the male sex drive, is here transported to the less aggressive realm of sisterhood.

(Hyland and McPherson 1989: 30)

While Allard's criticism established influential patterns with respect to analyzing Laurencin's subject-matter, Apollinaire's writings on the artist during the early phase of her career (from 1908 until 1914 when she left Paris for Spain) had a large impact on how the artist's style was interpreted. According to him, Laurencin demonstrated the essentially feminine formal qualities of grace and serpentine line (Apollinaire 1972: 230).[14] This tendency to describe Laurencin's style as feminine became even more pronounced in the critical discourses surrounding her mature work following her return to Paris in 1921. During the 1920s, tangible evidence of her femininity was confirmed by her palette: "nun's gray, and robin's egg blue, all of them married to lavender, cerise and rose" (Crowninshield 1937: 1).

As noted earlier, in her interview with Buffet Laurencin stated she was unsure whether she could paint men but she loved painting women. Repeatedly she stressed that her art was intuitive and non-rational in contrast to the rigorous work of the Cubists. Evidently she felt it imperative to distance herself from her male contemporaries when she passionately responded to the question "What do you think of Cubism?"

Cubism has poisoned three years of my life, preventing me from doing any work. I never understood it. I get from cubism the same feeling that a book on philosophy or mathematics gives me. Aesthetic problems always make me shiver. As long as I was influenced by the great men surrounding me I could do nothing.

(Buffet 1923: 394)

Marie Laurencin's description of the "great men" of Cubism should be read with some degree of irony since, in many respects, her notion of the feminine involved radically rejecting the male-dominated cultural status quo, a strategy evident in Dorothy Todd's interview with the artist in *Arts and Decoration*. Todd noted that Marie Laurencin's "insistent preoccupation with purely feminine qualities" resulted in a "peculiarly exaggerated division of all known experience into masculine or feminine," all of which led the interviewer to conclude that "she is a feminist, probably the strangest feminist the world has ever seen" (Todd 1928: 92). While the interviewer obviously supported feminism and treated Laurencin more seriously than most of her peers – praising her practicality, modernity, and interest in physical activities – Todd was nonetheless disconcerted by what we might today call Laurencin's radically essentialist and separatist position. In Todd's words, Laurencin displayed "an almost frantic determination not to allow the pure ether in which her own essentially feminine sensibility wanders to become clouded by any admixture of a heavier, more masculine quality" (92). Throughout the interview Laurencin turned conventional wisdom upside down by applying a logic that at points worried Todd. A typical instance was her argument that painting was logically a feminine pursuit:

> I conceive a woman's role to be of a different nature; painting to be essentially a "job" for a woman (one who sits so long quiet on a chair); and a painter's ideal inspiration to be life and that of a natural sensibility rather than the outcome of intellect or reason. There is something incongruous to me in the vision of a strong man sitting all day [Marie Laurencin always sits to paint – the majority of men painters, as a matter of fact, mostly prefer to stand] manipulating small paint brushes, something essentially effeminate.
>
> (92)

Significantly, Todd felt obliged to intervene and in the midst of recording Laurencin's comments reassured readers that there was an appropriate way for men to paint (standing) thereby defusing Laurencin's charge that painting was a job for women. Here Laurencin's choice of the word "job" is worth noting since it reveals her underlying sense of professionalism – her belief that painting was work from which women could earn money in much the same way that they were paid for sitting at office desks meticulously typing and filing.[15] Later in the interview Todd stressed that Laurencin saw work as a feminist issue: "Her Anglo-Saxon sympathies are particularly noticeable in all matters concerning the emancipation of women. 'I only like people who work,' she says, 'I have no use for idlers'" (95). We might also remember that in her accusation that the "great men" (or geniuses) of Cubism prevented her from working, Laurencin set the notion of genius against, or outside, the demands of the workaday world.

In contrast to Stein, who – in Bourdieu's terms – was initially willing to invest in the longer-term dividends of genius, Marie Laurencin was more interested in seeing her career flourish as soon as possible. She needed the money. Describing her situation at the time of her first exhibition at the Salon des Indépendants in 1907, Hyland and McPherson note that "she was not a success financially, only barely managing to survive while living with her mother in a tiny two-room apartment" (Hyland and McPherson 1989: 54). She continued to live at home until her mother's death in 1913 – partly because she was unmarried and not earning enough to support herself, and partly because, as the illegitimate daughter of a seamstress, her family capital was limited. Initially Laurencin's mother had hoped she would become a secondary school teacher; when that failed she enrolled Laurencin in porcelain painting classes at the Sevres factory. Such practical early training indicated that Laurencin was expected to earn her own livelihood. Later, during her wartime exile in Spain after she had married the German painter Otto von Watjen, an alcoholic, Marie Laurencin was financially assisted by her wealthy friend Nicole Groult, a sister of Poiret, the fashion designer (Stein 1960: 62).

Finally in 1921 when she returned to Paris at the age of 36, Marie Laurencin divorced her husband and managed to set her career on a firm financial footing. During the twenties Laurencin capitalized on her prewar critical acclaim by turning to the highly lucrative fields of society portraiture, costume and set design, and graphic illustration.[16] Two particularly successful commissions included her costumes and sets for *Les Biches*, a ballet choreographed by Nijinsky and set to music by Poulenc which was performed by the Ballets Russes in 1924, and her contribution to the *Chambre de Madame* designed by André Groult for the *Exposition des arts décoratifs* in 1925, which was one of the first important exhibitions of Art Deco works.

Part of Laurencin's success stemmed from the combination of influences that critics detected in her mature style, all of which complemented the new Art Deco aesthetic. Although the degree to which Laurencin deliberately developed her style to suit prevailing aesthetic tastes remains a matter of speculation, the art critics of her generation often observed that

> no one better than she gives the flavour of the period.... [Her] dove-grays, light Boucher blues and delicate rose colours combine, with a certain subtle naughtiness, to convey the Paris of the pre-war years and of the early twenties in one of her most enchanting moods. Perhaps in France, they will talk of the "Laurencin period," towards the end of this century, much as we now talk of the "Beardsley period."
> ("Two Marie Laurencin exhibitions" 1937: 103–4)

The suggestion of a Laurencin period and the comparison with Beardsley, a graphic designer, imply that Laurencin's art reached a public that extended beyond the confines of the art world. Another critic (albeit disparagingly) compared her work to that of Jules Cheret, the popular art nouveau poster designer: "Somme toute, l'artiste auquel elle fait le plus penser, c'est Jules Cheret. Même attrait capricieux, voluptueux sans sensualité, tout en mousse, vite evente, dont la monotonie, avec le recul du temps, étonnera" (Fosca 1925: 122).[17] More favourably, a third critic pointed out just how effectively the artist had adapted her style to the technology of mass-produced images (J.L. 1937: 19). In fact, during the 1920s coloured reproductions of the artist's paintings – an English advertisement for these reproductions appearing in *Colour* (November 1929: 32) indicated a starting price of three pounds – were sold through numerous galleries catering to a wide range of middle-class consumers interested in owning Laurencin's images.

A further indication of her commercial viability was the fact that until 1940 Laurencin's work was handled by the Galerie Rosenberg, a leading contemporary dealer who also exhibited the works of Matisse, Picasso, and Braque.

However, Laurencin preserved her autonomy when it came to portraiture which she contracted directly with her clients (Hyland and McPherson 1989: 33; Marchesseau 1986: 13).[18] Few of her female contemporaries were as widely exhibited or collected, as Dorothy Todd emphasized:

> Since the time of her famous compatriot Berthe Morisot, no woman painter has earned the world-wide endorsement of art connoisseurs to so great an extent as Marie Laurencin. Her pictures hang in almost every national gallery and no private collection is considered complete without one.
>
> (Todd 1928: 92)

Indeed, between 1912, the date of her first major exhibition which she shared with Robert Delaunay at the Galerie Barbazanges, and 1939 Marie Laurencin had eleven solo exhibitions in Paris, London, Dusseldorf, and New York. All but the 1912 exhibition took place after her return to Paris in 1921. Success had its rewards. Laurencin owned a large, comfortable apartment on the rue Savorgnan and in 1925 bought a country house at Champrosay. She could afford to live alone, travel, and accept work that suited her. In 1930 she was invited to a lunch organized by the art dealer René Gimpel for the four "queens" of French culture: herself (painting), Colette (literature), Valentine Tessier (theatre), and Coco Chanel (fashion). Often photographed in the popular press of the period, Laurencin was usually identified as a famous woman painter (Gimpel 1966: 72).[19]

In different ways, Marie Laurencin's attitudes towards professionalism and the emancipation of women were as complex and contradictory as those of Gertrude Stein. By using the separate spheres rationale to argue that painting was a feminine pursuit, Laurencin was, in part, reviving strategies that conservative bodies of female artists such as the *Union des femmes peintres et sculpteurs* had mobilized in their campaign for equal access to male artistic institutions during the 1880s and 1890s. This group had mounted the influential argument that women, as the natural preservers of tradition, should be artistically enfranchised to protect traditional French values and styles of painting against the threat of avant-gardism (see Garb 1989: 39–65). Evidently, this argument worked less successfully for a female avant-garde artist, a construct which was a contradiction in terms. Although avant-garde critics often praised what they constructed as her femininity (for example, her perceived proximity to nature and the primitive), for the most part Laurencin was doubly marginalized. On the one hand, she did not fit into the mainstream category of female painters, who tended to be more traditional; on the other, she was nearly always cast as an outsider, or non-competitor, when it came to discussions of the male avant-garde. John Quinn, one of her most important patrons, typically summed up the problem: "One of the things that I like about Marie Laurencin is that she paints like a woman, whereas most women artists seem to want to paint like men and they only succeed in painting like hell" (Reid 1968: 470). As we have already observed, although Quinn may have found Laurencin's feminine style appropriate, when it came to ranking her genius, he considered her a third-rate talent. One cannot help suspecting that part of Quinn's enthusiasm for Laurencin's work was the fact that it reinforced prevailing conceptions of femininity as belonging to the lesser categories of taste and talent as opposed to genius.

In an article examining the formation of the critical category of "*l'art féminin*" in late nineteenth-century France, Tamar Garb has pointed to the difficulties facing women artists who were "measured not only in terms of a difference from 'masculinity,' conceived as normative, but also in terms of their difference from a fantasy of femininity, constructed in relation to 'masculinity.'" Women's art had to be not only technically adequate, but to "express an essential femininity" (Garb 1989: 48). As our case study of Marie Laurencin and Gertrude Stein suggests, not much had changed in the first few decades of the twentieth century. Women artists were still negotiating an impossible situation, caught between the conflicting discourses of gender and genius. By proclaiming her femininity, Laurencin had it turned against her as proof of her third-rate talent; in staking her own early claim to "genius," Stein adopted a largely masculine persona, entered into a traditional bourgeois marriage, and asserted her difference from other women.

FEMINA ACADEMICUS, OR, CAN(N)ON FODDER

In *Homo Academicus* Pierre Bourdieu sardonically provides a privileged insider's view of the way power works in academic systems:

> Academic capital is obtained and maintained by holding a position enabling domination of other positions and their holders, such as all the institutions entrusted with controlling access to the corps.... [T]his power over the agencies of reproduction of the university body ensures for its holders a statutory authority, a kind of function-related attribute which is much more linked to hierarchical position than to any extraordinary properties of the work or the person ...
>
> (Bourdieu 1988: 84)

Within academic institutions and systems, certain disciplines are privileged over others, just as the objects and issues of study in various fields are also hierarchically ranked according to acceptable disciplinary criteria. In the fields of literary studies and art history this latter operation is generally known as canon formation. In this section we will consider the ways in which the gendering of Stein's and Laurencin's genius has positioned them within literary and art historical canons.

First of all, some important differences between the fields of literature and art history should be acknowledged. Admittedly, the discipline of art history has a certain prestige value which is largely derived from the precious and usually unique nature of the objects it studies (the original artefact costs more and carries more weight in the visual arts than in literature) as well as the field's ostensible distance from everyday life, at least according to the widely held aesthetic hypothesis that to perceive the artistic one must transcend the mundane. Furthermore, the discipline is appealing to many precisely because it seems to offer a pleasureable, intuitive, and irrational refuge from conscious intellectual life. This is because the literary domain of words and texts has been more closely associated with thought than has the artistic domain of icons and images. In other words, we believe that we think verbally and not visually. Perhaps partly for this reason, the development of critical theory in the discipline of art history has been slow and painful. It is hardly an exaggeration to say that most art historians have been reluctant to address the rapid proliferation of new theories within such fields as literary studies. On the rare occasions where theory has been needed, it has usually been borrowed from those working elsewhere. According to Norman Bryson,

> What is certain is that while the last three decades have witnessed an extraordinary and fertile change in the study of literature, of history, of anthropology, in the discipline of art history there has reigned a stagnant peace; a peace in which – certainly – a profession of art history has continued to exist, in which monographs have been written, and more and more catalogues produced: but produced in an increasingly remote margin of the humanities, and almost in the leisure sector of intellectual life.
>
> (Bryson 1983: xi)

As a consequence of art historical conservativism, the discipline – which, in any case (and for well-documented historical reasons), had never achieved the hegemonic centrality of English studies (see Baldick 1983, Doyle 1989, Viswanathan 1989) – diminished in prestige in the post-1968 academy. The discipline's resulting failure to secure academic centrality has had important consequences for the recovery of "lost" women artists. Just as it was somewhat easier for modernist women writers to take themselves seriously, due in large part to the existence of nineteenth-century female precursors of recognized "genius," so both the centrality of English studies within the academy and its acknowledged "social mission" (the phrase is Baldick's) have led to a greater concentration of theoretical and feminist work – and, consequently, to an earlier challenging of received canons than was evident in art history. Certainly what might be called a visual inferiority complex (especially *vis à vis* the supposedly more intellectual nature of literary or language-based studies) has marked Western culture since the Enlightenment, and the two fields have been privileged, and gendered, accordingly: the profession of literary criticism was increasingly "masculinized" during the first three decades of this century, while that of art history was increasingly "feminized."

In addition, the relative privileging of literary over visual texts – a characteristic, as we have already noted, of modernity – made available different strategies of self-representation to Stein and Laurencin, as is evident in the different patterns of their careers. Stein was associated with the privileged terms of masculinity, genius, and avant-garde culture while Laurencin was seen as feminine, talented, and popular. Significantly, conventional wisdom has characterized the differences between Stein and Laurencin as qualitative – relating to the nature of their ability and the calibre of their work. In fact, as we might recall, Stein herself was quick to differentiate between the contemporary genius (which was how she characterized herself) and the "precious" or minor poet who lived in the shadow of the past or in the imagination (terms which evoke the critical discourses on Laurencin's painting). Furthermore, in 1925 Stein directly contributed to Laurencin's devaluation in elite cultural circles when she expressed her reservations about the quality of the Group of Artists and sold the picture (Hyland and McPherson 1989: 54). One wonders whether it was significant that Stein sold the picture just as Laurencin's popularity peaked after her return to Paris in 1921. Perhaps Stein felt that Laurencin had lost her avant-garde edge; this would have tarnished her reputation for Stein who liked to think of herself as a particularly progressive patron. In any event, Stein profited financially given the rising prices of the art market in general and of Laurencin's paintings in particular.

However, before we are seduced by the appealing simplicity of judging individuals, it is useful to reconsider Bourdieu's cautionary observation which warns us that symbolic capital is more immediately linked to hierarchical position than to extraordinary properties in the work or person. Here we want to move beyond the rather obvious point that Stein's work was more formally innovative within its field than Laurencin's. Although undoubtedly this has played a role in assessments of their work, we think it is important to place their critical reputations in a broader institutional framework that takes into account their positions and available options. This approach enables us to raise a number of often neglected questions which should be factored into value judgements of these artists' work: why have formal innovation and masculine models of genius been fetishized by critics? what other criteria should feminists consider in evaluating the work of women writers and artists? should such notions as genius and the canon be perpetuated? and finally, how might Stein and Laurencin be usefully re-positioned in feminist cultural histories of the period?

Of immediate concern to feminists are the problems associated with overvaluing the strategies of Gertrude Stein and denigrating those of Laurencin. Ironically, both women experienced striking reversals of critical fortune in the later years of their careers and after their deaths: Stein acquired a significant position within the canon, while Laurencin virtually disappeared from view. Even feminist cultural criticism has tended to perpetuate these

evaluations by promoting Stein's work as not only formally but sexually
innovative while anxiously casting around for ways to justify the rediscovery
of Marie Laurencin. Indeed, Laurencin herself was highly ambivalent and
inconsistent in the way she constructed her femininity and its relation to her
work during the heyday of her career in the twenties and thirties. As we have
seen, sometimes she used her femininity to criticize the male-dominated
profession of painting while at other times she felt it cast her in a subordinate
position. On occasion her oscillation between the two positions was
painfully schizophrenic, indicating that she found it hard to look against the
grain of patriarchal culture consistently. For instance, in *Le Carnet des nuits*
after complaining that male genius was too much for her, she ended up
expressing her reverential admiration for it:

> Le peu que j'ai appris m'a été enseigné par ce que j'appelle les grands
> peintres, mes contemporains: Matisse, Derain, Picasso, Braque. Ils ne
> seront pas contents que je cite leur nom, ils sont comme cela. Je les
> compare à l'air de Carmen: "Si tu ne m'aimes pas, je t'aime..."
> Si je ne suis pas devenue peintre cubiste, c'est que je n'ai jamais pu.
> Je n'en étais pas capable, mais leurs recherches me passionnent.
>
> (Laurencin 1956: 22)[20]

It is perhaps because she constructed her femininity in such ambivalent
ways, as well as the fact that she developed a light and decorative style during
her maturity, that feminists have felt so uncomfortable about reviving
Laurencin's painting. Indeed, the artist virtually disappeared from the early
twentieth-century canon of painters for some thirty years from the period
after her death in 1956 until the 1980s when the Marie Laurencin museum
was established in Tokyo.[21] It seems significant that her rediscovery has been
mainly promoted by feminist art historians and Japanese scholars, both of
whom are largely outsiders to the tradition of Western European painting
and art criticism. Perhaps this is because Laurencin herself always remained
something of an outsider *vis à vis* the art historical canon, as Hyland and
McPherson emphasize:

> The question can no longer be put off. What place does Marie
> Laurencin occupy in the constellation of twentieth-century French
> painting? Within what art historical context should her work be
> viewed? ... As *femme peintre*, Laurencin was doubly an outsider – as
> artist and as woman. Unaffiliated with any major modern movement
> Laurencin took refuge in an imaginary world inhabited by dreamy
> women and peaceful animals.
>
> (Hyland and McPherson 1989: 39)

Hyland and McPherson go on to argue that in art historical terms she should
be placed within the School of Paris along with such painters as Chagall,
Modigliani, Douanier Rousseau, Soutine, Pascin, and Utrillo. While this

might be a useful preliminary stylistic classification, it also seems necessary to place her, as we have done in this chapter, within the larger field of women writers and artists working in Paris. It is only by doing so that one can start to understand how the pressures of her position, like those of Gertrude Stein's – which finally led Stein to acknowledge the degree to which "genius" exists only in public discourse – motivated Laurencin to accept certain premises that might seem disturbing to women of the later twentieth century.

5

MEDIATING MODERNISM
Djuna Barnes and Nina Hamnett

On February the fourteenth, 1890, I was born.

Everybody was furious, especially my Father, who still is. As soon as I became conscious of anything I was furious too, at having been born a girl; I have since discovered that it has certain advantages.

Nina Hamnett, *Laughing Torso*, 1932

Everybody seems to be "remembering" us – *that's the fine state of affairs we are in!* ... K. Burke being r[i]diculous on *Nightwood*, idiot children working on PhD's, Who's Who and dictionarys [sic], requests from colleges, and platforms, and all the time, not a soul really cares a damn – the children have it. They've run off with the world, – and *we* have let them!

Djuna Barnes to Natalie Barney, 28 March 1967 (emphasis in original)

As the epigraphs to this chapter suggest, Djuna Barnes and Nina Hamnett were enormously self-conscious about not only their positioning specifically as *women* writers and artists during the modernist period, but also about the ways in which they were represented in the popular and, later, the academic press. It is, of course, not surprising that any writer or artist would attend to her reputation within always fluctuating literary and art markets. However, for reasons of both gender and economic status, Barnes and Hamnett were especially sensitive to the monetary and emotional price attached to being public figures within an artistic community. Unlike most of the women we have already discussed (with the exception of Marie Laurencin), neither of the women who are the focus of this chapter had a private income. Each had to work to support herself and, in Barnes's case, her family; each was also frequently dependent upon the sometimes unpredictable patronage of women like Peggy Guggenheim and Natalie Barney.[1] Unlike such male modernists as James Joyce, neither of these women was the beneficiary of sustained and sufficient patronage; ironically, many potential women patrons instead focused their efforts on securing an income for male artists. Natalie Barney's sponsorship, with Ezra Pound, of the Bel Esprit project to "free

Valéry and [the unwilling] Eliot from their financial cares so that they might devote themselves fully to their writing" (Sieburth 1976: 286) is one example.[2] From 1913 until the early 1930s, Djuna Barnes worked as a journalist while in the 1910s and 1920s Nina Hamnett worked in Roger Fry's Omega Workshops and as an artist's model, with a brief stint as an art teacher. However, although Barnes and Hamnett worked, sometimes sporadically, in areas that were tangential to their work as artists, neither achieved the kind of highly prestigious paying work – like T.S. Eliot's editorship at Faber & Faber – that could empower her to influence the course of "modernism." Instead, much of their paying work involved "popularizing" avant-garde modernism for consumption by a broader public: Barnes through her sketches of bohemian life for mass circulation dailies and weeklies like the *New York Morning Telegraph Sunday Magazine* and glossy magazines like *Vanity Fair*, and Hamnett through her work in the Omega Workshops, whose function was "to provide young artists with the opportunity to earn some money and to allow the influence of Post-Impressionism to invigorate decoration" (Spalding 1983: 122).

Significantly, popularizing avant-garde modernism – selling it to a broader paying public – frequently also meant selling themselves as prototypes of the modern, thus lending authority or, in Bourdieu's terms, symbolic capital to their products.[3] Since, however, in the cultural field the accumulation of symbolic capital depends upon maintaining distance from the world of everyday bourgeois reality, the question which must be asked is whether, in *investing* their symbolic capital in short-term appeals to the bourgeois public, these women ultimately held less symbolic capital in avant-garde and academic circles? We will argue that, in their mediating position between the avant-garde and the bourgeoisie, Barnes and Hamnett were valued less for the uniqueness of their work than the fact that they *stood in for* the bohemian. As a result, they were enormously aware of the degree to which their subjectivity could be manipulated through representation and performance, by others and by themselves. Hamnett accomplished this manipulation most spectacularly in her best-selling and scandalous autobiography, *Laughing Torso* (1932). In his introduction to the 1984 Virago Press reissue of *Laughing Torso*, Hamnett's nephew, Edward Booth-Clibborn, remarks that "Those who knew Nina Hamnett later in her life will know that whatever she did in painting she was a complete success as a socialite" (ix), and indeed Hamnett – like Barnes – figures repeatedly in memoirs of the period as a "character." Both are evoked by numerous memoirists as part of (to use Sylvia Beach's phrase) "the Crowd," the list of background names which authenticates the memoirist's claim to participation in expatriate modernism. Thus Barnes and Hamnett may be more familiar to many of today's readers as bit players in the modernist pageant than as artists in their own right.[4] This may help to explain the bitterness of Barnes's indignant 1967 observation to Natalie Barney that "Everybody seems to be 'remembering' us" – the unspoken addition might be, "but not our work." It may also help to explain another of Barnes's comments, this one from a 1971 interview:

> Years ago I used to see people, I had to, I was a newspaperwoman, among other things. And I used to be rather the life of the party. I was rather gay and silly and bright and all that sort of stuff and wasted a lot of time. I used to be invited by people who said, "Get Djuna for dinner, she's amusing." So I stopped it.
>
> (quoted in Kannenstine 1977: 11–12)

While their work as mediators between the modernist avant-garde or bohemia and the bourgeois public may partially explain the lack of critical attention accorded the work of Barnes and Hamnett, the fact that each worked in two media – the textual and the visual – is also significant. Barnes was a writer, illustrator, and portraitist; her illustrations accompanied many of her newspaper and magazine articles, and several of her books – most notably *The Book of Repulsive Women* (1915), *Ryder* (1923), and *Ladies Almanack* (1928) – can only be fully understood by reading the visual *against* the literary text. Nina Hamnett was primarily a painter, and sometime illustrator, whose best-selling autobiography catapulted her to public attention as the "Queen of Bohemia," a reputation which has continued to block serious critical attention to her painting. The cross-disciplinary work of these women has led to their relative critical neglect for a number of reasons. Their "vacillation" between two media has been read as lack of commitment; the entrenchment of academic criticism in rigidly defined fields has created critics ill-equipped to interpret the full range of their work; and, most importantly, "modernism's" self-defining emphasis upon formal experimentation militated against genuinely cross-disciplinary work. As is articulated most consistently in the work of art critic Clement Greenberg and in the continuing influence of the American "New Critics," the "modernist" critical enterprise has emphasized disciplinary purity.

The kind of work performed by Barnes and Hamnett sheds light not only on the conditions of the woman writer or artist without a private income – making it clear that even so narrow a critical category as white Anglo-American women's modernism must acknowledge privilege as an important site of difference – but on the nature of the modernist avant-garde. The efforts of these two women to secure a livelihood which would also satisfy desires for artistic expression and a "bohemian" lifestyle force us to rethink the gendered economies of "modernism" at the same time as blurring "modernist" distinctions between "the avant-garde" and "the popular," "the professional" and "the commercial," and "genius" and "talent." In this chapter, we will argue, firstly, that the modernist venture required the mediating or border-crossing work of apologists who could bring modernism to a wider public while at the same time assuring that the (male) modernist practitioner could remain visibly committed to "the absolute" and to "ultimate values" (Greenberg 1961: 5, 15); and secondly, that these apologists (editors, booksellers, gallery owners, journalists) were typically women, many of whom were artists in their own right and whose more "serious" work would suffer critical neglect as a result of its association with "the popular." To do this, we will discuss primarily Djuna Barnes's sketches of Greenwich Village life and articles about James Joyce and Nina Hamnett's autobiography and café sketches.

THE PRESS FOR WAFER

The speaker of Ezra Pound's *Hugh Selwyn Mauberley* (1920) bemoans the decline of modern life, in which "We have the press for wafer / Franchise for circumcision" (ll. 51–52). Although these lines would seem to suggest that it is the secularization of modern life which constitutes its downfall, Pound elsewhere in the poem makes it clear that it is modernity's commitment to mass production and consumption (in which "the Beautiful" is "Decreed in the market place" (l. 48)), which is the real cause of cultural decline. It is only the "stylist" who, in retreat with his "placid and uneducated mistress" (ll. 174, 178), can attempt to revive genuine culture through his art. This argument is obviously not unique to Pound and it would be further developed by, for example, Clement Greenberg in "Avant-garde and kitsch." However, Pound's description of the substitution of mass forms of communication and political participation for more "genuine" rites of communion and initiation is telling. Given that questions of franchise during this period were more specifically questions of women's suffrage (in Great Britain women over the age of 30 achieved the vote in 1918, in the United States women achieved the federal vote one year later), his description of the substitution of franchise for a markedly phallocentric religious ritual makes it clear that Pound saw the decline of culture as rooted in its feminization, a feminization which is here metonymically linked to mass or popular culture specifically in the form of the popular press.[5] The association of mass culture with the feminine has been discussed by Andreas Huyssen who notes that: "It is indeed striking to observe how the political, psychological, and aesthetic discourse around the turn of the century consistently and obsessively genders mass culture and the masses as feminine, while high culture, whether traditional or modern, clearly remains the privileged realm of male activities" (Huyssen 1986: 47).[6] The association of mass culture with the feminine and high culture with the masculine obviously grows from the same cultural economy which associates "genius" with masculinity and "talent" with femininity, as discussed in our last chapter. Huyssen's seven-point summary of "what the modernist art work has become" as a result of its antagonistic stance toward mass culture and its subsequent canonization (53–54) is enormously useful and succinct; here we will draw from his seventh and final point: "Only by fortifying its boundaries, by maintaining its purity and autonomy, and by avoiding any contamination with mass culture and with the signifying systems of everyday life can the art work maintain its adversary stance: adversary to the bourgeois culture of everyday life as well as adversary to mass culture and entertainment which are seen as the primary forms of bourgeois cultural articulation" (54).

Although Huyssen and, in *Sentimental Modernism*, Suzanne Clark focus primarily on popular or pulp fiction as paradigmatic of feminine mass culture, the newspaper, together with other forms of mass periodical literature, is obviously a central forum for "the bourgeois culture of everyday life." Moreover, it is through the newspaper and the magazine that avant-garde culture is brought to the attention of the bourgeoisie. The willingness of many modernist and avant-garde writers and artists to be featured, like Mina Loy, in daily newspapers or, like Romaine Brooks and Gluck, in glossy magazines provides some evidence that while bourgeois culture might be a primary focus of criticism or satire in modernist art production, it nonetheless represented an important potential market.[7] That many artists attended carefully to this market is evident in the following 1925 letter from Man Ray to Gertrude Stein:

> Your photo appeared in this month's Vanity Fair very effectively. If you haven't a copy, I'll send you mine. Another publication "Shadowland" has just written me that they will publish the photo of the interior, next month. So you see I am doing my share to keep the pot boiling.[8]

Certainly, modernist and avant-garde artists were not homogenous in their attitudes toward mass circulation periodicals. As Marjorie Perloff has pointed out, European avant-garde movements like the Cubists and Futurists made frequent use of the newspaper – both as object and as typographic style – in their collages and manifestos. The insertion of newspaper fragments into Cubist collage, for example, allowed referentiality to be "reasserted even as it [was] called into question," while the *avant guerre* Italian Futurists used newspapers in their collages to reinforce their commitment to populism (Perloff 1986: 49, 73). Such appeals to the transitory and the populist – in effect, to the politics of everyday life – were less common among Anglo-American modernists who were more likely to make use of upmarket weekly or monthly periodicals like *Vanity Fair*, *Vogue*, and *Sketch* for mostly publicity purposes. In either case, we must be careful not to confuse modernist and avant-garde *use* of mass circulation periodicals, either to open up new markets or to integrate art and praxis, with *endorsement* or validation of the bourgeois ideology of these publications. As Bourdieu has shown, the very *periodicity* of these publications (daily, weekly, monthly) is at odds with an avant-garde cultural economy which depends on long- rather than short-cycle production. That is, the "consecration" of avant-garde art depends to an enormous degree on its apparent disinterestedness, its *distance* from a profit motive. Bourdieu uses the example of commercial as opposed to avant-garde publishing firms; the commercial firm invests in the short-term (i.e. in "best-sellers") while the avant-garde firm invests in the long-term (i.e. in "classics"): "it is the *intervening time* which provides a screen and disguises the profit awaiting the most disinterested investors" (Bourdieu 1986: 154). A safe rule of thumb might be, the shorter the turn-around time, the less symbolic capital; this would put daily newspapers at the bottom of the cultural hierarchy with monthly magazines slightly higher. In order to maintain their symbolic power within the cultural field, avant-garde artists can have, at best, an ironic relation to mass circulation periodicals whose life is purposely brief and whose commitment to the profit motive (through their reliance on advertising revenue) is unashamed.

Given the determination of modernist and avant-garde artists to remain at a highly critical arm's length from the production of newspaper and magazine copy, together with their partial reliance on such copy, how could a woman like Djuna Barnes negotiate the mediating or border-crossing work of journalism? How could she ensure herself a living wage while at the same time protecting her more serious avant-garde work? Ultimately, she couldn't. Several of Barnes's critics have argued that she abandoned journalism in the early 1930s *because* she was becoming successful as a novelist (see Levine 1991: 28; Plumb 1986: 33). However, it seems more likely that success as an avant-garde novelist was compromised as long as she continued to publish widely in the popular press. Barnes may have gambled and lost; in any event, she spent the last thirty years of her life in an often humiliating and largely unproductive poverty. The gamble for men who were both journalists and literary writers seems to have been less chancey, largely because the *kinds* of stories they were assigned carried more cultural weight than stories "about what the crowned heads of Europe liked for dinner" (Levine 1991: 28). An analysis of modernist engagement in journalistic and editorial practice suggests hierarchies that were organized on the basis of "transitoriness" *and* of gender. While newspaper writing occupied the lowest rungs, and magazine writing the middle rungs, the usually unpaid and subsidizing editorship of the "little magazines" which influenced the course of modernism constituted the upper rungs of the hierarchy. In terms of newspaper reporting, "yellow journalism" ("stunts, advice columns, and sob sisters" (Marzolf 1977: 45)) was at the bottom of the hierarchy, followed by crime and city reporting, with foreign and war correspondence at the top.

It may be useful here to compare Djuna Barnes's career with that of a male modernist writer, Ernest Hemingway, similarly remembered for the degree to which his literary style was influenced by his newspaper training.[9] Hemingway credited the Kansas City *Star* – which hired him in 1917 to cover first the federal and then the police and ambulance beats — with providing "the best rules I've ever learned for the business of writing" (quoted in Lynn 1987: 68). By 1920, after a stint of feature writing for the *Toronto Star Weekly*, Hemingway was sent to Paris as the *Toronto Star*'s first European correspondent: "Whenever he was on assignment, he would be paid seventy-five dollars a week, plus expenses, and for every unassigned piece that the paper accepted he would be paid at the rate of a penny a word" (Lynn 1987: 147). Although Barnes was at least as financially successful – by 1917 "she was earning five thousand dollars a year as a free-lance feature writer" (Levine 1991: 28) – her career as a woman reporter took a slightly different shape. When she began work for the Brooklyn *Daily Eagle* in the summer of 1913, Barnes was assigned some straight city reportage; she was quickly moved to the kinds of quirky feature articles and interviews that would become her trademark. However, at the same time she also made her name as a "stunt girl" reporter, allowing herself to be hugged by a gorilla and rescued by firemen.[10] Her most famous stunt consisted of being forcibly fed, supposedly in an effort to understand what many English suffragettes were experiencing; a photograph of Barnes bound and restrained by four men, one of whom was a doctor, accompanied the article (the article is reproduced in Barnes 1989; the photograph in Broe 1991).[11] As Marion Marzolf indicates, stunt reporting, together with "sob sister" and sensationalist reporting and advice columns, was one of the most accessible routes to a career in journalism for women during this period (Marzolf 1977: 32–73). Like Hemingway, Barnes also went to Paris sometime around 1920, in her case on what has been described as a "loose" commission for *McCall's* magazine (Field 1985: 104). However, while Hemingway was grumblingly called away to cover the 1922 International Economic Conference in Genoa or to interview Benito Mussolini, Barnes was publishing interviews with fashion designers and articles on "American wives and titled husbands."[12] From the early 1920s until 1928, she published primarily literary sketches in such mass circulation magazines as *McCall's*, *Charm*, *Vanity Fair*, and the *New Yorker*; from 1929 until 1931, when she effectively gave up journalism, she published a monthly column in *Theatre Guild* magazine (Plumb 1986: 19–33).[13] A huge proportion of her mature journalism, then, involved interpreting artistic and expatriate communities for a variety of readerships in the United States. A comparison of several profiles of artist figures and sketches of bohemian life produced within a six-year period for three different readerships will reveal something of the function and strategy of Barnes's position as mediator between avant-garde and bourgeois culture. We will discuss below her 1922 interview with James Joyce, published in *Vanity Fair*; a 1922 sketch of Paris, including discussions with Joyce, published in the little magazine, *The Double Dealer*;[14] and four sketches of bohemian Greenwich Village, published in *Bruno's Weekly*, *Pearson's Magazine*, and the *New York Morning Telegraph Sunday Magazine* in 1916.

Like bookselling and publishing (Sylvia Beach and Harriet Weaver, who brought Joyce's works to print, are important examples here) or gallery-directing (Vanessa Bell was one of three co-directors, with Roger Fry and Duncan Grant, of the Omega Workshops), journalistic coverage of the arts and of the arts community requires its practitioners to be able to identify more immediately with the marketplace and with bourgeois sensibilities, at least to the degree of knowing limits of toleration.[15] In his introduction to *Vanity Fair: Photographs of an Age, 1914–1936*, John Russell indicates that journalists and publishers were highly and strategically aware of these limits. Frank Crowninshield, editor of *Vanity Fair*, determined that modern art and literature should be featured in the magazine, but "without frightening its readers away" (Russell 1982: xv). One strategy was not to "tackle the work head on;" if, for example, Crowninshield "reproduced one of [Picasso's] paintings, it was what we would now consider a safe and tame example" (xvii). Russell cites Djuna Barnes's interview with James Joyce, which appeared in the April 1922 issue of *Vanity Fair*, as a "classic instance" of how to introduce a difficult modern writer to a readership unfamiliar with his work.[16] As Russell points out, Barnes accomplished this by focusing on the man – how he spoke and dressed – rather than on *Ulysses*, published that year. Crowninshield, in other words, "dealt in gossip" but "gossip of high quality from the best possible source" (xvi). Only one month later, Barnes published a *second* article featuring Joyce, this time in *The Double Dealer*, a little magazine published in New Orleans.[17] A comparison of the two articles should help to reveal something of Barnes's strategies for popularizing so difficult a writer, but it will first be useful to consider the status of *Vanity Fair* for which, in 1922, Barnes published five pieces within a six-month period: her Joyce article, three satiric pieces under the pen-name Lydia Steptoe, and one poem.[18]

Frederick J. Hoffman has argued that "It is hard to imagine a magazine more appropriate to the decade [of the twenties] than *Vanity Fair*" which he describes as both "sophisticated and philistine" (Hoffman 1955: 86, 88). *Vanity Fair*'s spoofs, parodies, and satires – especially of the youth culture of debutantes, flappers, and Ivy League undergraduates – are considered its most characteristic and successful offerings, and these were certainly forms in which Barnes excelled. The three short satires published by her under the name of Lydia Steptoe combine the witty and epigrammatic comedy of Oscar Wilde with an acid awareness of the forms and effects of social constructions of femininity. The 14-year-old narrator of "The diary of a dangerous child," for example, notes in her diary that:

> I am debating with myself whether I shall place myself in some good man's hands and become a mother, or if I shall become wanton and go out into the world and make a place for myself.
> Somehow I think I shall become a wanton.
> It is more to my taste. At least I think it is.
>
> (Barnes 1922c: 56)

Just one year later, however, the "dangerous child" – barely teetering on the edge of self-affirmation – has already become more fully disciplined and feminized, a feminization Barnes represents as regression: "In another year I shall be fifteen, a woman must grow young again. I have cut off my hair and I am asking myself nothing. Absolutely nothing" (Barnes 1922c: 94). Significantly, it is the mother who is the disciplinary vehicle of the daughter's socialization, a theme Barnes would return to in her 1958 play *The Antiphon*. The older and considerably more jaded narrator of "Against nature" (significantly, this is the usual English-language title of Huysmans's influential decadent novel *À Rebours*), whose primary target is the "jeune fille,"[19] describes herself in terms which can perhaps be read as reflecting Barnes's awareness of her own performance as a woman arts reporter for the bourgeois press:

> [Y]ou can tell by the way my nostrils quiver that I have suffered delicately over such subjects as whether Conrad got more out of women or the sea.
>
> I hold advanced ideas, but not vulgarly advanced. I just keep prettily ahead of the times, where I show to best advantage, half turned head over shoulder, beckoning the generation.
>
> (Barnes 1922d: 60)

However, although *Vanity Fair* specialized in such "lighthearted" fare, it also attracted a considerable number of modernist heavyweights: Aldous Huxley wrote on Marie Laurencin, Tristan Tzara on Dada, Gertrude Stein on Picasso, Ezra Pound on Paris (Hoffman 1955: 86). And in 1922 the magazine became involved in a virtual bidding war with *The Little Review* and *The Dial* for first American publishing rights to T.S. Eliot's still unfinished *The Waste Land*.[20] Russell suggests that *Vanity Fair* "aimed to combine the characteristics of both the little and the big magazine" (x). The magazine's interest in Eliot's poem – which was touted by Pound, acting as Eliot's agent, as "the justification ... of our modern experiment, since 1900" (quoted in Rainey 1989: 24) – represented its bid for a greater degree of symbolic capital. *Vanity Fair*'s obvious interest in Barnes's work during this period can be read as a sign of her growing status as writer and interpreter of the modernist avant-garde. However, a comparison of Barnes's profiles of James Joyce published in *Vanity Fair* and *The Double Dealer* suggests that she saw the magazine as fairly firmly entrenched in bourgeois sensibilities.

Although in her private correspondence Barnes maintained an ironic posture toward her career as a journalist, her published articles reveal a different deployment of irony and "sincerity." The more bourgeois she thought her audience, the more sincerely, even romantically, she represented bohemian or avant-garde culture, saving her most savage irony for her peers. Her *Vanity Fair* article on Joyce ("James Joyce: A portrait of the man who is, at present, one of the more significant figures in literature") treads a middle ground between romantic celebrations of artistic genius and a very slight and sly undercutting of the masculinism of such traditions. The article falls loosely into three parts: four introductory paragraphs, then two sections which constitute the interview proper – "Joyce, the man" and "His appearance." Joyce's stature as a writer of enormous significance is reinforced by the paragraphs (one full column of what is essentially a four-column article) which build up to his meeting with Barnes in the café of the Deux Magots in Paris. His legendary reputation precedes him, as Barnes stresses in her opening sentences, laying out what will become the theme of the interview, the lyricism of Joyce's writing: "There are men in Dublin who will tell you that out of Ireland a great voice has gone; and there are a few women, lost to youth, who will add: 'One night he was singing and the next he wasn't, and there's been no silence the like of it!'" (Barnes 1922a: 65). The degree to which Joyce is a focus of intense international interest is reinforced by the fifth and sixth paragraphs which set up a chorus of speculation and rumour: "I had seen ... I had been told ... I had heard that ... And then, one day, I came to Paris" (65). The remainder of the article both reinforces and undercuts the legend of Joyce, primarily through the use of Romantic, even decadent, stereotypes of the artist. Like the Romantic artist he sacrifices himself to his vocation: "A man who has been more crucified on his sensibilities than any writer of our age," with something of "the look in the throat of a stricken animal" (65). And yet he is also a bit of a dandy with his "delightful waistcoat" and "eternal cigar." Throughout the article Barnes hints at decadence, most obviously in the following paragraph: "Yes, then I realized Joyce must indeed have begun life as a singer, and a very tender singer, and – because no voice can hold out over the brutalities of life without breaking – he turned to quill and paper, for so he could arrange, in the necessary silence, the abundant inadequacies of life, as a laying out of jewels – jewels with a will to decay" (65). This passage clearly evokes such well-known decadent texts as Arthur Symons's 1893 article, "The decadent movement in literature," which described decadent writing as "a new and beautiful and interesting disease." Barnes's emphasis on Joyce's voice and the musicality of his writing similarly invokes Symons's argument that "to be a disembodied voice, and yet the voice of a human soul: that is the ideal of Decadence" (Symons 1981: 136, 141). Elsewhere in the article Barnes describes Joyce's enervation ("His hands, peculiarly limp in the introductory shake and peculiarly pulpy"), the paleness of his eyes ("the same paleness seen in plants long hidden from the sun"), and suggests that he is "a little afraid of women." And yet, once the reader has become accustomed to Joyce the Decadent, she is suddenly introduced to Joyce the Family Man, with a wife and two great strapping children at his side: "Large children, almost as tall as he is himself, and Nora walks under fine red hair, speaking with a brogue that carried the dread of Ireland in it" (104). The article closes with the now famous passage from *Portrait of the Artist as a Young Man* in which Stephen Dedalus determines to "express myself in my art as freely as I can and as wholly as I can, using for my defense the only arms I allow myself to use: silence, exile and cunning" and with Barnes's suggestion that, in Joyce, "at last Ireland has created her man" (104).

How are we to read Barnes's allusions to decadent genius in this article? That decadence had an early appeal for her seems evident from her first chapbook, *The Book of Repulsive Women: Eight Rhythms and Five Drawings* (1915), with its highly stylized black-and-white illustrations and its depiction of "diseased" lesbianism. And certainly the illustrations that accompanied many of Barnes's articles during the period up to 1920 are more reminiscent of illustrators from the 1890s such as Aubrey Beardsley. For instance, her drawing of an extravagantly dressed dandy (Figure 5.1), which appears with a republished form of her essay "Becoming intimate with bohemians" (Barnes 1989: 236),[21] closely resembles some of Beardsley's more decadent male figures in terms of elaborate pose, elongated limbs, sensuously exaggerated lips, and theatrical costume.[22] In this typical drawing from the period Barnes directly borrowed a number of Beardsley's well-known stylistic hallmarks including the juxtaposition of outlined and solid form, trails of ink dots diminishing in size, repetitive decorative shapes (for example, the curls of hair or folds of the jacket), and spiky-edged forms. Even her signature rendered in an imitation Japanese calligraphy echoes that of Beardsley's early period.

Yet by 1922 her more serious work was moving away from an almost purely decadent aesthetic toward the more muted style of *A Book*, her 1923 collection of one-act plays, short stories, lyric poems, and six charcoal and pencil portraits. As Kannenstine notes, the extreme stylization, both verbal and visual, of *The Book of Repulsive Women* has given way in *A Book* to visual understatement and stories "characterized by a carefully limited scope and an economical quasi-naturalistic manner" (Kannenstine 1977: 25, 33). Although Barnes returned (exuberantly) to decadence in *Ladies Almanack* (1928) and *Nightwood* (1936), it was with a heightened and parodic sense both of the limitations and the usefulness of the discourse. In her later works decadence was no longer a privileged tradition, but one among many, including Elizabethan and Restoration.

In contrast, her allusions to decadence in the Joyce article seem almost naive. And that may be the point. Although a fin-de-siècle decadence was certainly outmoded within avant-garde communities by the 1910s and 1920s, it was still used within the popular press as a kind of shorthand to invoke all that was outrageous and artistic. Moreover, two of Barnes's mentors in the New York publishing community, Guido Bruno and Frank Harris (publisher of *Pearson's Magazine*), maintained emotional, historical, and material attachments to a decadent aesthetic.[23] Frank Harris had been an avid early collector of Beardsley's work and had discussed the artist in his autobiography as well as his book on Wilde.[24] Given these interests, he may well have encouraged Barnes to adopt Beardsley's illustrative style. It was Guido Bruno, furthermore, who popularized Barnes in 1915 as "the American

Figure 5.1 Djuna Barnes, untitled (figure of a male dandy, n.d.). Location of original unknown. Medium unknown, probably pen and ink. Reprinted in Djuna Barnes, *New York* (Los Angeles: Sun & Moon Press, 1989).

Figure 5.2 Djuna Barnes, *Self-Portrait* (1919). Location of original unknown. Medium unknown, probably pen and ink. Published with an interview of Barnes by Guido Bruno, "Fleurs du mal à la mode de New York – An Interview with Djuna Barnes," *Pearson's Magazine* (December 1919). Reprinted in Djuna Barnes, *Interviews* (Washington, D.C.: Sun & Moon Press, 1985).

Beardsley" (quoted in Kannenstine 1977: 23) and who published her first chapbook. As Douglas Messerli notes in his foreword to a collection of Barnes's interviews, Bruno was one of the "greatest charlatans and pretenders to participate in the Greenwich Village Bohemianism of 1912–1918," a man who "preached the *fin de siècle* aesthetics of Oscar Wilde and Aubrey Beardsley while promoting his own name and reputation as an impressario and dealer of experimental literature and visual art" (Barnes 1985: 383). In his Greenwich Village memoir, *The Improper Bohemians*, Allen Churchill is blunter, claiming that "Bruno won the undying hatred of most Villagers" for his promotional gimmicks aimed at turning Greenwich Village into a tourist attraction (Churchill 1961: 150–55). The Village's main selling features were its artists and bohemian reputation, and it is likely that Bruno promoted decadence as a lure to the potentially huge uptown bourgeois market. Bruno's commitment to reproducing decadence in Greenwich Village is evident in his 1919 interview with Djuna Barnes, published in Frank Harris's *Pearson's Magazine* and titled "Fleurs du mal à la mode de New York." His interview stresses Barnes's "morbidity" and concludes: "She is only one of many: a new school sprung up during the years of the war. Followers of the decadents of France and of England's famous 1890s, in vigorous, ambitious America" (Barnes 1985: 388).

Significantly, though, Barnes's self-portrait (Figure 5.2) accompanying the article somewhat ambivalently takes up the decadent morbidity that Bruno attaches to her. Certainly Barnes still uses Beardsley's characteristic black-and-white vocabulary by juxtaposing the white ground of her face and dress with the dark black mass of her hair, emphasizing the decorative drops of her art-nouveau earrings and dress pattern, and, finally, stylizing her facial features and signature in a way that is reminiscent of many of Beardsley's "portraits" and signatures. And yet, in spite of its obvious stylistic debt to the 1890s, Barnes's rather crude self-portrait (which is certainly much more roughly rendered than anything by Beardsley) disrupts the languidly elegant and decadent tone of the text. Certainly Barnes's own comments in the interview stress her unhappiness and sense of futility:

> Often I sit down to work at my drawing board, at my typewriter. All of a sudden my joy is gone. I feel tired of it all because, I think, "What's the use?" Today we are, tomorrow dead. We are born and don't even know why. We live and suffer and strive, envious or envied. We love, we hate, we work, we admire, we despise.... Why? And we die, and no one will ever know that we have been born.... Joy? I have had none in my twenty-six years.
>
> (Barnes 1985: 386)

Although Bruno claims to find Barnes's work "morbid," he cannot reconcile such work and the attitudes she expresses with the "real" Djuna he claims to know:

You have never met Djuna. The picture reproduced on this page is a self-portrait. She insists that it looks like her real self. I think it is contemptibly bad. Not a shadow of likeness. There isn't a bit of that slovenly doggedness in the real Djuna.

Red cheeks. Auburn hair. Gray eyes, ever sparkling with delight and mischief. Fantastic earring in her ears, picturesquely dressed, ever ready to live and to be merry; that's the real Djuna as she walks down Fifth Avenue, or sips her black coffee, a cigarette in hand, in the Café Lafayette.

(387–88)

Perhaps by inserting this rather crude image, Barnes wanted to disrupt the growing myth of her glamorous beauty which was depicted by numerous photographers of the period, including Man Ray. As her comments suggest, she may have wanted to appear more seriously intellectual. And yet, she was probably also aware of how such images would be circulated in the popular press when she had agreed to be interviewed. Bruno certainly seems to have made the most of the differences he detected between Barnes's verbal and visual representations of herself and his appreciative male view of her. By emphasizing such discrepancies, Bruno turns Barnes into an exotic, mysterious (and really beautiful) female puzzle for his readers. In a piece such as this, one imagines that Barnes's motives may well have been mixed: she would have needed the money, probably welcomed the publicity at this early stage of her career, but resented such superficial treatment.

This depiction of Barnes should alert us to the fact that Bruno was offering his readers a particularly appealing construction of the Village as a decadently navel-gazing and even paralyzing bohemian refuge. As already suggested, this was a particularly non-threatening and marketable view of the Village which largely ignored other politically engaged activities going on in its midst, such as Emma Goldman's feminist activism or various forms of resistance to the Sedition Act. Significantly, as Floyd Dell would later recall in his *Homecoming: An Autobiography*, the authenticity of village life was disappearing in the wake of tourism entering the Village.

> Greenwich Village had become commercialized during the war. The little basement and garret restaurants, decorated according to their own taste, proved a lure to up-towners, who came to the Village with their pockets full of money and their hearts full of a pathetic eagerness to participate in the celebrated joys of Bohemian life. The restaurants responded by laying on Village quaintness in thick daubs, to tickle the fancy of the visiting bourgeoisie....
>
> I loathed what the Village had now become. It was a show-place, where there was no longer any privacy from the vulgar stares of an up-town rabble....
>
> The Villagers were beginning to leave the Village; and those that still

remained were hard to find, so closely did they secrete themselves. To fill the gap left by their disappearance from their old haunts, there now appeared a kind of professional "Villager" playing his antics in public for pay. It was doubtless an honest way of making a living; but it was shocking to one who had been a Villager. It was a bitter thing to have to look at these professionals, and realize that this was the sort of person oneself was supposed to be.

(Dell 1933: 324–26)[25]

Allen Churchill suggests that the succession of chapbooks and little magazines published by Guido Bruno from "Bruno's garrett" were intended to function primarily as promotional literature: "These provocative little magazines were strenuously hawked uptown, where the gay and immoral Bohemian life pictured within made buyers itch to journey southward" (Churchill 1961: 151). This suggests that Barnes's commitment to the decadent vision of *The Book of Repulsive Women* (1915) – published by Guido Bruno – was probably ambivalent. Like Natalie Barney, who would become a close friend and occasional benefactor, Barnes found in decadence a ready-made language for articulating alterity; unlike the wealthy Barney, Barnes had to consider the financial repercussions of adopting a fully alternative lifestyle. Even within the bohemian communities in which she moved, Barnes could not risk alienting her patrons. Certainly *The Book of Repulsive Women* has presented a critical challenge, particularly to feminist readers, partly because it is rather unlike Barnes's other serious work but also because of its Baudelairian depiction of diseased and "repulsive" lesbian sexuality. Carolyn Burke has suggested that Barnes published the volume "almost as if it were necessary to kill off the old images of women before a different vision might become possible," but she concludes by wondering "whether Barnes was also writing, in part, to *épater le bourgeois*" (Burke 1991: 70, 71); Shari Benstock suggests that the book may have been intended, like *Ladies Almanack*, "for an audience of women" (Benstock 1986: 240).

However, attention to its publishing history suggests that the book may have functioned (whatever Barnes's complicated intentions, and it is worth noting that she did not include any of its poems in her 1962 *Selected Works*) not so much to *épater le bourgeois* as to sell him on the kinkiness of bohemian life. An examination of four sketches of bohemian life published in three different magazines suggests that when Barnes was writing for Guido Bruno, she laid the decadence on with a trowel. "The last petit souper (Greenwich Village in the air – Ahem!)," published in the 29 April 1916 issue of *Bruno's Weekly*,[26] describes a day in the life of a typical Greenwich Village "character," the dilettante. Barnes outlines three whimsically named versions of this character, each of whom is associated with a stereotypically decadent talisman: Vermouth who carries "a heavy blond cane and a pair of yellow gloves," Yvette, carrying his own "now-famous, silver-wattled cane," and

Absinthe, whose long fingernails are "silvered or gilded with gold" (Barnes 1989: 218–21). Vermouth, Yvette, and Absinthe are depicted as connoisseurs of exquisitely imagined pain and (through a reference to Marcus Aurelius) disciples of Walter Pater. In this article, Barnes addresses her intended readership explicitly and, by identifying herself with them, reassures them that they have nothing to lose and everything to gain by making the journey to Bohemia: "The public – or in other words that part of ourselves that we are ashamed of – always turns up the lip when a dilettante is mentioned, all in a patriotic attempt to remain faithful to that little home in the Fifties with its wax flowers, its narrow rockers, and its localisms and, above all, to that mother whose advice was always as correct as it was harmful" (219). Significantly, when Barnes published "Greenwich Village as it is" six months later for Frank Harris's *Pearson's Magazine*, her identification was squarely with the Villagers, now no longer wistful (male) aesthetes, but robust visionaries of both sexes: "And so you of the outer world, be not so hard on us, and above all, forbear to pity us – good people. We have all that the rest of the world has in common commodities, and we have that better part: men and women with a new light flickering in their eyes, or on their foreheads the radiance of some unseen pleasure" (Barnes 1989: 232).[27] "Greenwich Village as it is" is a relatively straightforward catalogue of Village restaurants, clubs, personalities, and little magazines; however, in her two sketches for the *New York Morning Telegraph Sunday Magazine* Barnes again returns to selling the bourgeoisie, here caricatured as "Madam Bronx," a suitable vision of bohemian life. That she expected the readership for these articles – "Becoming intimate with the Bohemians" and "How the Villagers amuse themselves"[28] – to be different from that of *Pearson's Magazine* is suggested by the fact that, only a month later, she was recycling some bits of her "Greenwich Village as it is" piece. Furthermore, her allusions to decadence are slightly more ironic than in "The last petit souper," and are usually counterpointed with references to the material difficulties of life as an artist. The following passage from "Becoming intimate with the Bohemians" is long but worth quoting in full, because it illustrates the degree to which Greenwich Village was in the early stages of becoming (to use today's phrase) gentrified; that this gentrification was the result of selling the bourgeoisie a "decadent" Village is also suggested in the contrast between the studio of the "consumer" of bohemian culture – with its incense and its Japanese prints – and that of the cultural "producer:"

> There are many evenings in the studios, blue and yellow candles pouring their hot wax over things in ivory and things in jade. Incense curling up from a jar; Japanese prints on the wall. A touch of purple here, a gold screen there, a black carpet, a curtain of silver, a tapestry thrown carelessly down, a copy of *Rogue* on a low table open at Mina Loy's poem. A flower in a vase, with three paint brushes; an edition of Oscar

Wilde, soiled by socialistic thumbs. A box of cigarettes, a few painted fans, choice wines (this here the abode of the more prosperous).

And then – a small hall bedroom under the eaves, a dirty carpet lying in rags; a small cot bed with a dirty coverlet. A broken shaving mug with a flower in it, a print of a print on the wall, a towel thrown in a corner, a stale roll and a half-finished cup of tea. A packing box with a typewriter on it, some free verse, a copy of a cheap magazine with a name in the table of contents that corresponds to the name written at the top of the sheet of paper in the machine.... A pair of torn shoes, a man's body on the bed, with arms thrown out, breathing slowly the heavy breath of the underfed.

(Barnes 1989: 242)

It is obvious that Barnes produced a number of different Bohemias, each carefully tailored to meet the requirements of a different editor or audience. Her representations of individual artists also varied considerably. It is significant that the Joyce of "Vagaries malicieux," published only one month later, is not the enervated and self-immolating genius of Barnes's *Vanity Fair* article. Although "Vagaries malicieux" draws on the same meeting at the café of the Deux Magots, this Joyce is, instead, "sad, quiet, and eternally at work" (Barnes 1922b: 254). He is also – an interesting variation on the "great voice" of *Vanity Fair* – a bit of a windbag:

His memory is said to be perfect (I had little chance to find out) and it has some of the slow dragging quality of an inland mist....

My mind wandered a little, I looked out into the square and wondered if I would ever come to this café again.

Just how long it was before I realized that Joyce had been talking to me I do not know, but when I gave him my attention again he was in the middle of a sentence whose conclusion was – "and that is how I missed seeing Tagore; another one of the world's misconceptions of the mystic. Because I had no evening clothes."

(253–54)

Here Barnes colludes with Joyce in deflating "the world's misconceptions of the mystic" or artist-genius. The article itself, addressed to a "little magazine" readership,[29] is a not-so-gentle deflation of the Paris of expatriate lore and a demonstration of the impossibility of achieving a "Paris" of full presence:

I said that the multiplication of Paris had been its destruction, and when [the Professor] asked me what I meant, I said that too many people had reported Paris, – it had the fame of a too beautiful woman. One should never come within hailing distance of beauty in women, cities or religion.

"We have too many thousands of opinions to discard, and in the event of the inevitable discard too much goes. There is hardly a shred left."

(256)

139

Significantly, the most vivid character of "Vagaries malicieux" is not Joyce, who figures in the article only briefly, but the middle-aged bourgeois wife of "the nation's most remarkable obstetrical surgeon," to whose home Barnes is invited when she expresses a wish to see a "real" French family. As she waits in "Madame's salon" she thinks that "Over it hung the silence that is in one's heart for all women who have come in and out of boudoirs to no end but the grave, and have done it so bravely, with lace and scent and timely fashions of all sorts, running on satin slippers which left the heel at every step" (255). The situation of the bourgeois wife is set alongside two other brief sketches of French women: three "interpretive dancers" in a French nightclub who "kicked a little ... but they showed only very soiled frills," and the chambermaid of Barnes's hotel in the rue Jacob who cries "Toujours travaille!" Barnes's exposure of the other side of the Paris of the modernist imagination reveals the degree to which expatriate dreams of freedom and licence were founded on the sexual and domestic labour of women.

The concluding paragraph of "Vagaries malicieux" cynically queries whether Barnes will "tell the world what Paris meant to me" or whether she will instead "let [the world] sit in its clubs, and its libraries and its homes with Mark Twain and Arthur Symons on its knee" (260). As is evident from "Vagaries malicieux" and "James Joyce," she did both.

HOW THAT TORSO ... DOES GET ABOUT!

September 1981. I have an hour before catching my train at Victoria. I go in to wander around the National Portrait Gallery.... Here the fun quickly gives way to nightmare. Heads, heads, heads.... What bizarre obstinacy to endlessly paint and repaint, for centuries, the same thing, all those heads of animals protruding from lace collars or fabric, hair done, all dressed up, and all so profoundly serious. That's it: the seriousness of the head that is posing, and that everyone makes a big deal about. Because the portrait doesn't work without the following assumption: this individual has a social value, and, more fundamentally, man [sic] has a value.

(Lejeune 1989: 114)

Although Nina Hamnett drew and painted her share of heads – in this chapter we will focus on her self-portraits of 1913 and 1918 – when she *wrote* her self-portrait, *Laughing Torso: Reminiscences* (1932), she titled it after the tiny, headless, marble *Torso* (1913) by Henri Gaudier-Brzeska for which she was the model. The title of her autobiography is curious. Why would she name her own "life" after a representation of her by someone else? Moreover, a torso is by definition headless and limbless; how can it laugh – and why? Philippe Lejeune's description, in *On Autobiography*, of his "nightmare" experience in London's National Portrait Gallery provides some clues. The genre of the (auto)biography, like that of the (self-)portrait, assumes "this individual has a social value, and, more fundamentally, man has a value." Although Lejeune is here using "man" in its "traditional" generic sense to refer to "the human being," feminist theorists of autobiography have pointed out the degree to which the genre assumes "male" models of selfhood and social value. Sidonie Smith, for example, argues that what we now regard as traditional autobiography emerged from an eighteenth- and nineteenth-century ideology of metaphysical selfhood, valorizes public life and discourse, and works to sustain sexual difference. She suggests that it is only with the emergence of modernism that the female autobiographer "begins to grapple self-consciously with her identity as a woman in patriarchal culture" (Smith 1987: 56) and that "twentieth-century women have used autobiography as one prominent ground for cultural critique" (Smith 1990: 21). Among her examples are Virginia Woolf's "A sketch of the past" (1939, in Woolf 1976), which experiments with the instability of "history, memory, self, sexuality," and Gertrude Stein's *The Autobiography of Alice B. Toklas* (1933), which "renegotiates generic conventions" through its use of Toklas as narrator and its reformulation of "the conventional patriarchal marriage" (Smith 1990: 19). Smith calls these women "autobiographers of the margins," a term which is accurate, but also, in some ways, inaccurate. After all, the great attraction of Hamnett's *Laughing Torso* and Stein's *The Autobiography of Alice B. Toklas*, published only a year later, was their promise of access to the bohemian and avant-garde worlds of expatriate Paris. The authority of their autobiographies depended upon Hamnett and Stein representing themselves as intimates of the major artists and writers of their period. Stein accomplished this by insisting on the centrality of her own literary "genius," and, by aligning it with that of the artist Pablo Picasso and the philosopher Alfred North Whitehead, she managed to lay discursive claim to a huge chunk of Western culture.

Although there are some similarities between Stein's and Hamnett's autobiographies – both, for example, are massively *peopled* – Hamnett's strategy was quite different. In *Laughing Torso* she frequently seems to occupy the margins even of her own life. Although some of her sketches and three of her portraits are reproduced in her book, she scarcely mentions her own work or concerns as an artist; when she does, it is often self-deprecatingly, as in the following passage:

> On the evening of my arrival I showed [Walter Sickert] my pictures, hoping that he would like them. He was, unfortunately, horrified and hated them. This filled me with gloom. I rather admired them myself at that time, but, having seen some of them recently, am inclined to think that he was right.
>
> (Hamnett 1932: 166)

One of her reviewers noted that "Philistines will be cheered to know that there is hardly a line of explicit art criticism in *Laughing Torso;*" instead her autobiography is described as "the most complete and captivating picture of Bohemianism which any modern has yet drawn" (Pippett 1932: 13). As this quote suggests, the real subject of *Laughing Torso* is not Nina Hamnett but an image of Bohemia that will titillate the *sale bourgeoisie* she occasionally invokes. One suspects that she knew her social value was strategic and relational; or, to put it cynically, she knew that her social value was as an object of exchange and representation.

When Rebecca West reviewed Nina Hamnett's *Laughing Torso: Reminiscences* in the 10 June 1932 issue of the *Daily Telegraph*, the headline promised "The Racy Autobiography of a Woman Artist." The American edition of the book, a best-seller on both sides of the Atlantic, was advertised as "the frankest autobiography ever written by a woman" (Booth-Clibborn 1984: vi). That the appeal of the book lay in its sexual promise is also evident from West's initial summary of the narrative: "How that torso, which is not only cheerful but excessively willing and active, does get about! It spins and spins from London to Paris, from studio to studio, from party to party, from night club to night club, and if not from pole to pole, at least from Swede to Pole" (6). Nina Miller has explored the degree to which, in the Greenwich Village of the 1920s, the "two central ideals of Village bohemia, the 'artist' and 'free love,' produced a deeply contradictory position for women writers" (Miller 1991: 38), and the same was certainly true for women artists in London and Paris throughout the 1910s and 1920s. In effect, Hamnett has been critically "disciplined" for assuming and representing *both* prerogatives of male bohemianism: sexual freedom and artistic vocation. That her self-representation as a "bohemian" woman had repercussions on her critical reputation is evident in subsequent memoirs and in her almost complete absence from art historical consideration. For example, in their history of the Café Royal (subtitled "Ninety Years of Bohemia"), Guy Deghy and Keith Waterhouse describe Hamnett as one of the "female element" (primarily models) who frequented the Café in the prewar Georgian era. Hamnett's work is not mentioned; instead, Deghy and Waterhouse focus on her friendship with various male avant-gardists and on her sexuality:

> To all these she spoke as man to man. She wore her hair cut short, and hid her beautiful legs in trousers at a time when legs were becoming more and more into evidence. She was the Modern Woman, who had discarded all the coynesses and pruderies that Shaw had apostrophized as "roguey-poguey." She would burst in, still excited by the discovery, announcing to Sickert that Verlaine and Rimbaud had shared the same rooms in Great College Street where she had lost her virginity! And shouldn't the L.C.C. put a blue plaque up? "My dear," said the painter, "they will put up one on the front for you, and one on the back for them."
> (Deghy and Waterhouse 1955: 131)

In *Is She A Lady? A Problem in Autobiography*, published more than twenty years later, Hamnett suggests that at least one of her motives in writing a memoir was to earn money: "I said that I was not writing a book to show up people or to propagate scandal, but partly I thought I owed it to some of my friends who were dead, partly to amuse myself, and incidentally to earn an honest penny" (Hamnett 1955: 87). While throughout the 1910s and 1920s, Barnes earned her living, in part, by selling the bourgeoisie suitably familiar sketches of bohemian life, together with interviews with other artists or entertainers, Hamnett sold herself as "a character," a madcap woman bohemian. Rebecca West seemed to realize the degree to which Hamnett based her autobiographical persona on a non-threatening, recognizable (and marketable) female "type," claiming in her review that *Laughing Torso* was really written by Agatha Runcible, a character from Evelyn Waugh's 1930 novel *Vile Bodies*, who spins through life madly socializing. Later in the review, West attempts to slightly undermine Hamnett's self-representation by noting similarities between Hamnett and such recognizably significant artists as Modigliani and Jean Cocteau, and by stressing the difference between such bohemians and the ordinary comfort-loving bourgeoisie. The bohemians are like religious aesthetes; both seek intense experiences which require painful regimes of discipline:

> Modigliani and Cocteau and Miss Hamnett knew that their aims were too diverse from the aims of monasticism to make them good monks and nuns. But for a plank bed substitute a bed rendered unsuitable for its primary purpose by books and insects ... for the cell substitute the café (equally ill-suited for permanent use as a home and abounding in a most wearisome type of lay brother); and for pulse and water substitute an equally monotonous diet of the cruder forms of alcohol. Then one gets an existence as far from fulfilling the voluptuous demands of the natural man as any monastic rule.
>
> (West 1932: 6)

In *Laughing Torso*, Hamnett refuses to deliver – except in an occasional and seemingly unwary aside, as in her discussions of her father's abusive behavior – her "self." The book's subtitle, "Reminiscences," with its allusion to a kind of Proustian aesthetics, promises instead a milieu and a fictional "character," the impossible laughing torso. In other words, according to Lejeune's analysis of the effects of self-portraiture, Hamnett's autobiography cannot be considered a self-portrait because Hamnett does not assign herself any social value. Instead, she functions as a mirrored surface, reflecting back the images of other, more important bohemian personalities. Such is not the case, however, in her painted *Self-Portrait* of 1913 (Figure 5.3) in which Hamnett asserts a much greater presence. Unlike Djuna Barnes, who in 1917 described herself as both an artist (at the drawing board) and writer (at the typewriter) and published a number of illustrated articles, Hamnett primarily

Figure 5.3 Nina Hamnett, *Self-Portrait* (1913). Original was destroyed. Published in *Colour* (June 1915).

saw herself as a painter, only later taking up writing in the thirties in order to make ends meet. Certainly her *Self-Portrait* of 1913 (done shortly after she had finished her schooling and secured her own studio) demonstrates her early confidence as she gazes out directly at the world. The wide-brimmed hat, up-to-date short haircut, and workman's smock assert her identity as a modern and independent woman.[30] According to her biographer, Denise Hooker:

> She unashamedly delighted in the rather romanticized image of herself as a Bohemian artist. She was consciously adopting the time-honoured pose for a self-portrait of the artist, jauntily confronting the male tradition head-on with no concessions to her femininity and no attempt to charm. The picture ... is powerfully self-assertive. It is a declaration of faith; a wager with herself and the world.
>
> (Hooker 1986: 37)

Like the later self-portraits of Vanessa Bell from c. 1915 (Figure 3.7, page 87) and Romaine Brooks from 1923 (Figure 2.1, page 32), the artist's body is situated in a shallow picture plane disconcertingly pressed up against the viewer. Similarly, in all three portraits the figure of the artist dominates a flatly painted background space. Clearly Hamnett was satisfied with this image of herself because she had the painting published in *Colour* magazine two years later in 1915.[31]

During the 1910s and 1920s, Hamnett received much favourable press coverage for her portraits which critics considered interestingly modernist in their surface arrangement and psychologically perceptive. For instance, *Colour* hailed her as "one of the few women artists in London of the contemporary movement" while the *Cambridge Magazine* noted that she had been influenced by Cézanne.[32] Numerous writers also favourably commented on Hamnett's probing analysis of personality and social types, emphasizing how much she shaped her material. An article by Mrs. Gordon-Stables entitled "Nina Hamnett's psychological portraiture" opened with Hamnett's own comment that "My ambition is to paint psychological portraits that shall represent accurately the spirit of the age" (Gordon-Stables 1924: 112). According to Gordon-Stables, Hamnett represented people not as they superficially appeared but rather as she knew them to be. Hamnett's vision was described as frank, unflinching, and uncompromising, all of which contrast with the rather ingratiating expressions of admiration which characterize her autobiographies. In this sense, Hamnett's painting of portraits (at least from the 1910s and 1920s) is treated much more seriously by reviewers. Much as in the case of Romaine Brooks, Hamnett's work in an old-fashioned genre like portraiture is praised on the grounds that she asserts her independence and genius by choosing who she will paint and how they will be represented. For instance, Walter Sickert noted:

Her portraits are not those of an employé. She seems to have no disposition to enter into competition with the *valetaille* of the already somewhat over-stuffed Society super-goose. Like Hogarth she picks her sitters, rather than suffers them gladly to pick her, so that in the end her gallery of portraits is likely to form an interesting sequence.

(Eldar Gallery 1918: [3])

Interestingly, Gordon-Stables observed that in contrast to writers who create impressions by adding as many details as they can, painters omit them wherever possible provided such omissions do not sacrifice their image's veracity. It is perhaps in this respect that Djuna Barnes's detailed textual character sketches and descriptions of places differ from Hamnett's rather spare and simplified modernist visual forms. And yet, at times, their visual self-representations were strikingly similar. This is perhaps best demonstrated by comparing Barnes's self-portrait of 1919 (Figure 5.2) published with Bruno's interview of her in *Pearson's Magazine* and a self-portrait sketch by Hamnett (Figure 5.4) executed in 1918 and published in the *Coterie* in 1920. Hamnett had published several images in the *Coterie*, perhaps because she was on the editorial committee of this small avant-garde magazine which appeared after the war.[33] It should be pointed out that the published context of the Barnes and Hamnett self-portraits differed in that Hamnett's image was not played off against textual representations of her, nor against a reputation for beauty. While Hamnett's style is sketchy when compared with the solidly massed black-and-white technique of Barnes, both artists emphasize impersonal, masklike features which make their faces seem heavily expressionless. Significantly, this masklike anonymity also characterized many of Vanessa Bell's portraits of women from the same years which makes it tempting to speculate whether such stylized modernist conventions appealed to women artists of this period because they allowed them to interpose a certain psychological distance between themselves and their viewers and to refuse traditional expectations that images of women would function as sites of visual pleasure. Again, such masklike qualities characterize a number of Hamnett's portraits of women from this period, including *The Student – Madame Dolores Courtney* from 1917 (Figure 5.5). Although Hamnett's forms are more solidly rendered, her painting echoes the arrangement of Bell's earlier self-portrait from c. 1915 (Figure 3.7, page 87) where the figure was similarly posed and set against a background of decorative geometric patterning. The differences between the two paintings – Hamnett's painting is more conventionally structured than Bell's in terms of its finer brushwork, careful modelling, and realistic details in the background (which is composed of real cushions and shelves rather than Bell's abstract patterning) – may partly be explained by the fact that one is a self-portrait which may have allowed greater artistic license. However, as we have seen in the case of *Mary Hutchinson* (Figure 3.1, page 62), Bell

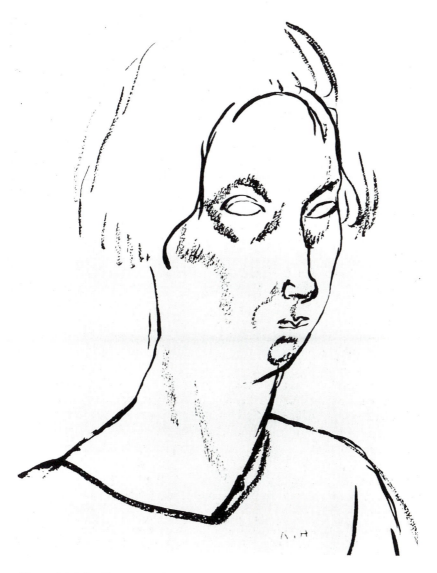

Figure 5.4 Nina Hamnett, *Self-Portrait* (1918). Medium unknown. Location of original unknown. Published in *Coterie* 4 (Easter 1920).

Figure 5.5 Nina Hamnett, *The Student – Madame Dolores Courtney* (1917). Oil on canvas. 32 × 24 inches. Ferens Art Gallery, Hull City Museum and Art Galleries.

depicted other women in much the same style as her self-portrait. Instead, Bell's more extensive use of modernist devices was probably a result of her longer associations with the avant-garde circles of Fry and Grant (as oppposed to Hamnett, who was still quite friendly with artists like Walter Sickert despite her participation in the Omega Workshops after 1913 and her affair with Roger Fry) and, probably more importantly, her greater economic and symbolic capital which meant that she was less pressured to sell work and thus freer to experiment with potentially unpopular avant-garde forms.

Moreover, Hamnett's desperate financial situation often made her quite anxious to sell work which in turn might explain her preference for certain subjects.[34] Despite the simplification of Hamnett's visual language, her portraits clearly seem to have been recognized as "types", according to several reviewers. As in her later autobiographies, the types that Hamnett most often depicted were fellow artists and café dwellers – the same sort of material that Djuna Barnes had found marketable. Although Hamnett saw her choice in independent terms – "I am more interested in human beings than in landscape or still life. That is why I live in Paris and sit in cafés" (Gordon-Stables 1924: 112) – there was also a significant market for such material. Like Barnes, Hamnett sold a number of her drawings to little magazines including the *Coterie*, *Colour*, and the *Transatlantic Review*.[35] She was also commissioned to do the illustrations for Seymour Leslie's first novel, *The Silent Queen* (1927). Hamnett's illustrations were quick pen and ink sketches depicting scenes of the hero's adventures in North America and Europe, including various views of London, the Armistice celebrations, a boxing match at Blackfriar's ring, the pier at Greenwich Village, the terrace at the Rotunde, and various cafés. A café scene depicting four people around a table (Figure 5.6) is a typical example of Hamnett's bohemian types who exhibit something of the decadent extravagance and languor found in Djuna Barnes's descriptions of Greenwich Village life for the uptown New York bourgeoisie (Seymour 1927: facing 114). As subsequent memoirs of the period – together with the photographs (for example, "In my local today") which accompany her 1955 autobiography, *Is She A Lady?* – show, Nina Hamnett came increasingly to *stand in for* the dissolute life of expatriate Paris and bohemian London. As Hamnett's biographer suggests, her increasingly caricatured public persona caused her enormous pain at the end of her life.[36]

MEDIATING MODERNISM

Djuna Barnes and, to a lesser though still significant extent, Nina Hamnett are liminal figures who negotiated with varying degrees of success the borders between the avant-garde and the popular, the textual and the visual. Their experiences reveal much about the conditions of "modernist" women writers and artists without a private income, and the various strategies they adopted in compensation. However, their work also contributes to our

Figure 5.6 Nina Hamnett, *Café Scene* (1927). Pen and ink. Published in Seymour
Leslie's, *The Silent Queen* (London: Jonathan Cape, 1927): facing p. 114.

understanding of the ways in which the avant-garde negotiates its relations with the larger bourgeois public. As many theorists of the avant-garde have pointed out, the problem of the avant-garde (to use Suleiman's phrase) "is how to avoid the impasse of recuperation" (Suleiman 1990: xvi), or, in other words, how to avoid the co-optation and reification of avant-garde work by bourgeois culture. What our case studies in this chapter reveal is that the relationship between the two "cultures" is far more complex than one of purely oppositional critique. We can draw two tentative conclusions: the avant-garde requires such mediating figures as Barnes and Hamnett to publicize its project; and the position of the mediator or liminal figure – the object of exchange between the two cultures – is "feminine."

6

CONCLUSION
Enabling strategies

As we observed at the outset of this study, the question of the relationship between "modernism" and various political formations already has a long and vexed history. Theorists of the avant-garde, like Peter Bürger, would argue that the project of the historical avant-gardes – their critique of the autonomy of art in bourgeois society and their attempt to "organize a new life praxis from a basis in art" (Bürger 1984: 49) – was *innately* political, as indeed the term "avant-garde," with its militaristic overtones, suggests. Many post-structuralist feminist theorists similarly argue, as does Alice Jardine in *Gynesis: Configurations of Woman and Modernity* (1985) or Laura Mulvey in "Visual pleasure and narrative cinema" (1989), for the necessity of a cultural politics involving a "radical reconceptualization of the speaking subject and language" (Jardine 1985: 47) capable of disrupting patriarchal psychic and symbolic processes. However, such approaches frequently run the risk of nostalgia or utopianism: a cultural politics was once, briefly, possible before its dynamics were appropriated by industrial capitalism; writing (or film-making) *in-the-feminine* will one day subvert dominant Western ideologies.

Without denying the importance of feminist utopianism, we want to suggest here that the institutional struggles that most of us are involved in on a daily level (in the family, at the work site, in local politics) are banal and contingent, but also pressing, and that feminist cultural studies can help us to understand our own positioning and theorize the options available to us. We need to learn from *our* cultural past: why did women cultural workers make the choices they did? what worked? what didn't? In a slightly different context, Nancy Fraser has called for a "pragmatic model" as the basis for a feminist politics. Pragmatic theories, she argues, "insist on the social context and social practice of communication, and they study a plurality of historically changing discursive sites and practices" (Fraser 1990: 100). What a pragmatic model offers us is the possibility of locating women's cultural and political agency within particular social and historical contexts. What options were available to wealthy women like Natalie Barney or to virtually impoverished women like Nina Hamnett? Why did or didn't women writers and artists describe themselves as feminists? Did they see their work as engaged in a cultural politics? Can *we* see their work as politically engaged? A pragmatic model also demands that women's cultural work and politics be located in as detailed a reconstruction of their socio-historical moment as possible. Therefore, in considering the question of modernist women's politics, we must consider a series of overlapping sites: the domestic, the cultural, and the political as they are normally understood.

What becomes clear in our case studies is the degree to which many of the women associated with various avant-gardes publicly and privately distanced themselves from any sort of direct political engagement, particularly feminism, in so far as feminism was associated with late nineteenth- and early twentieth-century suffragism. Thus, although Marie Laurencin has been described as a feminist, she is a most eccentric one who is not interested in politics, at least in the traditional sense of the word, since they belong to the world of men from which she entirely disassociates herself; Gertrude Stein points out that "causes" of any type are not her concern. And, as the following quote suggests, although Vanessa Bell clearly found the "new woman" intriguing to look at, she expressed little empathy with the person of Barbara Hyles who is described as a "specimen" and, although independent and cheerful, not very interesting:

> Barbara Hyles one of the young short haired generation is staying here now.... She is quite nice – not very interesting except as a specimen of the new school. Very independent & cheerful. She left home & went to the Slade & has refused to return. She rides a motorcycle & tried to get a job as a chauffeur but having failed to do so is taking to gardening.
> (Vanessa Bell to Virginia Woolf, 10 May [1916])[1]

Bell's judiciously balanced tone suggests she wanted to appear a detached and impartial judge.

Indeed, most of the women in this study tended to adopt individual rather than consistent politically aligned positions when it came to a number of the pressing issues which faced their generation. Of course, Virginia Woolf and Natalie Barney were deeply committed to feminism as many of their writings and activities indicate. It should be stressed, however, that their feminism usually took the form of independently written criticism or independently organized cultural activity rather than direct involvement with activist groups. Furthermore, both developed their own (sometimes highly idiosyncratic) feminist positions. As we discuss in Chapter 3, Woolf's feminism was the most fully articulated (as was her labour politics) and she was active on a number of fronts including lecturing to working women's guilds and women's colleges, laying the foundations for contemporary feminist literary criticism (in *A Room of One's Own*), and articulating the relationships between feminism and pacifism (in *Three Guineas*).[2]

Natalie Barney's feminism, on the other hand, was deeply informed by her lesbianism which gave it both a sentimental and a pragmatic orientation. Her romantic sentimentalism is most obvious in her epigrammatic *pensées* (e.g. "Let no woman renounce her natural crown lest man take her for his equal" (Barney 1963: 62)). Several of the poems from *Poems & Poèmes: autres alliances* (1920) similarly celebrate the primacy of romantic love and love poetry over even such cataclysmic contemporary events as war. "Apology," for example, makes the following argument: "While blue and khaki share the heroes' mud / And women tend in white or weep in grey, / Though all expressiveness seems over-dressed, / Yet some must wear the colours of their hearts / Upon their sleeves, like troubadours, of old; / And sing, and sometimes write their singing down" (Barney 1920: 9).[3] On the more practical side, Barney's feminism expressed itself in her material support of women's publishing ventures (she underwrote, for example, the publication of Djuna Barnes's *Ladies Almanack*), her founding of the *Académie des femmes* (which she describes in *Aventures de l'esprit* (1929)), and her occasional patronage of women writers like Barnes (though, as we discuss in Chapter 5, her support for women was unpredictable and not always sufficient). However, Barney's disregard for traditional politics also had its darker side for, although she participated mildly in pacifist activities at the time of the First World War, by the time of the Second World War she supported Mussolini's Fascism and spent the war in Italy.[4] Disturbingly, the class elitism evident in her salon and the *Académie des femmes* seems also to have formed the basis for her attraction to Fascism, an attraction which was perhaps reinforced by its association, for her, with an elite cadre of poets.

For the most part, the visual artists in this book resembled Stein in terms of adopting detached and highly individualistic points of view. This pattern might be explained, at least in part, by the greater barriers facing women entering visual arts as opposed to literary careers. Certainly women artists were fewer in number and faced the additional hurdles of acquiring a highly specialized training which required access to expensive equipment and large studios. Significantly, none of the artists in this study came from artistic families who could provide their daughters with such resources. In consequence, Laurencin and Brooks worked on a relatively small scale which required less in the way of special facilities; as we have seen, Laurencin even painted in her drawing-room. In contrast, Hamnett often borrowed other people's studios to avoid the expense of renting her own while Bell opted to set up house and studio with another painter.

While the sheer physical and financial struggle of maintaining professional necessities likely took more time for women artists, even more important was the way this struggle influenced their ideological outlook. By the time they had established themselves as painters, they seem to have accepted the view that they were extraordinary women for pursuing difficult careers. This was a point frequently reiterated by art critics of the period who almost invariably commented on their gender when reviewing their work. Despite the fact that they *were* unusual, the inordinate emphasis placed on their exceptional qualities created the impression that women were generally unsuited to artistic careers.[5] So, in addition to being isolated in their professions because they were women, as well as estranged from other women by their demanding careers, they were also seen as innately different or even deviant. Not surprisingly, most of the artists in this study seem to have internalized the resulting insecurities. As already mentioned, Brooks and Bell tended to withdraw from professional networks into their own smaller circles of friends, each going through paralyzing periods of self-doubt. Hamnett adopted an entirely different stance proclaiming early on in her autobiography that "a lady was the last thing that I wanted to be" (Hamnett 1932: 9). Laurencin seems to have been the most pragmatic – securing as many patrons and commissions as she could and working within traditionally accepted "feminine" parameters. Nevertheless, as we note in Chapter 4, the literature on Laurencin provides numerous glimpses both of her frustration and sense of humour on the occasions when she took her femininity to disturbingly parodic levels or suggested she preferred the world of women. Rather than any overt commitment to feminism, the struggle to reorganize daily life in a way that made a serious artistic career possible seems to have been the highest priority in these women's lives.

Of course events such as the First World War inevitably overshadowed the work of writing and painting and frequently forced women to take political stances. Both Marie Laurencin and Nina Hamnett were directly affected by the war – the former having married a German national with whom she fled from Paris to exile in Spain and the latter leaving Paris with her Norwegian fiancé to settle in London. Hamnett's husband was later arrested as an enemy alien and deported to France to fight for the Belgian army. Although neither had been active in pacifist movements, Laurencin and Hamnett were vastly relieved to return to Paris after the war, having left unhappy and short-lived marriages. Virginia Woolf and Vanessa Bell were more deeply committed to the pacifist cause. As we discuss in Chapter 3, Bell's move to Charleston in 1916 was initially to support Duncan Grant's farmwork as a conscientious objector. During the summer of 1915 Clive Bell had written a pamphlet entitled "Peace at once" which, according to Frances Spalding, alienated a number of former friends. After receiving letters from friends detailing their support for the war, Vanessa Bell observed to Woolf, "I see more and more that we are completely isolated from our kind" (quoted in Spalding 1983: 147). In contrast, Romaine Brooks, although initially opposed to the war soon found herself in Paris supporting the French war effort and even donating money for a fund to be named after a fallen artist (Brooks n.d.: 265). During this time she was closely associated with the Italian writer and poet, Gabriele d'Annunzio whom she painted in 1912 and 1916. The later portrait depicts his military role as *Il Commandante*, the heroic aerial combat fighter.

Similarly, she painted another allegorically patriotic scene of a red cross nurse who symbolized the heroic struggle and sacrifice of France. Probably in recognition of such contributions to the war effort, Brooks was awarded the Cross of the Legion of Honour in 1920. During her association with d'Annunzio, Brooks, like Barney, became progressively more interested in notions of the Nietzschean hero and occupied an increasingly isolated, conservative, and aristocratic socio-political position.

It would be a mistake, however, to conclude from this that most women writers and artists of this period were either apolitical or politically naive. The women of our case studies were active primarily in alternative or avant-garde cultural production in the metropolitan centres associated with "modernism." A fuller understanding of women's cultural politics during this period will require supplementary studies which focus on regions, genres, and audiences which are *not* privileged in "modernist" discourses; such studies will focus on women like Francis Marion Beynon and Georgina Sime in Canada (both of whom wrote accessible "realist" feminist novels), or Kathleen Innes in England (whose texts, devoted to pacifism and written for adults and children, were published by The Hogarth Press).[6] Furthermore, as Raymond Williams indicates, the modernist centres of London, Paris, and New York represent "the imperial and capitalist metropolis as a specific historical form, at different stages" (Williams 1989: 47); however, cultural critics have only recently taken up the question of modernism's relation to imperialism,[7] and supplementary work examining the specificity of women's cultural (im)positioning in various "outposts of empire" is needed.

Given all of the complexities of day-to-day life which created a multi-plicity of positions for the women of our case studies, how can we begin to re-conceptualize the field of modernism? One way of usefully approaching the question is to examine previous attempts to map the field. When looking at such maps it is useful to ask: what kinds of spaces were foregrounded by various modernist practitioners, historians, and critics? which spaces were enabling for women artists and writers? which were right off the map? and what do the *differences* between (and within) various maps reveal about cultural production during this period? Here we will draw on three quite different maps, two produced during the period under discussion, and one produced more recently by a feminist critic: Natalie Barney's map of 'Le Salon de l'Amazone' (Figure 6.1), the unfolding frontisleaf to her memoir, *Aventures de l'esprit* (1929); the cover design for Alfred H. Barr's Museum of Modern Art exhibition catalogue, *Cubism and Abstract Art* (1936) (Figure 6.2); and the street map of expatriate Paris which precedes Shari Benstock's *Women of the Left Bank* (1986) (Figure 6.3). Each of these maps makes substantially different assumptions about what should be represented and the relationship between represented items. Barney's hand-drawn map of her salon is the most "naive" of these representations; it collapses attendance during the six decades of her salon into one crude rendition of the interior

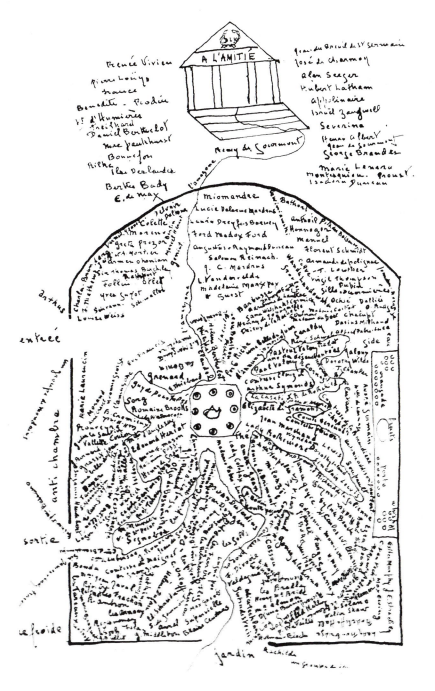

Figure 6.1 "Le Salon de l'Amazone." Frontisleaf to Natalie Clifford Barney, *Aventures de l'esprit* (Paris: Éditions Émile–Paul Frères, 1929).

of her drawing room at 20 rue Jacob. Her Temple à l'Amitié (Temple of Friendship) – an early nineteenth-century Doric temple in one corner of her garden (Wickes 1976: 104) – figures prominently at the top of the map together with the names of such foundational friends as Renée Vivien (who died just before Barney bought the house), Pierre Loüys, and, especially, Remy de Gourmont whose name is the pathway to the door of the Temple. The tea table occupies the centre of the map, while to one side Barney depicts a table bearing orangeade, fruits, port, and whisky. When mapping her life, together with a period of French literary and cultural history, Barney gave clear visual precedence to friendship – evidenced by the presiding Temple and suggested by her personal, handwritten commitment to naming individuals – and to domestic space. Barney's "modernism" is contained within the space of her drawing room, itself contained within the walled gardens of her home. The names of "the great" are buried within the names of the relatively unknown; the little hierarchy which is evident is established by claims of friendship rather than fame or cultural influence.

Alfred H. Barr's map of the development of abstract art (Figure 6.2), on the other hand, illustrates, as Griselda Pollock points out, "the way modern art has been mapped by modernist art history:"

> Artistic practices from the late nineteenth century are placed on a chronological flow chart where movement follows movement connected by one-way arrows which indicate influence and reaction. Over each movement a named artist presides. All those canonized as the initiators of modern art are men.
>
> (Pollock 1988: 50)

Pollock goes on to point out that the visual privileging of men as "initiators" indicates the degree to which "what modernist art history celebrates is a selective tradition which normalizes, as the *only* modernism, a particular and gendered set of practices" (50). Unlike Barney's non-hierarchical map of her salon, Barr's chart clearly sketches a visual narrative of art historical progress culminating in abstract art. While Barney collapses six decades into one visual representation, Barr traces the development of abstract art along a clear chronological grid; and while Barney's map consists almost entirely of proper names, Barr's chart names only nine men (and then only by their last names – an indication of their status), six of them with the dates of their deaths. The bulk of the chart is occupied with naming and dating various art movements although, significantly, three of the four boxed-in influences upon the development of modernist art – Japanese Prints, Near-Eastern Art, and Negro Sculpture – are charted not according to their historical development (as is the fourth, Machine Esthetic), but according to the historical moment at which they become visible or significant to the European imagination. Women are completely off the map of abstract art, while non-European "others" are significant only when their art can be absorbed by that of European men.

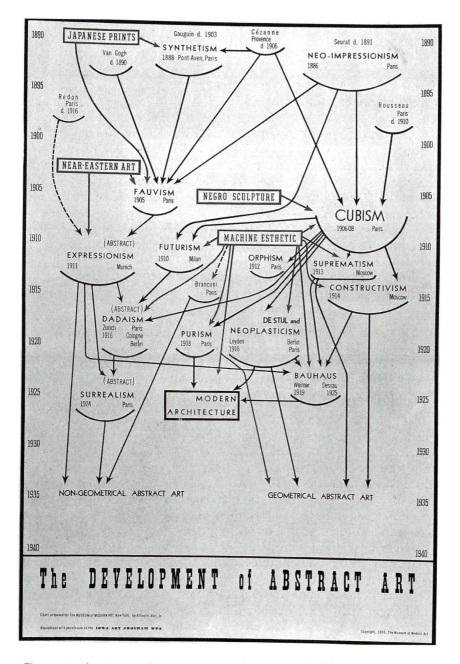

Figure 6.2 Chart prepared by Alfred H. Barr, Jr. for the jacket cover of the exhibition catalogue *Cubism and Abstract Art* by Alfred H. Barr, Jr. (New York: The Museum of Modern Art, 1936). Photograph courtesy of The Museum of Modern Art, New York.

Shari Benstock's map of expatriate Paris (Figure 6.3) is, of the three "maps" under discussion, the most familiar in terms of its organization. It is an ordinary street map with a legend of significant locations in the upper right-hand corner. The map orients the viewer by naming significant landmarks – Jardins des Tuileries, Palais du Louvre, Palais du Luxembourg, etc. – and by organizing itself along the axis of the River Seine. However, it upsets our expectations by *naming* primarily those streets which were associated with women's modernism, either as women's places of residence or places of business. The few men named in the legend (for example, Robert McAlmon or Jack Kahane) are there in relation to the women whose work they published. In this way, Benstock's diagram *maps over* traditional literary histories of modernism.

Each of these maps was obviously designed to serve a completely different function; nonetheless, it is possible to draw some tentative conclusions. The Barr map, for example, clarifies the degree to which (men's) "modernism" has traditionally been represented as an international and cosmopolitan field of competing movements, while both the Barney and the Benstock maps allegorize the ways in which women's "modernism" has been either invisible (hidden away in drawing-rooms and nurseries) or defined as local and vernacular. The fact that so many women modernists are clearly identified in the public imagination with their addresses – Barney's 20 rue Jacob, Bell's Charleston, Woolf's Asheham House, Stein's rue de Fleurus, Barnes's Patchin Place – is evidence of this tendency. Recent feminist reconstructions of women's "modernism" which reinforce the importance of women's communities (see Benstock 1986; Broe 1989; Hanscombe and Smyers 1987) similarly emphasize the local while putting it into a usually, and typically "modernist," metropolitan context. However, while "modernism" is traditionally defined as "an art of cities" (Bradbury 1976: 96) which offered access to commercial networks such as galleries, dealers, publishers, and avant-garde journals and magazines, as well as an opportunity to experiment with lifestyle, the modern city or metropolis also had different attractions for men and women of the period and it figures differently in their representations of "modernism."

One way in which men's and women's metropolitan experience *differed* relates to the gendered organization of social spaces and looking. As Janet Wolff reminds us, the canonized literature of modernity is largely based upon male experience, and many of the recognized tropes of literary and visual "modernism" have their roots in the nineteenth century. What is celebrated as "modern," according to most recognized modernist writers, artists, and literary critics, is the public gaze of the flâneur who freely moves about the city as a dislocated stranger sliding between various classes watching life on the streets and in the arcades (Wolff 1985: 40). Of course, as she points out, there is no female equivalent or "flâneuse" because the only women who inhabited the streets on a regular basis in the nineteenth

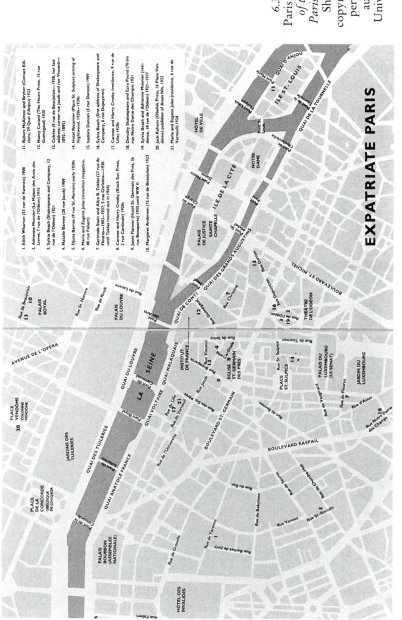

Figure 6.3 "Expatriate Paris." From *Women of the Left Bank: Paris, 1900–1940* by Shari Benstock, copyright © 1986. By permission of the author and the University of Texas Press.

EXPATRIATE PARIS

1. Edith Wharton (53 rue de Varenne) 1908

2. Adrienne Monnier (La Maison des Amis des Livres, 7 rue de l'Odéon) 1915

3. Sylvia Beach (Shakespeare and Company, 12 rue de l'Odéon) 1921

4. Natalie Barney (20 rue Jacob) 1909

5. Djuna Barnes (9 rue St.-Romain) early 1930s

6. Maria and Eugene Jolas (transition magazine, 40 rue Fabert)

7. Gertrude Stein and Alice B. Toklas (27 rue de Fleurus—1903–1937; 5 rue Christine—1938 until Toklas moved out in 1964)

8. Carese and Harry Crosby (Black Sun Press, 2 rue Cardinale) 1920s

9. Janet Flanner (Hotel St. Germain des Prés, 36 rue Bonaparte) 1925 until WW II

10. Margaret Anderson (15 rue de Beaujolais) 1923

11. Robert McAlmon and Bryher (Contact Editions, 29 Quai d'Anjou) 1923

12. Nancy Cunard (The Hours Press, 15 rue Guénégaud) 1930

13. Colette (9 rue de Beaujolais—1938, her last address; corner rue Jacob and rue Visconti—1892–1895)

14. Hotel Récamier (Place St. Sulpice) setting of *Nightwood*, 1920s–1930s

15. Isadora Duncan (5 rue Danton) 1909

16. Sylvia Beach (first address of Shakespeare and Company, 8 rue Dupuytren)

17. Carese and Harry Crosby (residence, 4 rue de Lille) 1920s

18. Dorothy Shakespeare and Ezra Pound (70 bis rue Notre Dame des Champs) 1921

19. Sylvia Beach and Adrienne Monnier (residence, 18 rue de l'Odéon) 1921–1937

20. Jack Kahane (Obelisk Press, 16 Place Vendôme) publisher of Anaïs Nin, 1932

21. Maria and Eugene Jolas (residence, 6 rue de Verneuil) 1924

century were prostitutes, destitutes, or women from the working classes – hardly those with the time and resources to write or paint.[8] Griselda Pollock takes up Wolff's argument when she considers how looking is gendered and valorized in the work of French mid to late nineteenth-century male and female painters. As she points out, the legacy of a well-entrenched separate spheres ideology meant that male and female artists (who, for the most part, were middle class) had different sorts of social mobility and consequently different points of view, hence subject-matter and viewpoints tend to differ in paintings by men and women of the period. For instance, Pollock rightly questions whether the domestic interiors of Mary Cassat or Berthe Morissot are any less "modern" than the public spaces of Edouard Manet (Pollock 1988: 66). But even more importantly, Pollock stresses it is not so much *what* is represented that registers gender differences but rather the *ways* in which space and the gaze are organized within particular pictures. Hence Cassat can paint the bodies of working women washing in ways that differ from her male counterparts who typically sexualized such subject-matter by seeing it through public stereotypes of the fallen woman. While Pollock notes that Cassat's images still inscribe her privileged middle-class point of view, they nevertheless provide evidence of the feminine spaces of modernity (88–89).

While early twentieth-century women writers and painters retained an interest in representing private and domestic spaces, they were also interested in radically redefining those spaces; the crowds of the metropolis – source of much male modernist angst[9] – provided for many women an anonymity and indifference that enabled the establishment of alternative domestic relations and communities. Certainly most of the women in this study felt that an independent urban lifestyle enabled them to take up creative enterprises that were impossible at home. Recalling the move, after the death of their father – whose theatrical display of grief and emotional need haunted their adolescence – from the former family home at Hyde Park Gate to 43 Gordon Square, Virginia Woolf recounted: "We were full of experiments and reforms. We were going to do without table napkins ... we were going to paint; to write; to have coffee after dinner instead of tea at nine o'clock. Everything was going to be new; everything was going to be different. Everything was on trial" (Woolf 1976: 162, 163). Sharing her sister's enthusiasm, Vanessa Bell remembered that "on the whole all that seemed to matter was that at last we were free, had rooms of our own and space in which to be alone or to work or to see our friends. Such things may come naturally to many of the present generation but to me at least in 1904 it was as if one had stepped suddenly into daylight from darkness" (quoted in Spalding 1983: 49).

Woolf's and Bell's relocation to a less respectable area of London after their father's death signified, for them, escape from a family oppression they explicitly identified as patriarchal. Their joy in altering small domestic rituals (no napkins, coffee instead of tea) clearly indicates the degree to which they identified the domestic as a political arena. Moreover, as Woolf makes clear in another of her contributions to the Bloomsbury Group's Memoir Club, the patriarchal home is frequently a place of sexual abuse.[10] The home was the site of abuse for at least three other women of our case studies: Djuna Barnes, whose journalistic career in New York City enabled her to escape her father's sexual abuse (see De Salvo 1991; Broe 1989); Nina Hamnett, whose ꞁtobiography notes with characteristic understatement her father's physical ꞁe and her own hysterical reactions;[11] and Romaine Brooks, whose unpublished autobiography details her emotional abuse by a mother whom she described as "a crazy ring-master directing her own small and private circus" (Brooks n.d.: 38). Although she was haunted by terrifying nightmares about her brother and mother, Romaine Brooks recorded feeling freed by their deaths; her inheritance underwrote her subsequent moves, first to London and then to Paris, cities she identified with freedom ("In those days Bohemia was the only refuge for the independent" (Brooks n.d.: 278)) and gender experimentation. Significantly, only Marie Laurencin – who, aside from Barnes, had the least orthodox family life – preferred to continue living at home. Laurencin's devotion to her mother caused her such extreme grief when the latter died in 1912 that she threw herself into an unhappy marriage with the German painter, Otto von Watjen, because, according to Gertrude Stein, Laurencin claimed that he was "the only one who can give me a feeling of my mother" (Stein 1960: 61).[12]

By moving to (or within) various metropolitan centres, the women of our case studies acquired not only the contacts and networks necessary for the pursuit of artistic work, but also the freedom to reorganize their domestic lives in ways that enabled them to find time to work and room to live experimentally. Their new domestic relations were frequently featured in their work. It is significant, for example, that all of the visual artists in this study were primarily interested in portraiture (often of personal friends) as well as domestic still life and genre subjects. In addition to painting selected friends and acquaintances, Romaine Brooks experimented with self-portraiture photography and the interior design of her own living spaces. As we have already discussed in our fourth chapter, Marie Laurencin was also fascinated by the "details of life," including costumes, hats, and fashions (Buffet 1923: 391). She too stressed the importance of her domestic environment to her work, preferring to paint at home in a drawing room (which greatly surprised one reviewer who commented on its careful "Anglo-Saxon" style of decoration: "unencumbered, gay chintzes and bowls of flowers on every table" (Todd 1928: 94)). Like Brooks, Laurencin professed a special interest in self-portraiture. The work of Vanessa Bell was similarly grounded in her everyday experiences; according to her biographer, Frances Spalding, Post-Impressionism (unlike abstract art) offered Bell "not only a more informal treatment but also a broader range of subjects," including the "casual and the everyday" (Spalding 1983: 125–26). And although Nina Hamnett's lifestyle was more public, most of her work consisted of painting and sketching her friends and café life. Gertrude Stein's experiment in living with Alice B. Toklas is partially documented in *The Autobiography of Alice B. Toklas* (1933), while the rhythm of their domestic lives is captured in the prose poems of *Tender Buttons* (1914). Although Stein moved to Paris in 1904 to join her much loved brother Leo (with whom she initially set up house at 27 rue de Fleurus) and not to escape an abusive home, she later understood her commitment to writing and to Alice as requiring a similar break from the patriarchal family. It was Leo who represented the traditional family and its claim to male prerogative. As she explains in *Everybody's Autobiography* (1937), "He had always been my brother two years older and a brother. I had always been following" (76). Significantly, as the following passage illustrates, identity for Stein was imaginatively bound up with domestic relations, themselves figured as location, place:

> It is a funny thing about addresses where you live. When you live there you know it so well that it is like identity a thing that is so much a thing that it could not ever be any other thing and then you live somewhere else and years later, the address that was so much an address that it was a name like your name and you said it as if it was not an address but something that was living and then years after you do not know what the address was and when you say it it is not a name any more but something you cannot remember. That is what makes your identity not a thing that exists but something you do or do not remember.
>
> (Stein 1937: 71)

The metropolis offered women the chance to construct alternative identities based on alternative domestic relations. However, it also offered an opportunity to establish alternative communities and social lives based on commonality of interest rather than family relations. In his essay "Metropolitan perceptions and the emergence of modernism," Raymond Williams stresses that the values of the modernist avant-garde were temporally specific reactions to early twentieth-century urban conditions. He stresses that the largely immigrant group of avant-garde artists tended to develop communities which focused on occupational media as "the only commonality available to them: a community of the medium; of their own practices" (Williams 1989: 45). Significantly, within such immigrant sectors of metropolitan centres, language starts to be perceived differently.

> It was no longer, in the old sense, customary and naturalized, but in many ways arbitrary and conventional ... more evident as a medium – a medium that could be shaped and reshaped – than as a social custom. Even with a native language, the new relationships of the metropolis, and the inescapable new uses in newspapers and advertising attuned to it, forced certain new productive kinds of strangeness and distance: a

new consciousness of conventions and thus of changeable, because now open, convention.

(45–46)

Certainly Stein and Barney were both highly aware of "productive kinds of strangeness and distance" in language, though in quite different ways. Living in Paris, immersed in the sound of French, allowed Stein to foreground the visual materiality of English and to regard it as an almost purely *literary* language rather than a language of everyday life.[13] Barney, on the other hand, regarded French as a more appropriately literary language, as she explained in her preface to *Quelques portraits-sonnets de femmes* (1900).[14] The French language would also have been associated for her – as Paris was for Stein – with the Napoleonic Code which did not recognize homosexuality as a crime and which enabled the formation of communities of lesbian women.

Williams concludes his essay "Metropolitan perceptions and the emergence of modernism" by urging critics to restore a sense of strangeness and distance to their analyses of early twentieth-century metropolitan culture by recognizing its specificity and limitations:

This means, above all, seeing the imperial and capitalist metropolis as a specific historical form, at different stages: Paris, London, Berlin, New York. It involves looking, from time to time, from outside the metropolis: from the deprived hinterlands, where different forces are moving and from the poor world which has always been peripheral to metropolitan systems. This need involve no reduction of the importance of the major artistic and literary works which were shaped within metropolitan perceptions. But one level certainly has to be challenged: the metropolitan interpretation of its own processes as universal.

(47)

Considering the gendered implications of modernist cultural production constitutes one such challenge. As our fifth chapter argues, the dividing lines between the metropolitan mass media and fine arts were often adversely gendered: women's contributions to the media were often dismissively feminized while the "purer" fine arts were validated as masculine preserves. Similarly, as our second chapter demonstrates, women's equal participation in the visual and literary arts was seriously hindered by numerous metropolitan avant-garde discourses which selectively hailed some radical visions as "modern" while completely ignoring others. Thus Picasso's formal innovations belong to the modernist canon while Romaine Brooks's sexual radicalism is excluded. Given such glaring inconsistencies and inequalities, Williams's strategy of challenging the metropolitan interpretation of its own processes is especially important for us as feminist critics since the women of our case studies often occupied an ambivalent place (not quite inside or outside of) the metropolitan avant-garde.

What does it mean to write about early twentieth-century women artists and writers of London, Paris, and New York from the position of very late twentieth-century feminist academics in one of those outposts of empire, Edmonton, Canada? At the turn of the century, Edmonton had fewer than 8,000 residents; Fort Edmonton, a fur-trading post, still stood on the grounds of our provincial legislature. When we look across the river from the university to the now expansive downtown skyline, history seems to extend no farther back than thirty years; yet when we travel through the badlands of southern Alberta, scattered with the fossils of dinosaurs, inscribed with the writing of first nations people, the modernist period and its culture seems a barely discernible scratch on the surface of history. On the one hand, the contiguity of our lives with those of the women we studied seemed very close this year, when one of our graduate students brought to class an Omega-style rug that her great-grandmother had hooked and displayed in a small farming town in southern Alberta. On the other hand, the really pressing social issues *here*, *now* are aboriginal land rights, the participation of women in the current constitutional debates, the protection of women and children from sexual and physical abuse. In our introduction we indicate that we want to appropriate the term "modernism" and put it to feminist use. How can feminist cultural studies, focusing on the cultural work of metropolitan women sixty to ninety years ago, help us here and now? We believe it can help us to imagine and, just as importantly, *recognize* a range of possible actions and responses.

In the course of our research we found ourselves very moved by the women we studied: by Hamnett's generosity of spirit, Laurencin's calm pragmatism, Woolf's visionary sweep. We were also dismayed by Barney's retreat into fascism, Barnes's bitter isolation for so many decades. Throughout this book we have insisted on the messiness of our case studies and the ways in which they disrupt received discourses of "modernism;" however, we also found that our case studies – even though they focus on a relatively homogenous group of relatively privileged women – resist easy feminist *evaluation*. Marie Laurencin, for example, produced representations of women that seem to our eyes hyperbolically "feminine" and certainly not progressive; and yet, when we examine the context of their production and the odds of her success, we see those same representations *differently*. Gertrude Stein identified with masculine models of artistic genius, publicly advocated conservative economic policies, and yet left an important and enabling body of lesbian love poetry. Virginia Woolf insisted on professional payment at the same time that she decried professional deformation. Clearly the stubborn (im)positioning of these modernist women opened up spaces for future women working in other cultural fields.

NOTES

1 WHOSE MODERNISM?

1 See also Pierre Bourdieu, "The production of belief:" "In short, what 'makes reputations' is not ... this or that 'influential' person, this or that institution, review, magazine, academy, coterie, dealer or publisher; ... it is the field of production, understood as a system of objective relations between these agents or institutions and as the site of the struggles for the monopoly of the power to consecrate, in which the value of works of art and belief in that value are continuously generated" (135).

2 For further analyses of various periodizations and characterizations of visual avant-gardes, see Diana Crane, *The Transformation of the Avant-Garde: The New York Art World, 1940–1985* (Chicago: University of Chicago Press, 1987): 11–17, 43–45, and the essays by Serge Guilbaut and Henri Lefebvre in *Modernism and Modernity*, ed. B. Buchloh, S. Guilbaut, and D. Solkin (Halifax: Nova Scotia College of Art and Design, 1983): ix–xv, 1–12.

3 Fry advances such arguments in "An essay on aesthetics," *Vision and Design* (Fry 1981: 12–27). This essay was first published in *New Quarterly*, April 1909. For an example of his attitudes towards the Victorian period, see "The ottoman and the whatnot," also reprinted in *Vision and Design*: 28–32.

4 See Bell 1987: 3–37. The first of many editions of *Art* was published in 1914.

5 For further discussion on these issues, see Harrison 1985: 217–32.

6 Originally published in 1939. It is interesting to note the parallels between Fry's and Bell's denigration of Victorian art, with its sentimental narratives and detailed rendering of contemporary life, and Greenberg's hostility to mass-produced kitsch. Bloomsbury's perhaps most famous disparagement of Victorian art can be found in Clive Bell's *Art*, where he dismisses Frith's *Paddington Station* as an amusing and interesting journalistic document which is certainly *not* "Art" (Bell 1987: 17–19).

7 See also Bradbury and McFarlane 1976.

8 See also Quinones 1985, who argues that "Modernism can be located historically in regard to those countries or individuals that enjoyed an advanced notion of time" (5).

9 Clement Greenberg makes a similar argument in "Modernist painting" (9).

10 See also Menand 1987.

11 See also Fredric Jameson's influential afterword – "Reflections in conclusion" – to Ernst Bloch, Georg Lukács, Bertolt Brecht, Walter Benjamin, and Theodor Adorno, *Aesthetics and Politics* (1977), where he describes "the fate of modernism in society itself": "For what was once an appositional and anti-social

phenomenon in the early years of the century, has today become the dominant style of commodity production and an indispensible component in the machinery of the latter's ever more rapid and demanding reproduction of itself" (209).

12 See, for example, Chapter 3 ("English as a masculine profession") of Brian Doyle's *English and Englishness* (1989).

13 See also Lunn 1982: 75–90, for background on the debate on realism and modernism.

14 We would note that although the English translator's choice of the term "man" makes Lukács' argument seem especially insensitive to questions of gender, Lukács himself was not particularly interested in women's involvement in cultural production during this period.

15 Lukács' work currently seems to be enjoying a small renascence. See, for example, Schenck 1989.

16 See also DeKoven 1991: 19–20 for a discussion of Anderson's essay.

17 For a more extended discussion of this essay, see Bridget Elliott and Jo-Ann Wallace, "Modernist anomalies: Bloomsbury and gender," *Feminist Art News* 3, no. 4 (1990): 21–24.

18 For other feminist uses of the strategy of "appropriation" see Laura Mulvey's "Visual pleasure and narrative cinema," (first pub. 1975) in *Visual and Other Pleasures* (Bloomington: Indiana University Press, 1989), which appropriates psychoanalysis as a political weapon, and Toril Moi's recent appropriation of Bourdieu (Moi 1991).

19 Our decision to focus on English-language literary texts means that the admittedly crucial presence of women in the avant-garde communities of Berlin is simply outside the scope of this study.

20 See, for example, Paul Mann, *The Theory-Death of the Avant-Garde* (1991).

21 The same sort of social withdrawal (at least from male modernist circles) was also practised by the English artists Gwen John and Gluck. However, as Jane Beckett and Deborah Cherry usefully caution, one should not exaggerate their reclusiveness thereby constructing these women as eccentric geniuses. All maintained meaningful personal friendships. Their withdrawals from the social networks of the art world were probably motivated by the desire for self-preservation rather than social perversity. For a further discussion of these issues in relation to Gwen John, see Cherry and Beckett 1988.

22 See also Bridget Elliott and Jo-Ann Wallace, "More than pin money: economies of representation in women's modernism," in Shirley Neuman and Glennis Stephenson (eds), *(Re)Imagining Women* (Toronto: University of Toronto Press, 1993).

23 The following observation from Raymond Williams's article, "The politics of the avant-garde," obviously applies to the situation of Barney and Brooks: "the son or daughter of a bourgeois family was financially in a position to lay claim to new forms of liberation, and in a significant number of cases could actually use the profits of the economic bourgeoisie to lead political and artisitic crusades against it" (Williams 1989: 56).

24 Significantly, the personae of "the page" and "the amazon" were first suggested to Barney by male artists. At age 11, Barney was painted by Carolus Duran as *The Little Page* (this painting is reproduced as the frontispiece to Barney's first collection of poems, *Quelques portraits-sonnets de femmes* (1900)), and in 1910 Remy de Gourmont celebrated her as "l'Amazone" in a series of letters published in *Le Mercure de France*.

25 A distinction should be drawn between photographs of Brooks that appeared in the press and her own experimental self-portrait photography done between the

years 1910 and 1920. A useful discussion and reproductions of her self-portrait photography are provided by Chavanne and Gaudichon 1987.

26 A segment of this photograph accompanied at least one French review of the Durand-Ruel exhibition, "L'Exposition des oeuvres de Mme Romaine Brooks" by Henri Frantz. The source of this review which appears amongst the newspaper cuttings in the Romaine Brooks Collection in the Archives of American Art, Smithsonian Institution, is not identified.

27 This press clipping from the Archives of American Art, Smithsonian Institution is also not clearly identified. However, the date of 1925 is accurate since that was when she held an exhibition at the Charpentier Gallery.

28 Leslie Stephen had left the substantial sum of £15,000 to his children which, as Vanessa Bell's biographer, Frances Spalding, points out, would, in 1983, amount to about £350,000. Furthermore, Jack Hills (the husband of their deceased half-sister, Stella) shared the income from Stella's marriage settlement with the Stephen children. For further information about their income at this time, see Spalding 1983: 48.

29 For further details about Vanessa Bell's income during the period 1913–18, see Spalding 1983: 160. Spalding notes that in 1917 Bell's total income exceeded £533 which was her expenditure for the year. Her income took the form of interest on her own investments of family capital (made on the advice of Maynard Keynes) and an allowance from Clive Bell.

30 These were The Hogarth Lectures on Literature, The Hogarth Living Poets, The Hogarth Letters, and The Hogarth Sixpenny Pamphlets.

31 Virginia Woolf's anxiety about the male-dominated publishing industry was probably exacerbated by the fact that her first two novels were published by her half-brother Gerald Duckworth. In the fourth volume of his autobiography, Leonard Woolf indicates that self-publishing eased many of Woolf's anxieties, but he seems unaware that these anxieties may have been associated with the sexual abuse Woolf suffered from her two half-brothers (see L. Woolf 1967: 68).

32 Janet Hobhouse provides an interesting account of Leo's and Gertrude's financial resources during this period. Leo recalls that they actually made fairly small sums of money go a long way. In his words, "Life was then cheap in Paris, rents were low, food was not dear, we had no doctor's bills.... We despised luxury except when someone else paid for it, and got what we most wanted. That made a satisfactory living" (quoted in Hobhouse 1975: 46). After Michael Stein moved his family to Paris to join Gertrude and Leo, he became interested in art collecting and sometimes gave them extra amounts for purchasing pictures. With such a windfall of eight thousand francs, Leo and Gertrude bought two Gauguins, two Cézanne figure compositions, two Renoirs, and a Maurice Denis from the dealer, Vollard.

33 See Collins 1989: 57–80 for a discussion of the many titled and monied acquaintances who visited Hamnett's exhibitions.

2 FLEURS DU MAL OR SECOND-HAND ROSES?

1 Regenia Gagnier points out that "the paradox and epigram, which criticized society by turning its own language curtly on its head ... were particularly appropriate techniques for a homosexual Irishman with socialist sympathies in nineteenth-century Britain" (Gagnier 1986: 28). Barney's own "double life" – she was a society lady *and* an unapologetic lesbian, an American who preferred to write in French – may also account for her attraction to the epigram.

2 An important exception to this tendency is Rita Felski's *Beyond Feminist Aesthetics* (1989) which argues that "the possibilty of a normative political aesthetic, the belief that certain forms are inherently more radical than others ... needs to be replaced by a sociologically based analysis of the reception of artworks in relation to specific audiences" (160).

3 On the feminizing of the marginal, see Jardine 1985. The implications of Jardine's study of the "woman effect" or how eminent male writers have introduced and used the term "woman" in discourse (she does not analyze the work of women writers) is discussed by Suleiman (1988). As Battersby (1990: 14) points out, the emphasis on originality is part of a long-standing conception of the artist as creator or God-like authority who imposes meaning and significance on formless matter.

4 For a critique of the ways in which the original/copy binary is applied to lesbian identity see Butler 1990: 31 ("gay is to straight *not* as copy is to original, but, rather, as copy is to copy"). See also Garber 1993: 141–46.

5 These are the words used enthusiastically by Charles Eldrege, Director of the Smithsonian Museum, in Breeskin 1986: 11. He fails to see any problem with having a legendary life.

6 Breeskin notes that portraits by Brooks were much sought after by members of fashionable society which gave her enormous leeway in her selection of subjects. She worked slowly, took on few commissions, and usually refused to sell her paintings.

7 Our reading of Barney's use of decadence differs from that of Benstock who argues that Barney turned to a pre-Raphaelite rather than a decadent model in her efforts to "divest ... the image of the lesbian of its homophobic implications" and "dissociate women's self-conception from the dark misogynous vision inherent in societal notions of homosexuality." Benstock further argues that "it was precisely the morbid fear of women, the association in the male mind of the 'femme fatale' with the 'vampire' figure, that Barney attempted to overturn" (Benstock 1986: 303). However, this reading does not account for such works as Barney's 1900 poem "Mlle L.S.," the last stanza of which reads: "Tu es la vampire des âmes / Toute sublime ou toute infâme. / Qui t'effleure te sent toujours!" (You are the vampire of souls, / Wholly sublime or wholly vile. / Whoever crosses you smells of you always!). Nor can it be argued that this is evidence of a youthful flirtation with decadence which is superseded in Barney's more mature works for, as we discuss in this chapter, even much later texts like *The One Who Is Legion* (1930) pay literary homage to their decadent precursors.

8 One of Barney's closest friends, Remy de Gourmont (who published his letters to her in *Le Mercure de France* and later in book form as *Lettres à l'Amazone* (1914)), said of Huysmans's *À Rebours*, "we should never forget what a huge debt we owe to this memorable breviary" (quoted by Baldick in Huysmans 1959: 11).

9 *The One Who Is Legion* also contains an epigraph from Milton's *Paradise Lost* which makes a similar argument:

> For Spirits, when they please,
> Can either sex assume, or both; so soft
> And uncompounded in their essence pure,
> Not tied nor manacled with joint or limb,
> Nor founded on the brittle strength of bones,
> Like cumberous flesh; but, in what shape they choose,
> Dilated or condensed, bright or obscure,

Can exercise their airy purposes,
And works of love or enmity fulfil.

10 A 1927 letter from Dolly Wilde to Natalie Barney, reproduced in part in Barney's
tribute to Wilde (Barney 1951: 118), suggests that Brooks had by that time
already completed a substantial portion of her memoirs. Wilde writes:

> Just as the French have appreciated Romaine as a painter, the English
> should appreciate her as a writer.... It is rare to find such purity of style,
> such sincerity and richness of thought combined in this *ms.* you showed
> me.
>
> Anyone who knows about writing would realize how well she blended
> straight narrative and abstract thought. The transition is never abrupt, one
> is never jerked into another key. It is not easy to balance simplicity and
> profundity. There is no wandering in byways, there is no disharmony, and
> the one follows the other with logical sequence.
>
> I only thought of this long after the reading. Only later an analysis made
> me aware of how beautifully she had maintained the balance through-
> out.... How easily the runaway horses of one's thoughts get beyond
> control, and how admirably she has handled the restive steeds in double
> harness.

Other readers have been less appreciative of the peculiarities of Brooks's style;
her biographer, for example, has noted that the inherently visual organization of
the autobiography gives it a "disjointed quality" and that it also suffers from "a
lack of perspective" (Secrest 1974: 313). Critics have also noticed similarities in
style between Barney's novel and Brooks's memoir. Wickes, for example, says of
The One Who Is Legion that "its dreamlike atmosphere seems to be haunted by
the same spirit that possessed Romaine in 1930, when she produced a series of
harrowing line drawings.... *The One Who Is Legion* sounds more like a work
of Romaine's imagination than of Natalie's and suggests that for a time, at least,
she made Natalie share her vision" (150). It is perhaps significant that many of
the same images and themes are evident in Barney's novel and Brooks's drawings
of the period. Although there is insufficient evidence to make the case
conclusively, it seems possible that Barney and Brooks planned a collaborative
work. An earlier collaborative effort resulted in a poem by Barney, "The weeping
Venus" (Barney 1920: 12), modelled upon an earlier painting of the same name
which Brooks completed between 1916 and 1917 (Chavanne and Gaudichon
1987: 143–45). A short excerpt from Brooks's memoir was published as "No
pleasant memories" in the summer 1938 issue of *Life and Letters To-day*; the
author is listed simply as "Romaine."

11 Sutherland and Nochlin (1976: 268) discuss the accuracy of Brooks's autobiography. While certain aspects of Brooks's life may have been difficult, her
emphatic depiction of herself as an outsider perpetuates the romantic mythology
of the creative artistic genius, particularly in decadent and early twentieth-
century avant-garde circles. This is something that is overlooked by such critics
as Secrest 1974, Langer 1981, and Gubar 1981.

12 From the National Collection of Fine Arts Research Materials on Romaine
Brooks, Archives of American Art, Smithsonian Institution.

13 For instance, although Joshua Reynolds was interested in elevating the status of
his portraits in late eighteenth-century England by introducing classical motifs
into them, he still ranked the genre below history painting. This is discussed in
his fourth discourse where he juxtaposes invention and copying. As far as the

avant-garde is concerned, the status of portraiture seriously declined after the emergence of commercial portrait photography in the mid-nineteenth century. For further discussion of this issue, see Saisselin 1963.

14 As indicated above, Barney was called "l'Amazone" by Remy de Gourmont who first published his "Lettres a l'Amazone" in the *Mercure de France* in 1913, and then published them in book form in 1914. Gourmont's elitist politics are evidenced in his "Sur la hierarchie intellectuelle," *La Plume* 124 (15–30 June 1894): 251–54, and had a profound influence on such American writers as Natalie Barney and Ezra Pound. See also Silverman 1989: 71.

15 Battersby further notes that "The originality of the art-work was not seen as a reflection of the external world, but of the mind and personality that brought that work into existence. Consequently the artist's own character also became significant" (Battersby 1990: 13).

16 "in fact, Romaine Brooks belongs to no time, to no country, to no circle, to no school, to no tradition; nor is she in revolt against these institutions; but rather, like Walt Whitman, neither for nor against them, she doesn't know what they are. She is the embodiment, the 'flowering heights' of civilization in decline, whose face she has managed to capture" (our translation).

17 In a 1926 letter to Gertrude Stein, Barney writes: "The other night 'au cameleon' I realized how little the french 'femme de lettres' know of the english and Americans and vice versa ... I wish I might bring about a better 'entente' and hope therefore to organize here this winter, and this spring, readings and presentations that will enable our mind-allies to appreciate each other" (errors in original). This letter traces the origins of the *Académie de femmes* which Barney instituted in 1927. (Letter dated 16 December 1926, in the Beinecke Rare Book and Manuscript Library, Yale University.)

18 This was observed by Norman Bryson in his lecture on the work of Gericault delivered as part of the Henry Kreisel Lecture Series in "Literature and the Visual Arts" held at the University of Alberta, January 1990.

19 See Garber 1993 for discussion of the ways in which female-to-male cross-dressers remain underrepresented in popular culture and psychological studies today.

20 Weeks goes on to argue that,

> It is striking that it is amongst the new professional women of the 1920s that the articulation of any sort of recognisable lesbian identity became possible for the first time, and it was indeed in the 1920s that lesbianism became in any way an issue of public concern, following a series of sensational scandals.
>
> (Weeks 1981: 116)

21 Rolley draws this quote from a contemporary newspaper review of Radclyffe Hall's evening attire which appeared in the *Newcastle Daily Journal*, 22 August 1928 (Rolley 1990: 57).

22 Significantly, Dollimore's examples suggest (perhaps unintentionally) a continuing lesbian discourse of authenticity while he emphasizes a continuing homosexual discourse (through Oscar Wilde, Jean Genet, and Joe Orton) which is committed to "the subversion of authenticity" (Dollimore 1986: 189). Our analysis of the case of Barney and Brooks indicates that the latter was a strategy adopted by at least some lesbians some years before the publication of *The Well of Loneliness*.

3 PROFESSIONALISM, GENRE, AND THE SISTER(S') ARTS

1 Unpublished letter; quoted by permission of Quentin Bell and R.A. Marler.

2 In the second volume of *Virginia Woolf: A Biography* Quentin Bell details Virginia and Leonard Woolf's income and expenditures (together with the sources of their capital) for the years 1914, 1915, and 1916. Virginia's invested capital of approximately £9,000, most of it inherited from her brother Thoby and her aunt Caroline Emelia Stephen, yielded less than £400 a year (Q. Bell 1972: 38–41).

3 See Reed 1991 for a recent analysis of the critical reception of Bloomsbury in England and the United States. Reed usefully delineates an underlying homophobia on the part of "traditional" and "leftist" critics as well as various feminist critics.

4 Reed notes that this has been the prevailing view of a number of feminist accounts of Woolf and Bell, as in Marcus 1983, Rose 1978, and De Salvo 1989.

5 It should be noted that portraits formed only a small part of Bell's oeuvre when compared to Brooks or Laurencin.

6 On imagery of the suffrage campaign see Tickner 1987.

7 In June 1926, for example, Woolf seems remarkably indifferent to her single meeting with Gertrude Stein, writing only: "We then went to a party at Edith Sitwell's (I in my new dress) 'to meet Miss Stein,' a lady much like Joan Fry, but more massive; in blue-sprinkled brocade, rather formidable" (Woolf 1980a: 89).

8 Dora Marsden edited *The Freewoman* which published its first issue in November 1911 and which later became *The New Freewoman* in June 1913 and *The Egoist* in December 1913; Harriet Weaver took over the editorship of *The Egoist* in June 1914. Harriet Monroe edited *Poetry: A Magazine of Verse* which published its first issue in October 1912, and Margaret Anderson and Jane Heap published the highly influential *The Little Review* between 1914 and 1929.

9 Of course, later during the twenties, Bell regularly travelled to Cassis where she took up temporary residence and mingled with various French and English artists; she also made several trips to Paris, staying in the artistic quarter. During such travels, however, most of Bell's contact was either with friends of her children or other acquaintances of the Bloomsbury Group. In other words, she took her existing social context with her. These travels are discussed in Spalding 1983, Chapter 10 ("Charleston in France 1927–30").

10 In addition to numerous press reviews, many of which included photographs of the artist, Gluck was interviewed and photographed for such society magazines as *Tatler*, *Royal Magazine*, and *Homes and Gardens*. See Souhami 1988. Romaine Brooks received similar extensive exhibition coverage and was also featured in a number of fashion magazines, including *Vogue*, *Arts and Decoration*, and the *Sketch*. See Breeskin 1986.

11 See "Women and fiction" (Woolf 1966). See "Professions for women" in *The Death of the Moth*, reprinted in Woolf 1966. All quotations are from *The Death of the Moth* (Woolf 1942). See also *The Pargiters: The Novel-Essay Portion of The Years* for the original and full version of the speech, and pp. xv–xviii of Leaska's introduction for a discussion of the evolution of "Professions for women" (Woolf 1978c).

12 Woolf's enormous pleasure in earning her own living while, at the same time, providing a living for others is amply documented in her diaries (see, for example, Woolf 1980a: 221, in which Woolf itemizes the bonuses she and Leonard have provided their staff from the profits of The Hogarth Press,

concluding "I think with pride that 7 people depend, largely, upon my hand writing on a sheet of paper").

13 That this was an argument Woolf found sympathetic is evident in the following passage from *A Room of One's Own*: "The news of my legacy reached me one night about the same time that the act was passed that gave votes to women. A solicitor's letter fell into the post-box and when I opened it I found that [my aunt] had left me five hundred pounds a year for ever. Of the two – the vote and the money, I own, seemed infinitely the more important" (Woolf 1929: 56).

14 In 1918 the United Kingdom granted the vote to women over the age of 30; in 1928 it extended the franchise to all women over the age of 21.

15 It should be noted that, despite the Omega Workshops' intention to reach a market beyond that of the existing picture-buying elite, the patrons of the Omega Workshops were few in number and, for the most part, relatively wealthy. For further discussion of Bell's participation in the Omega Workshops, see Anscombe 1981, and Collins 1983, 1984.

16 As Menand points out, G.H. Lewes articulated a noticeable shift in the status of literature when he announced in 1865 that "Literature ... has become a profession," thereby "claiming for it its proper place in the occupational structure of its time" (114). However, "in clearing out the dilettanti, he needed to clear out the gifted as well ... for, as we have seen, genius, that which is given and cannot be earned, is not the basis for the professional's claim to superiority" (115). Menand also notes that "If aestheticism might be said to belong to the phase of professionalism's first serious challenge to occupational values [e.g., inspiration, innocence of design], modernism belongs to the phase of its successful hegemony over them" (117–18).

See also Chapter 3 ("One round of a long ladder: gender profession, and the production of *Middlemarch*") of Feltes 1986, which argues that the founding of the Society of Authors in 1884 and of *The Author* in 1890 represents only the climax of a longer nineteenth-century collective movement towards gendered institutional professionalization.

17 For two different interpretations of the event see Pratt 1963: 20–21, and Hanscombe and Smyers 1987: 199–203.

18 See Celeste Schenck's discussion of the gendering of poetic form within modernist poetry in "Exiled by genre: modernism, canonicity, and the politics of exclusion."

19 Given the witty complications of Orlando's (en)gendering, we have not included him/her in our consideration of Woolf's representation of the *woman* artist.

20 Woolf was occasionally taken to task for her willingness to publish in the glossies, as her description of one such exchange (in a 1925 letter to Jacques Raverat) indicates:

> I've been engaged in a great wrangle with an old American called Pearsall Smith on the ethics of writing articles at high rates for fashion papers like Vogue. He says it demeans one. He says one must write only for the Lit. Supplement and the Nation and Robert Bridges and prestige and posterity and set a high example. I say Bunkum. Ladies' clothes and aristocrats playing golf don't affect my style; and they would do his a world of good. Oh these Americans! How they always muddle everything up! What he wants is prestige: what I want, money.
>
> (Woolf 1977: 154)

21 See also Pamela Caughie's discussion of the place of *Flush* within the Woolf and modernist canons, and of Woolf's fear of being "popular" (Caughie 1991: 55).

22 See Elizabeth Abel's discussion of the ways in which *To the Lighthouse*'s "fractured explorations of elegiac subjects resists consolidation as a single genre or theme" (Abel 1987: 171).

23 "If Woolf's portrait of the artist as an aging woman locates her so firmly in the middle class, that is in significant part because the old intellectual aristocracy and the new intellectual proletariat, the civilized past and the semi-civilized future, are seen equally as male preserves, alien lands for female creativity" (Levenson 1991: 203).

24 "This is going to be fairly short: to have father's character done complete in it; & mothers; & St Ives; & childhood" (Woolf 1980a: 18).

25 All of these portraits are reproduced in Gillespie 1988. Bell did three portraits of Woolf in 1912, two of which show Woolf with a book (one of her seated in a deckchair and one in a frontal pose with her hands on an open book), while the third depicts her knitting in an armchair.

26 For a fascinating account of Bell's interest in the domestic and her desire to create views of an idyllic family life, see Val Williams, "Carefully creating an idyll: Vanessa Bell and snapshot photography 1907–1946" in Williams 1986: 72–88.

27 It was only much later in her career, after she had become widely accepted in establishment circles, that she painted herself in her studio seated at her easel and surrounded by brushes and tubes of paint. See her *The Artist in Her Studio*, 1952 (Ex coll. Pamela Diamond), reproduced in Shone 1980: no. 74.

28 This portrait may be compared with Grant's more typical images of Bell posing rather than painting, such as *Portrait of Vanessa Bell*, c. 1914 (private collection, see Watney 1980: plate 7), *At Eleanor: Vanessa Bell*, 1915 (Yale Centre for British Art, New Haven), *Vanessa Bell*, c. 1916–17 (National Portrait Gallery, London), and *Vanessa Bell*, c. 1918 (National Portrait Gallery, London).

29 Significantly, it is the pervasive belief in the artist's cultural authority that makes Kirchner's unusual later painting, *Self-Portrait as Soldier* (1917), so poignant since the artist represents himself disempowered by the amputation of his right hand.

30 Unfortunately a reproduction of this work in the Tatham Art Gallery, Pietmaritzburg, Natal, South Africa was not available at time of publication.

31 See, for example, *Abstract Composition*, c. 1913–14 (Anthony D'Offay Gallery, London) and *Abstract Painting*, c. 1914 (Tate Gallery, London). These were exhibited as numbers 24 and 25 in the exhibition at the Royal Museum in Canterbury (1983).

32 Of course, it must be acknowledged that some of her male portraits also tend to dissolve when the male figures appear as part of a group portrait or conversation piece. See, for example, her *Conversation Piece* of 1912 (in the collection of the University of Hull, reproduced in Watney 1980: plate 71).

4 THE MAKING OF GENIUS

1 This translation appears in Steegmuller 1963: 157–58. The original French version of Laurencin's complete comment is as follows:

Si je me sens si loin des peintres, c'est parce qu'ils sont des hommes – et que les hommes m'apparaissent comme des problèmes difficiles à résoudre. Leurs discussions, leurs recherches, leur génie, m'ont toujours étonnée.

Quand un poète écrit, il dit si bien ce que je voudrais dire que, tranquillisée, je me tais.

Pour la peinture, c'est exactement pareil, et les grands peintres aussi bien mes contemporains ont travaillé à ma place.

Mais si le génie de l'homme m'intimide, je me sens parfaitement à l'aise avec tout ce qui est féminin ...

(Laurencin 1956: 16)

2 Edward Fitzgerald in a letter to James Russell Lowell, in John Bartlett, *Familiar Quotations*, ed. Emile Morison Beck (Toronto: Little, Brown, and Company, 1968): 631.

3 In many ways, the debates surrounding Weininger's book rekindled those initiated ten years earlier by Max Nordau's *Degeneration* (New York: Howard Fertig, 1895; rpt. 1968). Denouncing what he perceived as the degenerate nervous pathology of avant-garde aesthetes, Nordau had called for the revitalization of sane, healthy, and manly art forms. Significantly, Weininger's promotion of healthy male genius similarly seeks to culturally disempower any but white heterosexual Western males. Both writers were strongly influenced by theories of eugenics.

4 Quoted in Benstock 1986: 189 and Mellow 1974: 152. Mellow also notes that Stein recommended *Sex and Character* to Marian Walker, "her ardent feminist friend of Johns Hopkins days." Walker responded in a 1909 letter that "it was evidently before not after he wrote the book that he went insane.... [He] was really a very half-baked individual" (152). See also Walker 1984, passim, for discussion of Weininger's influence on Stein's theory of character.

5 *Atlantic Monthly* published 60 per cent of *The Autobiography of Alice B. Toklas* in four installments running from May to August 1933; the last two installments appeared in the same issue as the *first* two installments of another experiment in genre, Virginia Woolf's *Flush: A Biography*, the story of Elizabeth Barrett Browning's spaniel. In its "Contributors' column," *Atlantic Monthly* celebrated Gertrude Stein's "arrival" in the following laudatory, but also carefully ironic, terms:

Not since Wordsworth and Coleridge published the *Lyrical Ballads* has any writer been the subject of such heated controversy as has *Gertrude Stein*. Just now, when literature, in common with the other arts, is passing through a period of transition, someone has aptly observed that the whole English-reading world may be divided into two groups – those who understand and applaud Gertrude Stein and those who don't. Whatever the reader's sympathies on this question, there can be no disputing the fact that she is one of the remarkable women of our time.... Hers has been an extraordinary life, and under the characteristic title, "Autobiography of Alice B. Toklas," she records it all in amusing and colorful detail – and in the King's English.

(*Atlantic Monthly* 151, 5 (May 1933): 641)

As James Mellow points out, *The Autobiography* afforded Stein her first real income from writing. Her royalties from the book "amounted to $4,495.31," the Literary Guild paid her an additional $3,000 to bring it out as the September selection, and *Atlantic Monthly* paid her $1,000 for the four installments (Mellow 1974: 424–25). Stein purchased "a new eight cylinder Ford car and the most expensive coat made to order by Hermes ... for Basket the white poodle and two collars studded for Basket" (Stein 1937: 40). For further discussion of Stein's publishing history see Ford 1975: 231–52.

6   See McAlmon's spring 1926 letter to Stein part of which reads: "Contrary to your verbal statements that you would help rid us of your volume, you have done nothing.... You *asked* me to take on the book. You knew it was a philanthropic enterprise as the Ms. had been some twenty years on your hands.... If you wish the books retained, you may bid for them. Otherwise, by Sept. – one year after publication – I shall simply rid myself of them en-masse, by the pulping proposition" (Gallup 1953: 189–90).

7   Our argument here differs slightly from that of Dydo who suggests that Stein's sense of her own genius was coincident with a sense of professionalism (Dydo 1985b: 61); we see a conflict between the two discourses.

8   "Before I decided to write this book my twenty-five years with Gertrude Stein, I had often said that I would write, The wives of geniuses I have sat with. I have sat with so many. I have sat with wives who were not wives, of geniuses who were real geniuses. I have sat with real wives of geniuses who were not real geniuses. I have sat with wives of geniuses, of near geniuses, of would be geniuses, in short I have sat very often and very long with many wives and wives of many geniuses" (Stein 1960: 14).

9   According to Fagen-King (1988: 111, fn. 92) critics repeatedly noticed the influence of Botticelli in Laurencin's work.

10 Originally published as "Art news: the decorative arts and female painting," in *Le Petit bleu* (13 March 1912).

11 Significantly, it was *The Autobiography of Alice B. Toklas* – obviously a memoir – which allowed Stein to "try out some new theories of narrative" (Ford 1975: 246).

12 In particular, we are thinking of Picasso's 1906–7 study for *Les Demoiselles d'Avignon* in the Oeffentliche Kunstsammlung, Kupferstichkabinett Basel. Laurencin's study is reproduced as Figure 4.4.

13 "As I have said elsewhere, her egoist art draws everything to her so that she has no other subject but herself and no concern but to discover herself. Having only an inclination for natural forms and objects which resemble her, for animals and plants that have her vigorous flexibility, she discovers reflections of her own face everywhere and the most pressing unexpected reasons to love herself. This is Narcissus, but decent and without difficulty, rather capable of giving life and lasting qualities to her fugitive images" (our translation). See also Allard 1921.

14 From "Art news: women painters," *Le Petit bleu* (5 April 1912).

15 On the entry of women into the clerical professions see Holcombe 1973. Significantly, women were believed to be better suited for typing than men given that smaller fingers more easily fitted keyboards.

16 Contemporary reviewers used the high prices of her canvases (usually selling in the region of 20,000 francs in 1922) to demonstrate her success (see Roche 1922: 215–18).

17 "All in all, the artist who she makes one think of most is Jules Cheret. Both are capricious, voluptuous without being sensual, bubbly, and without depth, which will prove boring once their novelty is past" (our translation).

18 Dealing directly with her sitters would have given Laurencin more control over whom she painted as well as enabling her to collect the full price of the work rather than giving a percentage to the dealer. In this respect, her portrait practice was similar to that of Romaine Brooks.

19 Gimpel also mentions that in 1930 *Vu*, a chic Paris society review, published photographs of Marie Laurencin, Colette, and Mme Anna de Noailles with the caption "The three most famous women in France."

20 "The little that I have learned has been taught to me by what I call the great painters, my contemporaries Matisse, Derain, Picasso, Braque. They will not be happy that I am citing their names – that's the way they are. I compare them to the song from Carmen: 'Even if you don't love me I still love you.'

If I haven't become a cubist painter, it's because I've never been able to. I wasn't capable of it, but I find their research exciting" (our translation).

21 This disappearance is discussed in the foreword to Marchesseau 1986.

5 MEDIATING MODERNISM

1 Karla Jay discusses the emotional effects of this unpredictability on Djuna Barnes, and suggests that Barnes's satiric *Ladies Almanack* (1928) – with what Jay calls its "reductionist vision of lesbianism" – represents the writer's revenge against her sometimes patron, Natalie Barney (Jay 1991).

2 For contemporary representations of the Bel Esprit project see Alfred Kreymborg's "Bel Esprit" in the June 1922 issue of *The Double Dealer* and Ezra Pound's "Paris letter" in the November 1922 issue of *The Dial*. Kreymborg quotes from a letter from Pound: "What we want is not more books, but a better quality of book; and the modus is (1) to find the man [sic]; (2) to guarantee him food and leisure, by a co-operation of subscribers (individuals or groups) pledging themselves to give fifty dollars per year for life or for as long as the artist needs it." In his concluding paragraph, Kreymborg suggests that potential donors "can reach Bel Esprit at 20 rue Jacob;" in a significant double erasure of the woman artist *and* the woman patron, he does not mention that this is Natalie Barney's address (Kreymborg 1922: 326–28). See also W.G. Rogers's fatuous *Ladies Bountiful* (1968), which describes women's patronage of male literary modernism: "Beyond any question these openhearted women who heard and heeded had an ear already cocked for exactly such appeals; they were born with not only a silver spoon but also a generous streak. Far from having to be persuaded, they were just waiting for a chance to throw out the life line" (Rogers 1968: 4–5).

3 " 'Symbolic capital' is to be understood as economic or political capital that is disavowed, mis-recognized and thereby recognized, hence legitimate, a 'credit' which, under certain conditions, and always in the long run, guarantees 'economic' profits.... For the author, the critic, the art dealer, the publisher or the theatre manager, the only legitimate accumulation consists in making a name for oneself, a known, recognized name, a capital of consecration implying a power to consecrate objects (with a trademark or signature) or persons (through publication, exhibition, etc.) and therefore to give value, and to appropriate the profits from this operation" (Bourdieu 1986: 132).

4 Andrew Field surprisingly reinforces this view of Barnes by describing her position in the expatriate community as follows: "Hemingway and Barnes were breezy acquaintances, but she did not move in the expatriation's front circle of fame and money. She was among the poets and actors, mostly homosexual, and the many women artists of all manner and sort, who furnished the fascinating background texture of the expatriation" (Field 1985: 16).

5 The next stanza reinforces the implications of the loss of virile culture:

All men, in law, are equals.
Free of Pisistratus,
We choose a knave *or an eunuch*

To rule over us.

(11. 53–56, our emphasis)

See also Ann Douglas, *The Feminization of American Culture*, New York: Knopf, 1977.

6   See also Suzanne Clark's important *Sentimental Modernism* (1991) which discusses the ways in which American literary modernism defined itself in opposition to the domestic and the sentimental.

7   Avant-garde poet and artist Mina Loy appeared as the prototypical "modern woman" in the 13 February 1917 *New York Evening Sun* which had launched a city-wide search for the "creature." In his introduction to Loy's *The Last Lunar Baedeker*, Conover suggests that "the *Sun* profile of Mina Loy is reminiscent of newspaper coverage given Marcel Duchamp shortly after he landed in New York in 1915. He too was hailed as an exemplary Modern" (xlv). It is, however, significant that Duchamp was *not* hailed as "the modern man;" newspaper coverage of him stressed his exemplariness rather than his proto-typicality, a strategy not requiring the gimmick of a search.

   During the twenties and thirties articles on Gluck appeared in such society periodicals as *Sketch, Royal Magazine, Tatler, Illustrated Sporting and Dramatic News, Sphere, Bystander*, and *Harper's Bazaar*. Some of these are discussed in Souhami 1988. Romaine Brooks was featured in similar magazines, such as *Sketch, Cosmopolitan, Arts and Decoration, Vogue*, and *Truth*.

8   The Beinecke Rare Book and Manuscript Library, Yale University.

9   Most other critics who have discussed Barnes's journalism have regarded it primarily as a source for *Nightwood* (Kannenstine 1977; Plumb 1986; Herzig 1987; Levine 1991). Our own approach is different; we are more interested in what light Barnes's career as a journalist sheds on the gendered economies of "modernism."

10 "The Girl and the gorilla; Dinah at the Bronx Zoo, a weird little forty-five-pound bunch of femininity – not yet full-grown, but converses intelligently in language of the primates," *New York World Magazine*, 18 October 1914: 9; "My adventures being rescued; demonstrating, as Chief Larkin says, that new fangled life-saving devices are mostly impracticable, so it's safer to stick to the old methods of 'the rope, the fireman and the girl,'" *New York World Magazine*, 15 November 1914: 6 (see Messerli 1975).

11 "How it feels to be forcibly fed," *New York World Magazine*, 6 September 1914: 5, 17. See also Barnes 1989.

12 [Lydia Steptoe], "A French general of fashion; Madame Jenny sums up the secret of taste: simple line, excellent texture, skillful cut," *Charm* 2 (January 1925): 24–25, 95; "American wives and titled husbands; when American girls marry titled foreigners do they ever become happy wives? Are their husbands interested in them – or their money? And can American women ever become accustomed to foreign society, foreign customs? Are they homesick? Are they sorry? These and many other questions are answered in this important series of interviews with titled American wives," *McCall's* 54 (June 1927): 8–9, 62. See Messerli 1975.

13 It should be emphasized that, from the beginning, Barnes disavowed any serious engagement in her newspaper and magazine articles. It remains an open question how much of this disavowal was strategic, how much was born out of bitterness, and how much was genuine. In 1915 Guido Bruno wrote that Barnes was "one of the few young American artists who can walk their own way. Not willing to make concessions to publishers and art editors, she is using her pen to earn her

livelihood as a newspaper woman, and permits herself the luxury of being an artist just to please herself" (quoted in Kannenstine 1977: 1–2). In 1950 Barnes wrote to Dan Mahoney that she considered her magazine writing "utterly wasteful;" in 1977 she referred to her *Theatre Guild* pieces as the "bottom of the barrel" (quoted in Plumb 1986: 19).

14 For an earlier discussion of Barnes's articles on Joyce, see Bonnie Kime Scott, *Joyce and Feminism* (Bloomington: Indiana University Press, 1984).

15 For further information on women gallery owners and directors in England, see Grimes, Collins, and Baddeley 1989: 18–19.

16 Russell incorrectly identifies March 1922 as the issue in which Barnes's interview with Joyce appeared; he also hints, anachronistically, that Barnes was chosen to interview Joyce because of her status as author of *Nightwood*, which was not published until 1936 (xv).

17 The two articles have since been gathered in a single volume, *Vagaries Malicieux: Two Stories*, published in 1974.

18 "James Joyce: a portrait of a man who is, at present, one of the more significant figures in literature" was published in the April issue; "The diary of a dangerous child," "Against nature," and "Little drops of rain," all signed "Lydia Steptoe," were published in the July, August, and September issues respectively and should be considered a series; the short poem, "I'd have you think of me" was published in the October issue.

19 "I know every young creature is entitled to one coming out, but they come out too far. They take a sliding run and land right out here in the midst of women who have suffered and kept their cigarettes lit at the same time" (Barnes 1922d: 60).

20 The poem would be simultaneously published in England in *The Criterion*, of which T.S. Eliot was the new editor. As Lawrence Rainey argues in his important 1989 article, "The price of modernism," the American venue for the poem was of crucial importance to the entrenchment of literary modernism:

> By 1922 literary modernism desperately required a financial–critical success that would seem comparable to the stunning achievement of modernist painting, yet every step in this direction was hampered by market constraints less amenable to the kinds of pressures from elite patronage and investment that had secured the fortunes of cubism and modern painting.... Patronage could nurture literary modernism only to the threshold of its confrontation with a wider public; beyond that point, it would require commercial success to ratify its viability as a significant idiom. That was the question that permeated discussion about publication of *The Waste Land*.
>
> (28)

Rainey concludes that, in spite of obvious differences between the three magazines (in terms of, for example, advertising revenue, marketing, and circulation), ultimately they differed from each other primarily in tone, "not in substantive ideology."

> [T]hese journals, it is clear, are best viewed not as antagonists who represented alien or incompatible ideologies, but as protagonists who shared a common terrain, whose fields of activity overlapped and diverged within a shared spectrum of marketing and consumption. Their activity suggests that there was no single or essential feature that distinguished "the avant-garde" from "modernism."
>
> (36, 37–38)

Our argument goes in a slightly different direction to suggest that these journals were perceived as appealing to different audiences, and that writers like Barnes tailored their articles – and the depictions of the modernists/avant-garde – accordingly.

21 It is not clear whether this drawing was published with the original article in the *New York Morning Telegraph Sunday Magazine* (19 November 1916).

22 Barnes's illustration echoes some of Beardsley's work for the *Yellow Book* (e.g. *The Repentance of Mrs. . . .* published in the fourth volume) as well as his work for the publisher Leonard Smithers (e.g. *Six Drawings Illustrating Theophile Gautier's Romance Mademoiselle de Maupin by Aubrey Beardsley*). These drawings are reproduced in Brian Reade, *Aubrey Beardsley* (London: Studio Vista, 1967).

23 Barnes published in Frank Harris's *Pearson's Magazine*, and interviewed him for the 4 February 1917 *New York Morning Telegraph Sunday Magazine* ("Frank Harris finds success more easily won here in America than in England": 8). Reproduced in Barnes 1985.

24 These discussions appear in Frank Harris, *My Life and Loves* (New York: Grove Press, 1963 rpt. of 1925) and *Oscar Wilde: His Life and Confessions* (Garden City, N.J.: Garden City Publishing Co., 1930).

25 We are indebted to Marie Clifford for this reference. For a further discussion of representations of bohemian life in Greenwich Village, see her "Drawing on women: suffrage imagery and representations of women in the graphics of *The Masses*, 1911–1917" (unpublished M.A. dissertation, University of Alberta, Edmonton, Canada).

26 Reproduced in Barnes 1989.

27 Originally published in *Pearson's Magazine*, October 1916. Reproduced in Barnes 1989.

28 "Becoming intimate with the Bohemians; when the dusk of a musty hall has crept through the ever widening keyhole the Queen of Bohemia has arisen, for her day has begun; you will find her in Polly's, the Candle Stick, the Brevoort, the Black Cat or any other Greenwich Village place you care to visit," *New York Morning Telegraph Sunday Magazine*, 19 November 1916: 1, 4; "How the Villagers amuse themselves; the task is sordid and hard, but it must be done – so after an early breakfast out sets the Bohemian," *New York Morning Telegraph Sunday Magazine*, 26 November 1916: 1. See Messerli 1975. Reproduced in Barnes 1989.

29 As Hoffman, Allen, and Ulrich point out in *The Little Magazine: A History and a Bibliography*, *The Double Dealer* fell into the category of "The advance guard magazine devoted to experimentalism in one form or another" (Hoffman *et al.* 1947: 9, 10–13).

30 Both the pose and smock in Hamnett's portrait closely resemble those in a later self-portrait by Gluck, suggesting that young women artists found the assertion of such a practical workmanlike identity appealing. The self-portrait by Gluck is reproduced in Souhami 1988.

31 The reproduction is all that remains of this picture which Hamnett noted as destroyed in her records.

32 These comments appeared in *Colour* (May 1915): 118 and *Cambridge Magazine* (8 November 1919: 67).

33 The editor was Chapman Hall and other members of the editorial committee included: T.S. Eliot, Tommy Earp, Richard Aldington, Aldous Huxley, Russell Green, and Wyndham Lewis. Hamnett also contributed a café scene drawing for the cover of the Christmas 1920 issue as well as a drawing of a seated female nude during the brief life of the magazine (Hooker 1986: 126–28).

34 She often expressed the hope of making money from her exhibitions, such as the one at the Eldar Gallery in London in 1918 (see Hooker 1986: 131).

35 The *Transatlantic Review*, launched in Paris in December 1923 and edited by Ford Madox Ford, published one of Hamnett's drawings of a life class in June 1924. The magazine published writers such as Joyce, Hemingway, Cummings, Pound, McAlmon, and Stein as well as reproductions of works by Picasso, Brancusi, and John Storr (see Hooker 1986: 157).

36 A few days later, on Wednesday 5 December [1956], Bob Pocock's radio play *It's Long Past the Time*, about life in Charlotte Street in the thirties, was broadcast. Nina featured prominently as the fictional character Cynthia, and Pocock had managed to get her a fee of [ten pounds]. Cynthia was played by the doyenne of radio, Gladys Young, whom Pocock had coached to good effect in Nina's distinctive voice, complete with the indispensable "my deahs" and the odd "ducky." Those who knew Nina thought the impersonation was magnificent.

It was too good. Nina felt that the programme was a cruel caricature and parody. She was upset and furious and thought her friends had betrayed her. In her vulnerable state, anxious about the results of her hospital tests and the fact that Mounsey had not appeared, it must have seemed to Nina that she was being written off as a figure of the past, an artistic has-been who was merely an object of amusement to others.

(Hooker 1986: 256–57)

6 CONCLUSION: ENABLING STRATEGIES

1 Unpublished letter from Henry W. and Albert A. Berg Collection, New York Public Library; quoted by permission of Quentin Bell and R.A. Marler.

2 In spite of her consciously feminist politics, Woolf believed that the term "feminist" was no longer politically useful (see Woolf 1938: 184–85).

3 See also "A Parisian roof garden in 1918" (Barney 1920: 23).

4 See Jay 1988: 28–29, 34–35; Wickes 1976: 192–93; Sieburth 1976: 289.

5 This strategy of marginalizing women has been extensively discussed by a number of feminist art historians; see, for example, Rosika Parker and Griselda Pollock, *Old Mistresses: Women, Art and Ideology* (London: Routledge & Kegan Paul, 1981), Chapter 1. As mentioned in our fourth chapter, Marie Laurencin seems to have resisted this reasoning by insisting that women were, in fact, better suited to painting than men.

6 Jane Watt is currently completing a doctoral dissertation on Georgina Sime, and Kathryn Harvey is completing a doctoral dissertation on Kathleen Innes (both at the University of Alberta).

7 See, for example, David Trotter, "Modernism and empire: reading *The Waste Land*," *Critical Quarterly* 28 (Summer 1986): 143–53, and Fredric Jameson, "Modernism and imperialism," in Terry Eagleton, Fredric Jameson, and Edward Said, *Nationalism, Colonialism, and Literature* (Minneapolis: University of Minnesota Press, 1990).

8 For a discussion of the ways in which women gained access to public spaces in turn-of-the-century London see Judith Walkowitz, *City of Dreadful Delight: Narratives of Sexual Danger in Late-Victorian London* (Chicago: University of Chicago Press, 1992).

9 See, for example, T.S. Eliot's *The Waste Land* (1922) and its depiction of decay and death in the modernist Unreal City (ll. 60–68) which can be compared with

Virginia Woolf's *Mrs Dalloway* (1925) which uses many of the same images – particularly the sounding of London's clocks – to provide a completely contrasting view of the city which represents, to Clarissa Dalloway, "what she loved; life."

10 See Woolf 1976, "A sketch of the past."

11 In *Laughing Torso*, Hamnett recalled that "My Father was selfish and bad-tempered and beat me. I must admit that I was a dreadful child but I think he rather overdid it" (4); the remainder of the passage details the way in which her father beat her with bamboo canes. She also recalled her father's threat to "have [her] put into a lunatic asylum" if she continued to draw:

> What with this and my hopeless passion I became paralyzed. I lost the use of my hands completely. I was taken to a doctor friend of my Father's, an unpleasant man who might have been my Father's twin brother. What I really was suffering from was virginal hysteria and boredom, but this monster invented a disease called Spinal Adhesion and made me lie down for hours. This made me worse.
>
> (Hamnett 1932: 27–28)

12 Laurencin is purported to have lost all sense of emotional stability when her mother died. See Gray 1958: 12.

13 "When I first knew Gertrude Stein in Paris I was surprised never to see a french book on her table, although there were always plenty of english ones, there were even no french newspapers. But do you never read french, I as well as many other people asked her. No, she replied, you see I feel with my eyes and it does not make any difference to me what language I hear, I don't hear a language, I hear tones of voices and rhythms, but with my eyes I see words and sentences and there is for me only one language and that is english. One of the things that I have liked all these years is to be surrounded by people who know no english. It has left me more intensely alone with my eyes and my english. I do not know if it would have been possible to have english be so all in all to me otherwise" (Stein 1960: 70).

14 As George Wickes points out, "The author's apologetic preface presents her as an American who has been struggling to master the strict rules of French rhyme and meter in order to please a pedantic schoolmaster. The poems themselves, mostly sonnets, reveal that the author was an apt pupil whose schoolmaster had curbed every effort to experiment with versification and had probably stifled every attempt at original expression. The style, the imagery and the language of love are all familiar to anyone who has browsed through conventional nineteenth-century French verse" (Wickes 1976: 45).

BIBLIOGRAPHY

Abel, Elizabeth (1987) "'Cam the wicked:' Woolf's portrait of the artist as her father's daughter," in Jane Marcus (ed.), *Virginia Woolf and Bloomsbury: A Centennial Celebration*, Bloomington: Indiana University Press.

Allard, Roger (1921) *Marie Laurencin*, Paris: Éditions de la "Nouvelle Revue Française."

—— (1925) "Marie Laurencin," *L'Art d'aujourd'hui* 2: 49–51.

Anderson, Perry (1988) "Modernity and revolution," in Cary Nelson and Lawrence Grossberg (eds), *Marxism and the Interpretation of Culture*, Urbana: University of Illinois Press.

anon (1937) "The elfin maidens of Marie Laurencin," *Art Digest* 12 (15 November): 10.

Anscombe, Isabelle (1981) *Omega and After: Bloomsbury and the Decorative Arts*, London: Thames & Hudson.

Apollinaire, Guillaume (1972) *Apollinaire on Art: Essays and Reviews 1902–1918*, Leroy C. Breunig (ed.), trans. Susan Suleiman, New York: Da Capo Press.

Baldick, Chris (1983) *The Social Mission of English Criticism 1848–1932*, Oxford: Clarendon Press.

Barnes, Djuna (1915) *The Book of Repulsive Women: Eight Rhythms and Five Drawings*, New York: Bruno Chapbooks 2, November.

—— (1922a) "James Joyce: a portrait of the man who is, at present, one of the more significant figures in literature," *Vanity Fair* 18 (April): 65, 104.

—— (1922b) "Vagaries malicieux," *The Double Dealer* 3 (May): 249–60.

—— [Lydia Steptoe] (1922c) "The diary of a dangerous child," *Vanity Fair* 18 (July): 56, 94.

—— [Lydia Steptoe] (1922d) "Against nature," *Vanity Fair* 18 (August): 60, 88.

—— [Lydia Steptoe] (1922e) "Little drops of rain," *Vanity Fair* 19 (September): 50, 94.

—— (1923) *A Book*, New York: Boni & Liveright.

—— (1936) *Nightwood*, London: Faber & Faber.

—— (1958) *The Antiphon*, New York: Farrar, Strauss & Cudahy.

—— (1974) *Vagaries Malicieux: Two Stories*, New York: F. Hallman.

—— (1985) *Interviews*, Alyce Barry (ed.), Washington: Sun & Moon Press.

—— (1989) *New York*, Alyce Barry (ed.), Los Angeles: Sun & Moon Press.

—— (1990, orig. pub. 1928) *Ryder*, Elmwood, Illinois: Dalkey Archive Press.

—— (1992; orig. pub. 1928) *Ladies Almanack*, Elmwood, Illinois: Dalkey Archive Press.

Barney, Natalie Clifford (1900) *Quelques portraits-sonnets de femmes*, Paris: Société d'Éditions Littéraires et Artistiques, Librairie Paul Ollendorf.

—— (1920) *Pensées d'une amazone*, Paris: Emile-Paul Feres.

—— (1920) *Poems & Poèmes: autres alliances*, Paris: Emile-Paul Frères; New York: George H. Doran.

—— (1929) *Aventures de l'esprit*, Paris: Emile-Paul Frères.

—— (1930) *The One Who Is Legion, or A.D.'s After-Life*, London: Eric Partridge (privately subscribed). [A facsimile reprint, The National Poetry Foundation, University of Maine, 1987.]

—— (1939) *Nouvelles pensées de l'amazone*, Paris: Mercure de France.

—— (ed.) (1951) *In Memory of Dorothy Ierne Wilde*. Privately printed.

—— (1960) *Souvenirs indiscrets*, Paris: Flammarion.

—— (1963) *Selected Writings*, Miron Grindea (ed.), [London:] Adam Books.

Battersby, Christine (1989) *Gender and Genius: Towards a Feminist Aesthetics*, Bloomington: Indiana University Press.

Baudelaire, Charles (1993) *The Flowers of Evil [Les Fleurs du mal]* (orig. pub. 1857), trans. James McGowan, Oxford and New York: Oxford University Press.

Beach, Sylvia (1980; first pub. 1956) *Shakespeare and Company*, Lincoln: University of Nebraska Press.

Bell, Clive (1987) *Art*, J.B. Bullen (ed.), London: Oxford University Press.

Bell, Quentin (1972) *Virginia Woolf: A Biography*, 2 vols., London: The Hogarth Press.

Bell, Vanessa (1975) "Notes on Bloomsbury," in S.P. Rosenbaum (ed.), *The Bloomsbury Group: A Collection of Memoirs, Commentary and Criticism*, Toronto: University of Toronto Press.

Benstock, Shari (1986) *Women of the Left Bank: Paris, 1900–1940*, Austin: University of Texas Press.

—— (1989) "Expatriate modernism: writing on the cultural rim," in Mary Lynn Broe and Angela Ingram (eds), *Women's Writing in Exile*, Chapel Hill: University of North Carolina Press.

Berman, Marshall (1983) *All That Is Solid Melts Into Air*, New York: Simon & Schuster.

Bishop, Edward (1989) *A Virgina Woolf Chronology*, London: Macmillan.

Blaine, Virginia; Grundy, Isobel; and Clements, Patricia (eds) (1990) *The Feminist Companion to Literature in English: Women Writers From the Middle Ages to the Present*, New Haven: Yale University Press.

Bloch, Ernst; Lukács, Georg; Brecht, Bertolt; Benjamin, Walter; and Adorno, Theodor (1977) *Aesthetics and Politics*, London: NLB.

Booth-Clibborn, Edward (1984) "Introduction" to Nina Hamnett, *Laughing Torso: Reminiscences*, London: Virago.

Bourdieu, Pierre (1985) *Distinction: A Social Critique of the Judgement of Taste*, trans. Richard Nice, London: Routledge & Kegan Paul.

—— (1986) "The production of belief: contribution to an economy of symbolic goods," trans. Richard Nice, in Richard Collins *et al.* (eds), *Media, Culture and Society: A Critical Reader*, London: SAGE Publications.

—— (1988) *Homo Academicus*, trans. Peter Collier, Stanford: Stanford University Press.

Bradbury, Malcolm (1976) "The cites of modernism," in Malcolm Bradbury and James McFarlane (eds), *Modernism 1890–1930*, Harmondsworth: Penguin.

Bradbury, Malcolm and McFarlane, James (1976) "The name and nature of modernism," in Malcolm Bradbury and James McFarlane (eds), *Modernism 1890–1930*, Harmondsworth: Penguin.

Breeskin, Adelyn D. (1986) *Romaine Brooks*, Washington: National Museum of American Art, Smithsonian Institute.

Brodzki, Bella and Schenck, Celeste (eds) (1988) *Life/Lines: Theorizing Women's Autobiography*, Ithaca: Cornell University Press.

Broe, Mary Lynn (1989) "My art belongs to Daddy: incest as exile, the textual economics of Hayford Hall," in Mary Lynn Broe and Angela Ingram (eds), *Women's Writing in Exile*, Chapel Hill: University of North Carolina Press.

—— (ed.) (1991) *Silence and Power: A Reevaluation of Djuna Barnes*, Carbondale: Southern Illinois University Press.

Brooks, Romaine (undated) "No pleasant memories," unpublished typescript, National Collection of Fine Arts Research Materials on Romaine Brooks, Archives of American Art, Smithsonian Institution.

Bryson, Norman (1983) *Vision and Painting: The Logic of the Gaze*, New Haven: Yale University Press.

Buffet [-Picabia], Gabrielle (1923) "Marie Laurencin," *Arts* (June): 391–96.

Bürger, Peter (1984; orig. pub. 1974) *Theory of the Avant-Garde*, trans. Michael Shaw, Minneapolis: University of Minnesota Press.

Burke, Carolyn (1991) "'Accidental aloofness:' Barnes, Loy, and modernism," in Mary Lynn Broe (ed.), *Silence and Power: A Reevaluation of Djuna Barnes*.

Butler, Judith (1990) *Gender Trouble: Feminism and the Subversion of Identity*, London: Routledge.

Casteras, Susan (1984) *Vanessa Bell 1879–1961*, Poughkeepsie, N.Y.: Vassar College Art Gallery.

Caughie, Pamela L. (1991) "*Flush* and the literary canon: oh where oh where has that little dog gone?", *Tulsa Studies in Women's Literature* 10 (Spring): 47–66.

Caws, Mary Ann (1990) *Women of Bloomsbury: Virginia, Vanessa, and Carrington*, New York: Routledge.

—— Kuenzli, Rudolph E. and Raaberg, Gwen (eds) (1991) *Surrealism and Women*, Cambridge and London: The MIT Press.

Chadwick, Whitney (1985) *Women Artists and the Surrealist Movement*, London: Thames & Hudson.

Chalon, Jean (1979) *Portrait of a Seductress: The World of Natalie Barney*, trans. Carol Barko, New York: Crown Publishers.

Chamberlain, Lori (1988) "Gender and the metaphorics of translation," *Signs* 13: 454–72.

Chavanne, Blandine and Gaudichon, Bruno (1987) *Romaine Brooks (1874–1970)*, Poitiers: Musée de la Ville de Poitiers et la Société des Antiquaires de l'Ouest.

Cherry, Deborah and Beckett, Jane (1988) "Gwendolyn Mary John (1896–1939)," *Art History* 11 (September): 456–62.

Churchill, Allen (1961) *The Improper Bohemians: A Re-creation of Greenwich Village in Its Heyday*, London: Cassell.

Clark, Suzanne (1991) *Sentimental Modernism: Women Writers and the Revolution of the Word*, Bloomington: Indiana University Press.

Clutton-Brock, Alan (1940) "Vanessa Bell and her circle," *Studio* (October): 90.

Collins, Judith (1983) *The Omega Workshops*, London: Secker & Warburg.

—— (1984) *The Omega Workshops 1913–1919: Decorative Arts of Bloomsbury*, London Crafts Council.

—— (1989) "Nina Hamnett 1890–1956," in Teresa Grimes, Judith Collins, and Oriana Baddeley (eds), *Five Women Painters*, London: Lennard Publishing.

Colour (1915) "Palette and Chisel" (May): 118.

Connolly, Cyril (undated) "Adam and the Amazon" [unidentified press clipping in a box of clippings on Romaine Brooks in the Beinecke Library, Yale University].

Cott, Nancy (1987) *The Grounding of Modern Feminism*, New Haven: Yale University Press.

Crowninshield, Frank (1937) *Marie Laurencin*, New York: Findley Galleries.

Deghy, Guy and Waterhouse, Keith (1955) *Café Royal: Ninety Years of Bohemia*, London: Hutchinson.

DeKoven, Marianne (1991) *Rich and Strange: Gender, History, Modernism*, Princeton: Princeton University Press.

Dell, Floyd (1933) *Homecoming: An Autobiography*, New York: Farrar & Rinehart.

Department of Art History and Archaeology, Columbia University (1976) *Modern Portraits: The Self and Others*, introduction Kirk Varnadoe, New York: Wildenstein.

De Salvo, Louise (1989) *Virginia Woolf: The Impact of Child Sexual Abuse on Her Life and Work*, Boston: Beacon.

—— (1991) " 'To make her mutton at sixteen:' rape, incest, and child abuse in *The Antiphon*," in Mary Lynn Broe (ed.), *Silence and Power: A Reevaluation of Djuna Barnes*.

Dollimore, Jonathan (1986) "The dominant and the deviant: a violent dialectic," *Critical Quarterly* 28: 179–92.

Dowling, Linda (1977) *Aestheticism and Decadence: A Selective Annotated Bibliography*, New York and London: Garland Publishing.

—— (1979) "The decadent and the New Woman in the 1890s," *Nineteenth Century Fiction* 33, 4: 434–53.

Doyle, Brian (1989) *English and Englishness*, London: Routledge.

Duncan, Carol (1973) "Virility and domination in early twentieth century vanguard painting," *Artforum* (December); rpt. in her 1982 *Feminism and Art History*, New York: Harper & Row.

Dunn, Jane (1990) *A Very Close Conspiracy: Vanessa Bell and Virginia Woolf*, London: Jonathan Cape.

Duro, Paul (1986) "Demoiselles a copier during the Second Empire," *Woman's Art Journal*, Spring/Summer: 1–7.

—— (1988) "Copyists in the Louvre in the middle decades of the nineteenth century," *Gazette des Beaux-Arts* 111: 249–54.

Dydo, Ulla E. (1985a) "*Stanzas in Meditation*: the other autobiography," *Chicago Review* 35: 4–20.

—— (1985b) "To have the winning language: texts and contexts of Gertrude Stein," in Diane Wood Middlebrook and Marilyn Yalom (eds), *Coming to Light: American Women Poets in the Twentieth Century*, Ann Arbor: University of Michigan Press.

Eldar Gallery, London (1918) *Nina Hamnett: A Catalogue of Paintings and Drawings*, preface by Walter Sickert.

Faderman, Lillian (1981) *Surpassing the Love of Men*, New York: William Morrow.

Fagen-King, Julia (1988) "United on the threshold of the twentieth century mystic ideal: Marie Laurencin's integral involvement with Guillaume Apollinaire and the inmates of the Bateau Lavoir," *Art History* 2 (1988): 88–114.

F.E. (1919) "Contemporary portraits," *Cambridge Magazine* (8 November): 67.

Felski, Rita (1989) *Beyond Feminist Aesthetics: Feminist Literature and Social Change*, Cambridge, Mass.: Harvard University Press.

Feltes, Norman (1986) *Modes of Production of Victorian Novels*, Chicago and London: University of Chicago Press.

Field, Andrew (1985) *Djuna: The Formidable Miss Barnes*, Austin: University of Texas Press.

Flanner, Janet (1990; orig. pub. 1947) *Men and Monuments: Profiles of Picasso, Matisse, Braque, and Malraux*, New York: Da Capo Press.

Ford, Hugh (1975) *Published in Paris: A Literary Chronicle of Paris in the 1920s and 1930s*, New York: Collier Books.

Fosca, Francois (1925) "Marie Laurencin," *Art et decoration* XLVII (April): 119–22.

Frascina, Francis and Harrison, Charles (eds.) (1982) *Modern Art and Modernism*, New York: Harper & Row.

Fraser, Nancy (1990) "The uses and abuses of French discourse theories for feminist politics," *boundary 2* 17: 82–101.

Fry, Roger (1981; orig. pub. 1920) *Vision and Design*, J.B. Bullen (ed.), London: Oxford University Press.

Fussell, B.H. (1980) "Woolf's peculiar comic world: *Between the Acts*," in Ralph Freedman (ed.), *Virginia Woolf: Revaluation and Continuity*, Berkeley: University of California Press.

Gagnier, Regenia (1986) *Idylls of the Marketplace: Oscar Wilde and the Victorian Public*, Stanford: Stanford University Press.

Gallup, Donald (ed.) (1953) *The Flowers of Friendship: Letters Written to Gertrude Stein*, New York: Alfred A. Knopf.

Garb, Tamar (1989) "L'Art feminin: the formation of a critical category in late nineteenth century France," *Art History* 12: 39–65.

Garber, Marjorie (1993) *Vested Interests: Cross-Dressing and Cultural Anxiety*, New York: Harper Perennial.

Garnham, Nicholas and Williams, Raymond (1986) "Pierre Bourdieu and the sociology of culture: an introduction," in Richard Collins *et al.* (eds), *Media, Culture and Society: A Critical Reader*, London: SAGE Publications.

Gawthorpe, Mary (1911) "To the women's social and political union," *The Freewoman* 3, 7 December 1911: 42.

Gilbert, Sandra M. and Gubar, Susan (1988) *No Man's Land: The Place of the Woman Writer in the Twentieth Century. Vol. 1. The War of the Words*, New Haven: Yale University Press.

—— (1989) *No Man's Land: The Place of the Woman Writer in the Twentieth Century. Vol. 2. Sexchanges*, New Haven: Yale University Press.

Gillespie, Diane Filby (1988) *The Sisters' Arts: The Writing and Painting of Virginia Woolf and Vanessa Bell*, Syracuse: Syracuse University Press.

Gimpel, René (1966) *Diary of an Art Dealer*, New York: Farrar, Straus, & Giroux.

Gordon-Stables, Mrs. (1924) "Nina Hamnett's psychological portraiture," *Artwork* (October): 112–15.

Gray, Christopher (1958) "Marie Laurencin and her friends," *Museum Art News* (Baltimore) 21: 6–15.

Greenberg, Clement (1961) "Avant-garde and kitsch" (first pub. 1939), in *Art and Culture: Critical Essays*, Boston: Beacon.

—— (1984) "Modernist painting" (first pub. 1965), in F. Frascina and C. Harrison (eds), *Modern Art and Modernism*, New York: Harper & Row.

Grimes, Teresa; Collins, Judith; and Baddeley, Oriana (eds) (1989) *Five Women Painters*, London: Lennard Publishing.

Grindea, Miron (ed.) (1962) "The Amazon of letters: a world tribute to Natalie Clifford Barney," *Adam International Review*, 29: 3–162.

Gubar, Susan (1981) "Blessings in disguise: cross-dressing as re-dressing for female modernists," *Massachusetts Review* 22: 477–508.

Guggenheim, Peggy (1979; orig. pub. 1946) *Out of This Century: Confessions of an Art Addict*, foreword by Gore Vidal, introduction by Alfred H. Barr, Jr., New York: Universe Books.

Hamnett, Nina (1932) *Laughing Torso: Reminiscences*, London: Constable; reissued by Virago, 1984.

—— (1955) *Is She A Lady? A Problem in Autobiography*, London: Allan Wingate.

Hanscombe, Gillian and Smyers, Virginia L. (1987) *Writing for their Lives: The*

Modernist Women 1910–1940, London: The Women's Press.

Harrison, Charles (1985) "Modernism and the 'transatlantic dialogue,'" in *Pollock and After: The Critical Debate*, London: Harper & Row.

Herzig, Carl (1987) "Roots of night: emerging style and vision in the early journalism of Djuna Barnes," *Centennial Review* 31: 255–69.

Hobhouse, Janet (1975) *Everybody Who Was Anybody: A Biography of Gertrude Stein*, New York: G.P. Putnam's Sons.

Hoffman, Frederick J. (1955) *The Twenties: American Writing in the Postwar Decade*, New York: Viking.

Hoffman, Frederick J.; Allen, Charles; and Ulrich, Carolyn (1947) *The Little Magazine: A History and a Bibliography*, 2nd ed., Princeton: Princeton University Press.

Holcombe, Lee (1973) *Victorian Ladies at Work*, Hamden, Conn.: Archon.

Hooker, Denise (1986) *Nina Hamnett: Queen of Bohemia*, London: Constable.

Howe, Irving (1967) "The idea of the modern," in Irving Howe (ed.), *The Idea of the Modern in Literature and the Arts*, New York: Horizon Press.

Hulme, T.E. (1924) "Romanticism and classicism," *Speculations*, New York: Harcourt, Brace, & Co.: 113–40.

Huysmans, J.-K. (1959) *Against Nature [À Rebours]* (orig. pub. 1884), trans. Robert Baldick, Harmondsworth: Penguin.

Huyssen, Andreas (1986) "Mass culture as woman: modernism's other," in *After the Great Divide: Modernism, Mass Culture, Post-Modernism*, Bloomington: Indiana University Press.

Hyland, Douglas K.S. and McPherson, Heather (1989) *Marie Laurencin: Artist and Muse*, Birmingham, Ala.: Birmingham Museum of Art.

Jameson, Fredric (1977) "Reflections in conclusion," in Ernst Bloch *et al.*, *Aesthetics and Politics*, London: NLB.

—— (1981) *The Political Unconscious: Narrative as a Socially Symbolic Act*, London: Methuen.

Jardine, Alice (1985) *Gynesis: Configurations of Woman and Modernity*, Ithaca: Cornell University Press.

Jay, Karla (1988) *The Amazon and the Page: Natalie Clifford Barney and Renée Vivien*, Bloomington: Indiana University Press.

—— (1991) "The outsider among the expatriates: Djuna Barnes' satire of the ladies of the *Almanack*," in Mary Lynn Broe (ed.), *Silence and Power: A Reevaluation of Djuna Barnes*.

J.L. (1937) "Marie Laurencin: a famous exponent of femininity," *Art News* 36: 18–19.

Johnston, Judith L. (1987) "The remediable flaw: revisioning cultural history in *Between the Acts*," in Jane Marcus (ed.), *Virginia Woolf and Bloomsbury: A Centenary Celebration*, Bloomington: Indiana University Press.

Jullian, Philippe (1969) "Fresh remembrance of Oscar Wilde," *Vogue* (November): 176–79, 229–34.

Kannenstine, Louis (1977) *The Art of Djuna Barnes: Duality and Damnation*, New York: New York University Press.

Kaplan, Sydney Jarret (1991) *Katherine Mansfield and the Origins of Modernist Fiction*, Ithaca: Cornell University Press.

Karl, Frederick R. (1988) *Modern and Modernism: The Sovereignty of the Artist 1885–1925*, New York: Atheneum.

Kenner, Hugh (1984) "The making of the modernist canon," *Chicago Review* 34, 49–61.

Kirkpatrick, B.J. (1980) *A Bibliography of Virginia Woolf*, 3rd ed., Oxford: Clarendon Press.

Koestenbaum, Wayne (1989) *Double Talk: The Erotics of Male Literary Collaboration*, New York: Routledge.

Krauss, Rosalind E. (1981) "The originality of the avant-garde," in *The Originality of the Avant-Garde and Other Modernist Myths*, Cambridge, Mass.: MIT Press.

Kreymborg, Alfred (1922) "Bel Esprit," *The Double Dealer* 3: 326–28.

Langer, Sandra (1981) "Fashion, character and sexual politics in some Romaine Brooks lesbian portraits," *Art Criticism* 1: 25–40.

Laurencin, Marie (1929) "Fine coloured reproductions of Marie Laurencin", *Colour* (November): 32.

—— (1956; orig. pub. 1942) *Le Carnet des nuits*, Geneva: Pierre Cailler.

Lejeune, Philippe (1989) *On Autobiography*, trans. Katherine Leary, Minneapolis: University of Minnesota Press.

Leslie, Seymour W. (1927) *The Silent Queen*, London: Jonathan Cape.

Levenson, Michael H. (1984) *A Genealogy of Modernism: A Study of English Literary Doctrine 1908–1922*, Cambridge: Cambridge University Press.

—— (1991) *Modernism and the Fate of Individuality: Character and Novelistic Form from Conrad to Woolf*, Cambridge: Cambridge University Press.

Levin, Harry (1960) "What was modernism?," *Massachusetts Review* 1: 609–30.

Levine, Nancy J. (1991) "'Bringing milkshakes to bulldogs:' the early journalism of Djuna Barnes," in Mary Lynn Broe (ed.), *Silence and Power: A Reevaluation of Djuna Barnes*.

Lombroso, Cesare (1891) *The Man of Genius*, London: W. Scott; New York: C. Scribner's Sons.

Loy, Mina (1985; orig. pub. 1982) *The Last Lunar Baedeker*, Roger L. Conover (ed.), Manchester: Carcanet Press.

Lukács, Georg (1977) "Realism in the balance," in Ernst Bloch *et al.*, *Aesthetics and Politics*, London: NLB.

—— (1989) "The ideology of modernism," trans. John and Necke Mander, in David H. Richter (ed.), *The Critical Tradition: Classic Texts and Contemporary Trends*, New York: Bedford Books, St. Martin's Press.

Lunn, Eugene (1982) *Marxism and Modernism: An Historical Study of Lukács, Brecht, Benjamin, and Adorno*, Berkeley: University of California Press.

Lynn, Kenneth S. (1987) *Hemingway*, New York: Simon & Schuster.

McAlmon, Robert (1968) *Being Geniuses Together, 1920–1930*, rev. with additional material by Kay Boyle, Garden City: Doubleday.

McNamara, Annie (1983) *Vanessa Bell Paintings 1910–1920*, Canterbury: The Royal Museum.

Mackenzie, Compton (1928) *Extraordinary Women*, London: Secker.

Mann, Paul (1991) *The Theory-Death of the Avant-Garde*, Bloomington: Indiana University Press.

Marchesseau, Daniel (1981) *Marie Laurencin: Catalogue Raisonné de l'Oeuvre Grave*, Tokyo: Éditions d'art Kyuryudo.

—— (1986) *Marie Laurencin 1883–1956: Catalogue Raisonné de l'Oeuvre Peint*, Tokyo: Éditions du Musée Marie Laurencin.

Marcus, Jane (1983) "Liberty, sorority, misogyny," in Carolyn Heilbrun and Margaret R. Higonnet (eds), *Representation of Women in Fiction*, Baltimore: Johns Hopkins University Press.

Marzolf, Marion (1977) *Up from the Footnote: A History of Women Journalists*, New York: Communication Arts Books, Hastings House, Publishers.

Mauclair, Camille (1899) "La femme devant les peintres modernes," *La Nouvelle revue*, 2nd series, I: 190–213.

Meisel, Perry (1987) *The Myth of the Modern: A Study in British Literature and*

Criticism After 1850, New Haven: Yale University Press.

Mellow, James R. (1974) *Charmed Circle: Gertrude Stein and Company*, New York: Avon Books.

Menand, Louis (1987) *Discovering Modernism: T.S. Eliot and His Context*, Oxford: Oxford University Press.

Messerli, Douglas (1975) *Djuna Barnes: A Bibliography*, New York: David Lewis.

Miller, Nina (1991) "The bonds of free love: constructing the female bohemian self," *Genders* 11: 37–57.

Moers, Ellen (1977) *Literary Women: The Great Writers*, New York: Anchor Books.

Moi, Toril (1991) "Appropriating Bourdieu: feminist theory and Pierre Bourdieu's sociology of culture," *New Literary History* 22: 1017–49.

Mulvey, Laura (1989) *Visual and Other Pleasures*, Bloomington: Indiana University Press.

Newton, Esther (1984) "The mythic mannish lesbian: Radclyffe Hall and the New Woman," *Signs* 9: 557–75.

Nisbet, John Ferguson (1912) *The Insanity of Genius*, London: S. Paul.

Nochlin, Linda (1973) "The realist criminal and the abstract law," *Art in America*, September/November: 25–48.

Olivier, Fernande (1964) *Picasso and his Friends*, trans. Jane Miller, London: Heinemann.

Owens, Craig (1985; orig. pub. 1983) "The discourse of others: feminists and postmodernism," in *Postmodern Culture*, London: Pluto Press.

Pease, Donald E. (1990) "Author," in *Critical Terms for Literary Study*, Frank Lentricchia and Thomas McLaughlin (eds), Chicago: University of Chicago Press.

Perloff, Marjorie (1986) *The Futurist Moment: Avant-Garde, Avant Guerre, and the Language of Rupture*, Chicago: University of Chicago Press.

—— (1988) "(Im)Personating Gertrude Stein," in Shirley Neuman and Ira B. Nadel (eds), *Gertrude Stein and the Making of Literature*, Boston: Northeastern University Press.

Pierre, José (1988) *Marie Laurencin*, Paris: Éditions Aimery Somogy.

Pippett, Roger (1932) "When artist turns author...," *Daily Herald*, 9 June: 13.

Plumb, Cheryl (1986) *Fancy's Craft: Art and Identity in the Early Works of Djuna Barnes*, Selinsgrove: Susquehanna University Press; London and Toronto: Associated University Presses.

Poggioli, Renato (1968; orig. pub. 1962) *The Theory of the Avant-Garde*, trans. Gerald Fitzgerald, Cambridge, Mass.: Harvard University Press.

Pollock, Griselda (1988) *Vision and Difference: Femininity, Feminism and the Histories of Art*, London: Routledge.

Pougy, Liane de (1901) *Idylle Saphique*, Paris: Plume.

Pound, Ezra (1922) "Paris letter," *The Dial* 73: 507–8.

—— (1957, orig. pub. 1920) "Hugh Selwyn Mauberley" in *Selected Poems of Ezra Pound*, New York: New Directions.

—— (1958) "Postscript to *The Natural Philosophy of Love* by Remy de Gourmont," *Pavannes and Divagations*, New York: New Directions.

—— (1968) *Literary Essays*, T.S. Eliot (ed.), New York: New Directions.

—— (1975) *Selected Prose 1909–1975*, William Cookson (ed.), New York: New Directions.

—— (1976) "Letters to Natalie Barney," ed. with commentary by Richard Sieburth, *Paideuma* 5: 279–95.

Pratt, William (ed.) (1963) *The Imagist Poem*, New York: E.P. Dutton & Co.

Quinones, Ricardo J. (1985) *Mapping Literary Modernism: Time and Development*, Princeton: Princeton University Press.

Rainey, Lawrence (1989) "The price of modernism: reconsidering the publication of *The Waste Land*," *Critical Quarterly* 31: 21–47.

Reed, Christopher (1991) "Bloomsbury bashing: homophobia and the politics of criticism in the eighties," *Genders* 11: 58–80.

Reid, B.L. (1968) *The Man From New York: John Quinn and His Friends*, New York: Oxford University Press.

Robbins, Bruce (1983) "Modernism in history, modernism in power," in Robert Kiely (ed.), *Modernism Reconsidered*, Cambridge, Mass.: Harvard University Press.

—— (1993) *Secular Vocations: Intellectuals, Professionalism, Culture*, London and New York: Verso.

Roche, Henri-Pierre (1922) "Marie Laurencin," *Les Cahiers d'aujourd'hui*: 215–18.

Rogers, W.G. (1968) *Ladies Bountiful*, New York: Harcourt, Brace, & World.

Rogoff, Irit (1990) "The anxious artist: ideological mobilisations of the self in German Modernism," in Irit Rogoff (ed.), *The Divided Heritage: Themes and Problems in German Modernism*, Cambridge: Cambridge University Press.

Rolley, Katrina (1990) "Cutting a dash: the dress of Radclyffe Hall and Una Troubridge," *Feminist Review* 35: 54–66.

Rose, Phyllis (1978) *Woman of Letters: A Life of Virginia Woolf*, New York: Oxford University Press.

Rosenbaum, S.P. (1975) *The Bloomsbury Group: A Collection of Memoirs, Commentary, and Criticism*, Toronto: University of Toronto Press.

—— (1983a) "An educated man's daughter: Leslie Stephen, Virginia Woolf, and the Bloomsbury Group," in Patricia Clements and Isobel Grundy (eds), *Virginia Woolf: New Critical Essays*, London: Vision Press.

—— (1983b) "Virginia Woolf and the intellectual origins of Bloomsbury," in Elaine K. Ginsberg and Laura Moss Gottlieb (eds), *Virginia Woolf: Centennial Essays*, Troy, N.Y.: Whitston Publishing Company.

Rosenman, Ellen Bayuk (1989) "Sexual identity and *A Room of One's Own*: 'secret economies' in Virginia Woolf's Feminist Discourse," *Signs* 14 (Spring): 634–50.

Ruehl, Sonja (1982) "Inverts and experts: Radclyffe Hall and the lesbian identity," in Rosalind Brunt and Caroline Rowan (eds), *Feminism, Culture and Politics*, London: Lawrence & Wishart.

Russell, John (1982) "Introduction," in Diana Edkins Richardson (ed.), *Vanity Fair: Photographs of an Age, 1914–1936*, New York: Clarkson N. Potter.

Saisselin, Remy G. (1963) *Style, Truth and the Portrait*, Cleveland: Cleveland Museum of Art.

Sandell, Renée (1980) "Marie Laurencin: cubist muse or more?," *Women's Art Journal* 1: 23–27.

Schenck, Celeste M. (1989) "Exiled by genre: modernism, canonicity, and the politics of exclusion," in Mary Lynn Broe and Angela Ingram (eds), *Women's Writing in Exile*, Chapel Hill: University of North Carolina Press.

Scott, Bonnie Kime (ed.) (1990) *The Gender of Modernism: A Critical Anthology*, Bloomington: Indiana University Press.

Secrest, Meryle (1974) *Between Me and Life: A Biography of Romaine Brooks*, Garden City, N.Y.: Doubleday.

—— (1984) "Shades of gray," *FMR* 2 (July): 121–44.

Sedgwick, Eve Kosofsky (1985) *Between Men: English Literature and Male Homosocial Desire*, New York: Columbia University Press.

Shone, Richard (1975) "The Friday Club," *Burlington Magazine* CXVII: 279–84.

—— (1980) *Vanessa Bell 1879–1961*, New York: David & Long.

Showalter, Elaine (1990) *Sexual Anarchy: Gender and Culture at the Fin de Siècle*, New York: Viking.

Sieburth, Richard (ed.) (1976) "Ezra Pound. Letters to Natalie Barney," *Paideuma* 5: 279–95.

Silverman, Debra (1989) *Art Nouveau in Fin-de-Siècle France*, Berkeley: University of California Press.

Smith, Sidonie (1987) *A Poetics of Women's Autobiography: Marginality and the Fictions of Self-Representation*, Bloomington: Indiana University Press.

—— (1990) "Self, subject, and resistance: marginalities and twentieth-century autobiographical practice," *Tulsa Studies in Women's Literature* 9 (Spring): 11–24.

Souhami, Diana (1988) *Gluck: Her Biography*, London: Pandora.

Spackman, Barbara (1989) *Decadent Genealogies: The Rhetoric of Sickness from Baudelaire to D'Annunzio*, Ithaca and London: Cornell University Press.

Spalding, Frances (1983) *Vanessa Bell*, New Haven and New York: Ticknor & Fields.

Spender, Stephen (1963) *The Struggle of the Modern*, London: Hamish Hamilton.

Steegmuller, Francis (1963) *Apollinaire: Poet Among the Painters*, New York: Farrar, Straus & Company.

Stein, Gertrude (1914) *Tender Buttons*, New York: Claire-Marie.

—— (1934) "And now," in Cleveland Amory and Frederic Bradlee (eds), *Vanity Fair: A Cavalcade of the 1920s and 1930s*, New York: Viking, 1960.

—— (1937) *Everybody's Autobiography*, New York: Random House.

—— (1960; first pub. 1933) *The Autobiography of Alice B. Toklas*, New York: Vintage Books.

—— (1967) *Writings and Lectures 1909–1945*, Patricia Meyerowitz (ed.), Harmondsworth: Penguin.

—— (1974) *How Writing is Written: Volume II of the Previously Uncollected Works of Gertrude Stein*, Robert Bartlett Haas (ed.), Los Angeles: Black Sparrow Press.

Steiner, Wendy (1982) *The Colors of Rhetoric: Problems in the Relation Between Modern Literature and Painting*, Chicago: University of Chicago Press.

Stimpson, Catherine R. (1986) "Gertrude Stein and the transposition of gender," in Nancy K. Miller (ed.), *The Poetics of Gender*, New York: Columbia University Press.

Suleiman, Susan Rubin (1988) "A double margin: reflections on women writers and the avant-garde in France," *Yale French Studies* 75: 148–71.

—— (1990) *Subversive Intent: Gender, Politics and the Avant-Garde*, Cambridge, Mass.: Harvard University Press.

Sutherland, Ann and Nochlin, Linda (1976) *Women Artists: 1550–1950*, Los Angeles: Los Angeles County Museum.

Symons, Arthur (1981) "The decadent movement in literature" (first pub. 1893), in Karl Beckson (ed.), *Aesthetes and Decadents of the 1890s: An Anthology of British Poetry and Prose*, rev. ed., Chicago: Academy Chicago.

Terdiman, Richard (1985) *Discourse/Counter Discourse: The Theory and Practice of Symbolic Resistance in Nineteenth Century France*, Ithaca: Cornell University Press.

Thornton, R.K.R. (1979) "'Decadence' in later nineteenth-century England," in Ian Fletcher (ed.), *Decadence and the 1890s*, London: Edward Arnold.

Tickner, Lisa (1987) *The Spectacle of Women: Imagery of the Suffrage Campaign 1907–14*, London: Chatto & Windus.

Todd, Dorothy (1928) "Exotic canvases suited to modern decoration," *Arts and Decoration* (January): 64, 92, 94–95.

Todd, Janet (1988) *Feminist Literary History*, New York: Routledge.

Tuckwell, Gertrude M. (1919) "Equal pay for equal work," *Fortnightly Review* 105, 1 January: 63–76.

Turnbaugh, Douglas Blair (1987) *Duncan Grant and the Bloomsbury Group*, Secausus, N.J.: L. Stuart.

Twitchell, Beverley H. (1987) *Cézanne and Formalism in Bloomsbury*, Ann Arbor: UMI Research Press.

"Two Marie Laurencin exhibitions" (1937) *Studio* (London) 13 (February): 103–4.

Varnadoe, Kirk (1976) "Introduction," in Department of Art History and Archaeology, Columbia University, *Modern Portraits: The Self and Others*, New York: Wildenstein.

Viswanathan, Gauri (1989) *Masks of Conquest: Literary Study and British Rule in India*, New York: Columbia University Press.

Walker, Jayne L. (1984) *The Making of a Modernist: Gertrude Stein from Three Lives to Tender Buttons*, Amherst: University of Massachusetts Press.

Watney, Simon (1980) *English Post-Impressionism*, London: Studio Vista.

Weeks, Jeffrey (1981) *Sex, Politics and Society*, London: Longman.

Weininger, Otto (1907) *Sex and Character*, trans. from 6th German edition, London: Heinemann.

West, Rebecca (1932) "The racy autobiography of a woman artist," *Daily Telegraph*, 10 June: 6.

Wickes, George (1976) *The Amazon of Letters: The Life and Loves of Natalie Barney*, New York: G.P. Putnam's Sons.

Williams, Raymond (1980) "The Bloomsbury fraction," in *Problems in Materialism and Culture*, London: Verso.

—— (1989) *The Politics of Modernism: Against the New Conformists*, ed. and introduction Tony Pinkney, London: Verso.

Williams, Val (1986) *Women Photographers: The Other Observers, 1900 to the Present*, London: Virago.

Wolff, Janet (1985) "The invisible flâneuse: women and the literature of modernity," *Theory, Culture and Society* 2: 37–46; rpt. in her 1990 *Feminine Sentences: Essays on Women and Culture*, Berkeley: University of California Press.

Woolf, Leonard (1964) *Beginning Again: An Autobiography of the Years 1911 to 1918*, London: The Hogarth Press.

—— (1967) *Downhill All the Way: An Autobiography of the Years 1919 to 1939*, London: The Hogarth Press.

Woolf, Virginia (1915) *The Voyage Out*, London: Duckworth.

—— (1927) *To the Lighthouse*, London: The Hogarth Press.

—— (1929) *A Room of One's Own*, London: The Hogarth Press.

—— (1937) *The Years*, London: The Hogarth Press.

—— (1938) *Three Guineas*, London: The Hogarth Press.

—— (1941) *Between the Acts*, London: The Hogarth Press.

—— (1942) "Professions for women," *The Death of the Moth*, London: The Hogarth Press (also rpt. in Woolf 1966).

—— (1966) *Collected Essays*, Vol. 2, London: The Hogarth Press.

—— (1967) "Memories of a working women's guild," *Collected Essays*, Vol. 4, London: The Hogarth Press.

—— (1975) *The Letters of Virginia Woolf*, Vol. 1, 1888-1912, Nigel Nicolson and Joanne Trautmann (eds), New York: Harcourt Brace Jovanovich.

—— (1976) *Moments of Being: Unpublished Autobiographical Writings*, Jeanne Schulkind (ed.), Sussex: The University Press.

—— (1977) *The Letters of Virginia Woolf*, Vol. 3, 1923–28, Nigel Nicolson and Joanne Trautmann (eds), New York: Harcourt Brace Jovanovich.

—— (1978a) *The Diary of Virginia Woolf*, Vol. 2, 1920–24, Anne Olivier Bell and Andrew McNeillie (eds), New York: Harcourt Brace Jovanovich.

—— (1978b) *The Letters of Virginia Woolf*, Vol. 4, 1929–31, Nigel Nicolson and Joanne Trautmann (eds), New York: Harcourt Brace Jovanovich.

—— (1978c) *The Pargiters: The Novel-Essay Portion of The Years*, Mitchell A. Leaska (ed.), London: The Hogarth Press.

—— (1980a) *The Diary of Virginia Woolf*, Vol. 3, 1925–30, Anne Olivier Bell and Andrew McNeillie (eds), New York: Harcourt Brace Jovanovich.

—— (1980b) *The Letters of Virginia Woolf*, Vol. 6, 1936–41, Nigel Nicolson and Joanne Trautmann (eds), New York: Harcourt Brace Jovanovich.

—— (1984) *The Diary of Virginia Woolf*, Vol. 5, 1936–41, Anne Olivier Bell and Andrew McNeillie (eds), New York: Harcourt Brace Jovanovich.

—— (1986) *The Essays of Virginia Woolf*, Vol. 1, 1904–1912, Andrew McNeillie (ed.), New York: Harcourt Brace Jovanovich.

—— (1989) *The Complete Shorter Fiction of Virginia Woolf*, rev. ed., Susan Dick (ed.), London: The Hogarth Press.

Zach, Natan (1976) "Imagism and Vorticism," in Bradbury and McFarlane (eds), *Modernism 1890–1930*.

INDEX

original/copy; of name 102; public life *see under* domestic and private life; *see also* homosexuality
mass media, modernism mediated through *see* mediating modernism
mass production *see* materialism
materialism, mass production and commercialism 4, 8, 9–12, 67, 94; *see also* financial resources; kitsch; mediating modernism
Matisse, H. 82, 85, 91, 96, 103, 115, 120, 177
Mauclair, C. 46
mediating modernism 15, 16, 30, 122–51, 165, 178–82; Hamnett's self-portraits 140–9; secularization and mass production 125–40; *see also* Barnes; Hamnett
Meisel, P. 58
Mellow, J.R. 98, 176
men *see* masculinity
Menand, L. 67, 68–69, 94, 96, 167, 174
Messerli, D. 135, 179
middle class/bourgeoisie 25–7, 168; and avant-garde, mediating position between *see* mediating modernism; *see also* Bell, V.; Laurencin; professionalism; Stein, G.; Woolf, V.
Mill, J.S. 70
Miller, N. 60, 142
Milman, S. 63
Milton, J. 170
Minimalism 3
modernism 1–30, 167–9; dating of 3; diversity within 6, 8; feminist configurations *see* feminism; formal configurations 3–6; institutional configurations 6–9; materialist configurations *see* materialism; purity of 4, 9; *see also* avant-garde; enabling strategies; genius; mediating modernism; positionings; professionalism
modernity 10
Modigliani, A. 143
Moers, E. 49
Moi, T. 2, 168
money *see* financial resources
Monroe, H. 63, 173
Moralt, H. 61
Morisot, B. 116, 162
Mulvey, L. 152, 168

Mussolini, B. 52, 128, 154

naturalness/artificiality binary of genius 91–2
negation of art, modernism as 10
Newton, E. 51
Nicholson, W. 14
Nicholson, B. 67
Nisbet, E. 96
Noailles, A. de 177
Nochlin, L. 36, 38, 171
Nordau, M. 40, 96, 176

old genres revived by avant-garde 34, 42–8
Olivier, F. 27, 102, 103, 105, 109
Omega Workshops 80, 81, 88, 128, 174
original/copy binary 34–36, 45, 53, 170; imitations/imitators of men, women as 60, 80–1
originality of avant-garde 34, 35–7
Orphism 94
Orton, J. 172
"outsiders", women as *see* amateurs
Owens, C. 55

pacifism 153, 154, 155
Pailthorpe, G. 14
painting *see* visual arts
Parker, R. 182
patronage 11, 29, 69–70, 122–3, 154; and mediating modernism 92, 95, 115; *see also* Barney; Guggenheim
payment for work *see* professionalism
Pease, D.E. 94–5
Perloff, M. 92, 102, 126
persona, male 170–1; of Barney 20, 46, 48–9, 168; genius *see* Stein, G.; *see also* cross-dressing
personality cult 38; *see also* lifestyle
Picasso, P. 14, 88, 165; avant-garde 38, 42, 43; genius 90, 91, 94, 96, 98–100, 102–3, 105, 107, 109, 113, 115, 120, 177; mediating modernism 129, 130, 141, 182
Pierre, J. 109
Pippett, R. 142
place *see* location
Plumb, C. 127, 179, 180
poetry 74; *see also* Barney; literature
Poggioli, R. 7
political *see* culture, production and political